JDBC™: Java™ Database Connectivity

JDBC™ : Java™ Database Connectivity

Bernard Van Haecke

IDG Books Worldwide, Inc.
An International Data Group Company

Foster City, CA ◆ Chicago, IL ◆ Indianapolis, IN ◆ Southlake, TX

JDBC™: Java™ Database Connectivity

Published by
IDG Books Worldwide, Inc.
An International Data Group Company
919 E. Hillsdale Blvd.
Suite 400
Foster City, CA 94404
http://www.idgbooks.com (IDG Books Worldwide Web site)

Library of Congress Catalog Card No.: 97-74338

ISBN: 0-7645-3144-1

Printed in the United States of America

10 9 8 7 6 5 4 3 2 1

1B/SX/RQ/ZX/FC

Distributed in the United States by IDG Books Worldwide, Inc.

Distributed by Macmillan Canada for Canada; by Transworld Publishers Limited in the United Kingdom; by IDG Norge Books for Norway; by IDG Sweden Books for Sweden; by Woodslane Pty. Ltd. for Australia; by Woodslane Enterprises Ltd. for New Zealand; by Longman Singapore Publishers Ltd. for Singapore, Malaysia, Thailand, and Indonesia; by Simron Pty. Ltd. for South Africa; by Toppan Company Ltd. for Japan; by Distribuidora Cuspide for Argentina; by Livraria Cultura for Brazil; by Ediciencia S.A. for Ecuador; by Addison-Wesley Publishing Company for Korea; by Ediciones ZETA S.C.R. Ltda. for Peru; by WS Computer Publishing Corporation, Inc., for the Philippines; by Unalis Corporation for Taiwan; by Contemporanea de Ediciones for Venezuela; by Computer Book & Magazine Store for Puerto Rico; by Express Computer Distributors for the Caribbean and West Indies. Authorized Sales Agent: Anthony Rudkin Associates for the Middle East and North Africa.

For general information on IDG Books Worldwide's books in the U.S., please call our Consumer Customer Service department at 800-762-2974. For reseller information, including discounts and premium sales, please call our Reseller Customer Service department at 800-434-3422.

For information on where to purchase IDG Books Worldwide's books outside the U.S., please contact our International Sales department at 415-655-3200 or fax 415-655-3295.

For information on foreign language translations, please contact our Foreign & Subsidiary Rights department at 415-655-3021 or fax 415-655-3281.

For sales inquiries and special prices for bulk quantities, please contact our Sales department at 415-655-3200 or write to the address above.

For information on using IDG Books Worldwide's books in the classroom or for ordering examination copies, please contact our Educational Sales department at 800-434-2086 or fax 817-251-8174.

For press review copies, author interviews, or other publicity information, please contact our Public Relations department at 415-655-3000 or fax 415-655-3299.

For authorization to photocopy items for corporate, personal, or educational use, please contact Copyright Clearance Center, 222 Rosewood Drive, Danvers, MA 01923, or fax 508-750-4470.

is a trademark under exclusive
license to IDG Books Worldwide, Inc.,
from International Data Group, Inc.

ABOUT IDG BOOKS WORLDWIDE

Welcome to the world of IDG Books Worldwide.

IDG Books Worldwide, Inc., is a subsidiary of International Data Group, the world's largest publisher of computer-related information and the leading global provider of information services on information technology. IDG was founded more than 25 years ago and now employs more than 8,500 people worldwide. IDG publishes more than 275 computer publications in over 75 countries (see listing below). More than 60 million people read one or more IDG publications each month.

Launched in 1990, IDG Books Worldwide is today the #1 publisher of best-selling computer books in the United States. We are proud to have received eight awards from the Computer Press Association in recognition of editorial excellence and three from *Computer Currents'* First Annual Readers' Choice Awards. Our best-selling *...For Dummies®* series has more than 30 million copies in print with translations in 30 languages. IDG Books Worldwide, through a joint venture with IDG's Hi-Tech Beijing, became the first U.S. publisher to publish a computer book in the People's Republic of China. In record time, IDG Books Worldwide has become the first choice for millions of readers around the world who want to learn how to better manage their businesses.

Our mission is simple: Every one of our books is designed to bring extra value and skill-building instructions to the reader. Our books are written by experts who understand and care about our readers. The knowledge base of our editorial staff comes from years of experience in publishing, education, and journalism — experience we use to produce books for the '90s. In short, we care about books, so we attract the best people. We devote special attention to details such as audience, interior design, use of icons, and illustrations. And because we use an efficient process of authoring, editing, and desktop publishing our books electronically, we can spend more time ensuring superior content and spend less time on the technicalities of making books.

You can count on our commitment to deliver high-quality books at competitive prices on topics you want to read about. At IDG Books Worldwide, we continue in the IDG tradition of delivering quality for more than 25 years. You'll find no better book on a subject than one from IDG Books Worldwide.

John Kilcullen
CEO
IDG Books Worldwide, Inc.

Steven Berkowitz
President and Publisher
IDG Books Worldwide, Inc.

Eighth Annual
Computer Press
Awards ≥1992

Ninth Annual
Computer Press
Awards ≥1993

Tenth Annual
Computer Press
Awards ≥1994

Eleventh Annual
Computer Press
Awards ≥1995

IDG Books Worldwide, Inc., is a subsidiary of International Data Group, the world's largest publisher of computer-related information and the leading global provider of information services on information technology. International Data Group publishes over 275 computer publications in over 75 countries. Sixty million people read one or more International Data Group publications each month. International Data Group's publications include: **ARGENTINA:** Buyer's Guide, Computerworld Argentina, PC World Argentina; **AUSTRALIA:** Australian Macworld, Australian PC World, Australian Reseller News, Computerworld, IT Casebook, Network World, Publish, Webmaster; **AUSTRIA:** Computerwelt Osterreich, Networks Austria, PC Tip Austria; **BANGLADESH:** PC World Bangladesh; **BELARUS:** PC World Belarus; **BELGIUM:** Data News; **BRAZIL:** Annuário de Informática, Computerworld, Connections, Macworld, PC Player, PC World, Publish, Reseller News, Supergamepower; **BULGARIA:** Computerworld Bulgaria, Network World Bulgaria, PC & MacWorld Bulgaria; **CANADA:** CIO Canada, Client/Server World, ComputerWorld Canada, InfoWorld Canada, NetworkWorld Canada, WebWorld; **CHILE:** Computerworld Chile, PC World Chile; **COLOMBIA:** Computerworld Colombia, PC World Colombia; **COSTA RICA:** PC World Centro America; **THE CZECH AND SLOVAK REPUBLICS:** Computerworld Czechoslovakia, Macworld Czech Republic, PC World Czechoslovakia; **DENMARK:** Communications World Danmark, Computerworld Danmark, Macworld Danmark, PC World Danmark, Techworld Denmark; **DOMINICAN REPUBLIC:** PC World Republica Dominicana; **ECUADOR:** PC World Ecuador; **EGYPT:** Computerworld Middle East, PC World Middle East; **EL SALVADOR:** PC World Centro America; **FINLAND:** MikroPC, Tietoverkko, Tietoviikko; **FRANCE:** Distributique, Hebdo, Info PC, Le Monde Informatique, Macworld, Reseaux & Telecoms, WebMaster France; **GERMANY:** Computer Partner, Computerwoche, Computerwoche Extra, Computerwoche FOCUS, Global Online, Macwelt, PC Welt; **GREECE:** Amiga Computing, GamePro Greece, Multimedia World; **GUATEMALA:** PC World Centro America; **HONDURAS:** PC World Centro America; **HONG KONG:** Computerworld Hong Kong, PC World Hong Kong, Publish in Asia; **HUNGARY:** ABCD CD-ROM, Computerworld Szamitastechnika, Internetto online Magazine, PC World Hungary, PC-X Magazin Hungary; **ICELAND:** Tolvuheimur PC World Island; **INDIA:** Information Communications World, Information Systems Computerworld, PC World India, Publish in Asia; **INDONESIA:** InfoKomputer PC World, Komputek Computerworld, Publish in Asia; **IRELAND:** ComputerScope, PC Live!; **ISRAEL:** Macworld Israel, People & Computers/Computerworld; **ITALY:** Computerworld Italia, Macworld Italia, Networking Italia, PC World Italia; **JAPAN:** DTP World, Macworld Japan, Nikkei Personal Computing, OS/2 World Japan, SunWorld Japan, Windows NT World, Windows World Japan; **KENYA:** PC World East African; **KOREA:** Hi-Tech Information, Macworld Korea, PC World Korea; **MACEDONIA:** PC World Macedonia; **MALAYSIA:** Computerworld Malaysia, PC World Malaysia, Publish in Asia; **MALTA:** PC World Malta; **MEXICO:** Computerworld Mexico, PC World Mexico; **MYANMAR:** PC World Myanmar; **NETHERLANDS:** Computer! Totaal, LAN Internetworking Magazine, LAN World Buyers Guide, Macworld Netherlands, Net, WebWereld; **NEW ZEALAND:** Absolute Beginners Guide and Plain & Simple Series, Computer Buyer, Computer Industry Directory, Computerworld New Zealand, MTB, Network World, PC World New Zealand; **NICARAGUA:** PC World Centro America; **NORWAY:** Computerworld Norge, CW Rapport, Datamagasinet, Financial Rapport, Kursguide Norge, Macworld Norge, Multimediaworld Norge, PC World Ekspress Norge, PC World Nettverk, PC World Norge, PC World ProduktGuide Norge; **PAKISTAN:** Computerworld Pakistan; **PANAMA:** PC World Panama; **PEOPLE'S REPUBLIC OF CHINA:** China Computer Users, China Computerworld, China InfoWorld, China Telecom World Weekly, Computer & Communication, Electronic Design China, Electronics Today, Electronics Weekly, Game Software, PC World China, Popular Computer Week, Software Weekly, Software World, Telecom World; **PERU:** Computerworld Peru, PC World Profesional Peru, PC World SoHo Peru; **PHILIPPINES:** Click!, Computerworld Philippines, PC World Philippines, Publish in Asia; **POLAND:** Computerworld Poland, Computerworld Special Report Poland, Cyber, Macworld Poland, Networld Poland, PC World Komputer; **PORTUGAL:** Cerebro/PC World, Computerworld/Correio Informático, Dealer World Portugal, Mac*In/PC*In Portugal, Multimedia World!; **PUERTO RICO:** PC World Puerto Rico; **ROMANIA:** Computerworld Romania, PC World Romania, Telecom Romania; **RUSSIA:** Computerworld Russia, Mir PK, Publish, Seti; **SINGAPORE:** Computerworld Singapore, PC World Singapore, Publish in Asia; **SLOVENIA:** Monitor; **SOUTH AFRICA:** Computing SA, Network World SA, Software World SA; **SPAIN:** Communicaciones World España, Computerworld España, Dealer World España, Macworld España, PC World España; **SRI LANKA:** Infolink PC World; **SWEDEN:** CAP&Design, Computer Sweden, Corporate Computing Sweden, Internetworld Sweden, it.branschen, Macworld Sweden, MaxiData Sweden, MikroDatorn, Nätverk & Kommunikation, PC World Sweden, PCaktiv, Windows World Sweden; **SWITZERLAND:** Computerworld Schweiz, Macworld Schweiz, PCtip; **TAIWAN:** Computerworld Taiwan, Macworld Taiwan, NEW ViSiON/Publish, PC World Taiwan, Windows World Taiwan; **THAILAND:** Publish in Asia, Thai Computerworld; **TURKEY:** Computerworld Turkiye, Macworld Turkiye, Network World Turkiye, PC World Turkiye; **UKRAINE:** Computerworld Kiev, Multimedia World Ukraine, PC World Ukraine; **UNITED KINGDOM:** Acorn User UK, Amiga Action UK, Amiga Computing UK, Apple Talk UK, Computing, Macworld, Parents and Computers UK, PC Advisor, PC Home, PSX Pro, The WEB; **UNITED STATES:** Cable in the Classroom, CIO Magazine, Computerworld, DOS World, Federal Computer Week, GamePro Magazine, InfoWorld, I-Way, Macworld, Network World, PC Games, PC World, Publish, Video Event, THE WEB Magazine, and WebMaster; online webzines: JavaWorld, NetscapeWorld, and SunWorld Online; **URUGUAY:** InfoWorld Uruguay; **VENEZUELA:** Computerworld Venezuela, PC World Venezuela; and **VIETNAM:** PC World Vietnam. 3/24/97

Credits

ACQUISITIONS EDITOR
John Read

DEVELOPMENT EDITORS
Suzanne Van Cleve
Tracy Thomsic

TECHNICAL EDITOR
Michael Epstein

COPY EDITORS
Roger Shapiro
Richard Adin
Anne Friedman

PRODUCTION COORDINATOR
Katy German

BOOK DESIGNERS
Jim Donohue
Kurt Krames

**GRAPHICS AND PRODUCTION
SPECIALIST**
Mark Schumann

QUALITY CONTROL SPECIALIST
Mick Arellano

PROOFREADER
David Wise

ILLUSTRATOR
Jesse Coleman

INDEXER
Ty Koontz

About the Author

Bernard Van Haecke is a consultant at Sun Microsystems Professional Services. He specializes in systems and network integration projects, most particularly DBMS, UNIX, and cutting-edge Java issues.

To Laura

Preface

Welcome to the IDG professional series and to *JDBC™: Java™ Database Connectivity!* This book will help Java developers optimize their efforts with an integrated approach to database access. Java is a powerful general-purpose programming language that combines the qualities of many other modern languages. Many developers consider Java an invaluable programming tool because of its platform independence – probably the most important of Java's many interesting features. Java is more than a programming language, however. It has its own environment – the Java Environment – that makes this object-oriented language robust, secure, architecture-neutral and portable, and also dynamic and threaded. Furthermore, Java is small and can be distributed on networks. Extensions such as portable graphic libraries, portable networking, and I/O capabilities empower the language and make it unique.

Like many other languages, Java may be used to develop components of client/server environments. The client/server paradigm proved its suitability for various purposes and is still evolving today. Actually, the most-used client/server architecture involves relational database servers and light (or not-so-light) clients running on desktops, so this book will obviously focus on connectivity with databases. In fact, Sun engineers developed a set of standard Java classes to allow database queries and updates to be issued from Java. This set of classes, called the Java Database Connectivity classes, is better known under the name of the JDBC Package. It is a part of Java Enterprise, a set of features that will mostly be used in various enterprise-wide projects. Once you master developing platform-independent programs with Java, you will then discover how to develop projects that access corporate or customers' data mines in a DBMS-independent way.

In fact, many applications are now tightly linked to databases, especially in the business world. From employee records to financial data, from library catalogs to student scores, a robust data management system must include:

- Access protection
- Data integrity and consistency
- Concurrency management
- Availability
- Scalability

All professional database management systems have such qualities. They even offer transaction management and relational access to data, replication, mirroring, and live backup facilities. These databases are well suited for all kinds of real-world data repositories, and they are often used in mission-critical environments such as process control, medical record tracking, or financial data warehouses.

Whatever kind of data relational databases store, there is one common language to query these: Structured Query Language (SQL). Its main purpose is to allow the database user to store and retrieve his or her data seamlessly, whatever the data source, while taking part of strong relations being set between data structures. It is also independent of the host language in which it is embedded. SQL has been standardized in 1986, 1989, and 1992. The most recent specification is called SQL-92 and is still evolving. Since it is an industry standard, it will be the language used to query databases through the JDBC. Be they applets, servlets, or applications, your next Java projects will be able to communicate to Database Management Systems using a universal and widespread language. You will, however, have to know the basics of SQL to understand fully the book's examples. The book will focus on the mechanisms used to integrate Java projects with DBMSs and not on SQL.

Because Java and its environment are powerful enabling technologies, we believe an extra component such as JDBC will be widely accepted and used by the developer community. It is robust, simple, perfectly designed, and enables all of today's Java applets, servlets, or applications to interact with databases. On the Internet battlefield, JDBC will push Java a little more because it is tremendously more powerful than the usual solutions to access databases from World Wide Web pages.

Who Is This Book For?

The audience for this book covers database developers that need to port applications or create new applications for the Internet or an intranet using World Wide Web and Java techniques. Obviously, this book is also intended for Webmasters, Web designers, and content developers who want to take advantage of the possibilities of Java. The third category of readers covers all Java developers wanting to learn client/server programming with databases in a very simple, easy, yet very powerful way using the standard JDBC API.

What You Need Before You Begin

The reader should have a minimum knowledge of Java programming. If you are working with a specific DBMS such as Oracle, Sybase, Informix, or DB2, you should understand the administration of such databases (to create new user accounts, for example). Smaller databases for desktop computers will also work with JDBC, although the possibilities will be far more limited. Knowledge of SQL is preferred, although it is introduced and illustrated by many examples in the book.

What's in This Book

This book is divided into four parts:

- ◆ **Part I: Introduction to Java Database Programming** — Part I introduces Java, database architectures and standards, and explains the Java Database Connectivity Classes.

- ◆ **Part II: Exploring JDBC** — Part II teaches you JDBC step-by-step, with plenty of code listings throughout the chapters. Part II also covers the three-tier approach, security issues, and Internet/intranet topics.

- ◆ **Part III: Working Examples** — Part III includes comprehensive examples of JDBC, including the code samples both in the book and on the CD-ROM.

- ◆ **Quick Reference Guide, Appendixes, and CD-ROM** — The Quick Reference Guide covers the JDBC 1.2 API of JavaSoft, and the appendixes include answers to frequently asked questions and references for additional information about SQL and DBMSs and Objects and DBMSs and JDBC products and drivers. The CD-ROM contains the source code for all examples, JDBC products, Bongo 1.0 from Marimba, and the common Java utilities such as the JavaSoft, Inc., JDK. See Appendix D, "What's on the CD-ROM," for a detailed list of CD-ROM contents.

We hope the theory and examples explained in this book will convince you there is now a real alternative to World Wide Web common gateway interfaces and that you can work successfully with Java without being a Java guru. We hope you will be convinced of the tremendous benefits Java offers via its robustness, security, object orientation and platform independence, and universal database connectivity.

Acknowledgments

Among the many individuals who helped with this project, I first want to thank very sincerely those who played an instrumental role both before and during the writing. Thank you to Laura Sanderson, Christophe Peerens, Wim De Munck, many former UCL colleagues and more recent Sun Microsystems colleagues, and of course my family.

I also want to thank Peter Ham and Gionata Mettifogo of Connect, Inc., for providing one of the most interesting examples in this book; Klaas Waslander of Marimba, Inc., for many informative discussions regarding the advanced examples; and to all of the reviewers who contributed from the beginning.

Special thanks go to Laurence Vanhelsuwé, who played a key role in locating the right editor for this book and for submitting a perfect proposal to him. Special thanks, too, go to John Read, Acquisitions Editor at IDG Books Worldwide, and to all of the editors who turned the manuscript into a terrific published book. They deserve much credit for their work. I am infinitely grateful to them.

Contents at a Glance

Contents

Part 1

Introduction to Java Database Programming

Chapter 1: About Java
Chapter 2: Database Fundamentals
Chapter 3: Database

Part I presents general background information about Java. You'll learn about typical applications related to Java and JDBC and why Java is so hot for client/server application development. You'll then review some database fundamentals, including relational ones, the standards such as SQL, X/Open CLI, and ODBC, and client/server architectures involving DBMSs.

Finally, you'll learn how to integrate today's databases using various approaches, as well as with the state-of-the-art Java and JDBC.

Chapter 1

About Java

IN THIS CHAPTER

Java is a new programming language especially well suited for the Internet. It offers many built-in features in its run time environment. From TCP-IP (Transmission Control Protocol/Internet Protocol) socket networking to method invocation on remote objects, from portable code and graphic toolkit to universal database connectivity, Java embraces many of the the technologies ever invented in the open-systems computing industry. This chapter covers:

◆ Java's philosophy

◆ Typical uses of Java

◆ Java's being more than a natural evolution

JAVA AND ITS ENVIRONMENT were introduced in 1995 by Sun Microsystems, Inc. Java was designed to meet the challenges of development in incompatible but networked environments.

Most modern programming languages already have some of the features present in Java, but none have all of the features. A majority of developers, analysts, designers, administrators, and executives agree that Java is the "enabler" of the 1990s. Much of the early discussion on the need for a Java-like language happened in Usenet newsgroups on the Internet. Now every major player endorses the technology and plans to deliver Java programs or javatized hardware. The reason is simple — Java's features. Most of the features of Java and its environment are revealed in the next paragraphs; however, Table 1-1 summarizes Java's feature set.

TABLE 1-1 JAVA — THE BIG PICTURE

	Java	C	C++
Simple	☺	☺	☹
Object-oriented	☺	☹	☺
Robust	☺	☹	☹

(continued)

TABLE 1-1 *(Continued)*

	Java	C	C++
Secure	☺	☹	☹
Interpreted	☺	☹	☹
Dynamic	☺	☹	☹
Portable	☺	☺	☺
Neutral	☺	☹	☹
Threads	☺	☹	☹
Garbage collection	☺	☹	☹
Exception	☺	☹	☺

☺ *Fulfilled by the language*
☺ Not built in the language, but feasible
☹ Not feasible in this language without third-party libraries

First and foremost, Java is definitely object-oriented. It is somewhat similar to C++, but its programming supplants functional and procedural styles. Java programmers only manipulate objects, data members, accessors, and mutators. Extra features such as automatic garbage collection (a garbage collector keeps track of the object instances and frees them when no longer used), object references replacing arithmetic address pointers, and native or nonnative multithreading add to Java's simplicity and power.

Java is a true object-oriented programming language. It fully supports encapsulation, polymorphism, inheritance, and dynamic bindings. The main benefit for the programmer is that his or her programming model will be close to the real world objects, making them easier to implement. Software reuse also benefits from this orientation, as is the case, for example, with many well-known C++ libraries.

Java is architecture-neutral, portable, and robust in that it can run on various platforms, anywhere on a network, regardless of which graphic subsystem is in use. It is truly independent of hardware, operating systems, and GUIs. The design of the Java Virtual Machine and Java's Abstract Window Toolkit make it portable, much more portable than C or C++, greatly simplifying deployment issues. This is why Java has such presence on the Internet. While Java applications are stand-alone programs, "applets" are pieces of software that can be downloaded from the Internet or intranet and run inside a World Wide Web (WWW) browser like HotJava. "Servlets" are also pieces of software that run as extensions to WWW servers while "aglets" are software agents that live and persist in networks, moving from host to host to perform dedicated tasks.

Java is an interpreted language whose bytecodes run within a secure virtual machine that translates the bytecodes to native CPU instructions. In some cases, this bytecode is compiled "just in time" and cached, or even "flash-compiled" so no additional interpretation is needed. It is also very dynamic. Java application classes may be downloaded across networks automatically.

Before passing to the interpreter for execution, bytecodes are verified. Bytecode verification ensures that the code does not point where it cannot point, that it does not violate access and network restrictions, and that it correctly accesses objects. Security is a very important intranet and Internet issue, which is why it is addressed at many levels of the Java environment.

Java provides an exception mechanism to create and catch user program errors and to catch system errors. This mechanism is superior to the usual way of trapping errors — using and testing return codes everywhere in the programs. It also adds to the code's simplicity and readability, which decreases the risk of introducing errors into programs.

Finally, Java features multithreading in a manner that is mostly independent of the underlying operating system from a programmer's point-of-view. Threads allow client-server applications to perform multiple tasks, including animations, concurrently.

Typical Uses

Many computer enthusiasts once said Java was well suited for animating World Wide Web pages. Actually, its use within WWW pages, mostly in the form of Java applets, is more a consequence of its design than its ultimate goal. Java is a very complete language, and there are no limitations that make it unsuitable for corporate and enterprisewide professional and business applications. On the other hand, both Sun and other parties are continuously enhancing the Java environment. These enhancements always preserve investments so there is no reason to wait before developing your next greatest corporate application in Java.

Virtually any application can be developed using Java, including those that need to issue calls to "system services" such as TCP/IP sockets. Many Integrated Development Environments (IDE) or Rapid Application Development tools (RAD tools) are being announced and released. These tools are often called Java Development Environments (JDE). If you are looking for such products, browse the Usenet newsgroup `news://comp.lang.java`. Many netizens will be happy to help you locate the best products. You also will have the opportunity to read and post comments to the support people from the companies that develop such programming environments. It has never been easier to get help to make choices before purchasing a development tool.

The Future

The possibilities Java offers are limitless. In the near future, many astonishing applications will appear. You'll soon see, for example, portable network management tools, interactive communication tools using multimedia techniques, interactive education tools, and information booths. But Java already has impacted operating systems. Many leading industry vendors already endorse the Java technology and include it in their existing platforms. Java made an important impact on the hardware industry, too. Java chips have been announced. They will be used in home appliances and industrial equipment. Many companies have agreed on common network computer specifications. These network computers will have operating systems and operating environments written in Java. Among the main benefits of all these new devices, the most impressive are the low cost and the possibility of on-demand downloading from the network of new versions of the operating elements, for both systems and applications.

Java Technology

Java technology evolves quickly. A Java Electronic Commerce Framework (JEFC), distributable Java components (JavaBeans), and Java/COM (Microsoft's Compound Object Model) integration are under development. The Java Database Connectivity API (Application Programming Interface), Java Object Serialization, and Java Remote Method Invocation are already available.

Concerning JDBC (Java Database Connectivity), JavaSoft (Sun Microsystems) and partners have plans for a Java Object-Relational Mapping API and for a Java Transaction Service API. The ODMG (Object Database Management Group) has been working on a standard API for Java object databases. This standard will be finalized by the time you read this book.

Java Applications

Certain Java applications are worth mentioning. Both the Java-enabled Transaction Processing Monitor and the Java CASE Tool are of interest for the database developer going the Java way.

EXAMPLE: TRANSACTION PROCESSING MONITOR

One of the most interesting available products is a Transaction Processing (TP) monitor that works with Java clients. A client/server environment can include a TP monitor when the servers are Database Management System server. It solves the problems that arise when hundreds, or even thousands, of clients send requests to a database server at the same time. The product is Vortex Java Edition, from Trifox, Inc.

Transaction processing monitors have existed for a long time. They were available for every mainframe environment. When the X/Open XTP Group's DTP model appeared, these monitors evolved to systems that guarantee their integration with open environments and that guarantee their interfacing with various components of distributed systems. The TP monitor is a special kind of middleware that offers services related to the application level. These services are transaction oriented.

The TP Monitor is a middleware between clients and servers as shown in Figure 1-1.

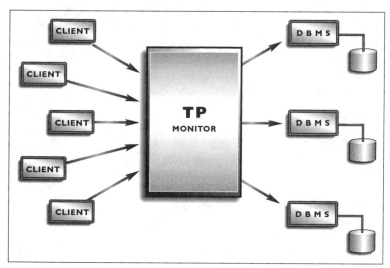

Figure 1-1: A TP monitor.

The TP monitor's roles are to:

♦ Manage and synchronize transactions

♦ Guarantee a sufficient level of performance and security

♦ Share the load of simultaneous transactions between different servers

♦ Handle heterogeneous DBMSs

The monitor's primary role is to dispatch transactions to one or multiple DBMS servers, allowing many clients to operate seamlessly. Common DBMSs are unable to handle thousands of simultaneous connections and process their queries. TP monitors solve the problem by reducing the number of active sessions necessary to process the client requests. They are probably the most advanced element of traditional client-server architectures where relational databases are involved. In the Internet scenario, the high number of clients that can potentially initiate a connection to a server makes the TP monitor middleware an interesting element of the client-server architecture.

The availability of Java-enabled TP monitors shows that there are no limits to what is possible using the Java language, the Java environment, and traditional elements of client-server systems.

ANOTHER EXAMPLE: A JAVA CASE TOOL

Another interesting product is Platinum Technology, Inc.'s Paradigm Plus code generator. It is a Computer Aided Software Engineering tool (CASE tool) that supports object-oriented analysis, design, and modeling, as well as reverse engineering from other languages. From conceptualization to deployment, it promotes component sharing and reuse across projects in the enterprise. The product supports all leading object-oriented methodologies and notations, and more — it allows developers to customize methods based on their specific requirements.

Among Paradigm Plus's many characteristics, the most interesting are its:

- Generation of Java code
- Highly graphical environment
- Object-oriented analysis and design
  - Support for OMT, Booch, Yourdon, and so on, methodologies and notation
  - Reverse engineering from C, C++, and SQL
- Generation of DBMS and ODBMS schema definitions
- Provision of an object repository
- Support for three-tier and n-tier architectures
- Promotion of Java component reuse

One feature, the generation of DBMS and ODBMS schema definitions, may be of particular interest to JDBC users. Indeed, the physical database design for persistent data may be done within this environment, and the result can then be applied within the DBMS.

JavaSoft's (Sun Microsystems) JavaPlan is a similar software engineering tool. There is no doubt that such complete, robust, and flexible products will help the analyst and developer during their Java projects. This is only the beginning of a new era and products like the CASE tool will soon emerge in all-Java or Java-enabled versions.

Summary

Java is definitely well suited for networked computing, and is complete enough to build robust, enterprise-class applications and applets.

The next chapter discusses fundamental database concepts such as SQL and database access interfaces.

Chapter 2

Database Fundamentals

IN THIS CHAPTER

This chapter discusses fundamental concepts such as relational databases, SQL, and database access programming interfaces. This chapter includes:

◆ Relational databases

◆ Software architectures

◆ Standard database APIs such as ODBC

ALMOST 100 PERCENT OF today's enterprise applications use a database. These databases are often managed by a Relational Database Management System (less often by an Object Database Management System). Whichever database management system (DBMS) is used, its role in the corporate information system is predominant. The DBMS offers a lot of features other than a centralized view of what may be a distributed database architecture. DBMSs ensure availability, integrity, consistency, concurrency, security of the corporate data through access control, and a lot more. Such DBMS facilities lighten all client programs since they are not involved in these issues. Furthermore, a lot of the query processing is done within the database management system itself, which makes optimized access plans to data when parsing client queries. Client programs are not able to do that.

The Java Database Connectivity (JDBC) interface allows Java applets, servlets, and applications to access data in popular database management systems. The standard for accessing data is SQL, which permits maximum interoperability. Of course, SQL is the language used with JDBC. JDBC is a software layer that allows developers to write real client-server projects in Java. JDBC does not concern itself with specific DBMS functions.

Relational Databases

Relational databases are the most common DBMS. A main characteristic of a relational database is the absolute separation between physical and logical data. Data is accessed through the associated logical model to avoid supplying physical storage locations and to reduce the limitations imposed by using physical information. Relational databases allow the definition of relations and integrity rules between data sets. E.F. Codd developed this model at the IBM San Jose Research Lab in the

1970s. A language to handle, define, and control data was also developed at the IBM lab: SQL. SQL stands for Structured Query Language. SQL is a query language that interacts with a DBMS. It allows data access without supplying physical access plans, data retrieval as sets of records, and the performing of complex computations on the data.

Software Architectures

The first generation of client-server architectures is called two-tiered. It contains two active components: the client, which requests data, and the server, which delivers data. Basically, the application's processing is done separately for database queries and updates, and for user interface presentations. Usually the network binds the back end to the front end, although both tiers could be present on the same hardware. For example, hundreds or thousands of airline seat reservation applications can connect to a central DBMS to request, insert, or modify data. While the clients process the graphics and data entry validation, the DBMS does all the data processing. Actually, it is inadvisable to overload the database engine with data processing that is irrelevant to the server, thus some processing usually also happens on the clients. The typical client-server architecture is shown in Figure 2-1.

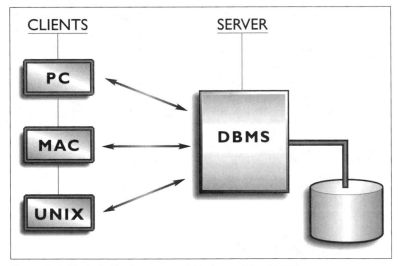

Figure 2-1: Typical client-server architecture with a DBMS.

Load balancing is sometimes necessary. The network becomes a bottleneck when too much data transits from the server to the clients. When this happens, it is necessary to limit the amount of data that comes back from the server. It is often unnecessary to display millions of data records on a client's screen (dynamic queries may return a lot of rows). If the database engine is overloaded, DBMS replication may be a good solution.

What is more important is that the real business logic is often located in the client's GUI logic and in the database at the same time. This occurs in many current applications and is a problem for code maintenance and code reusability. Indeed, applications evolve with time, but the GUI part, the data part, and the business logic part may not evolve concurrently. Figure 2-2 illustrates the two-tier architecture.

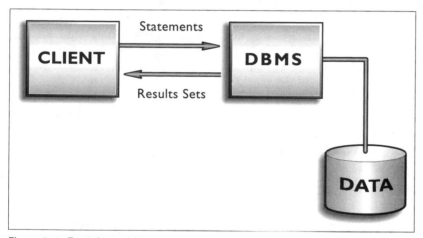

Figure 2-2: Two-tier architecture.

Although the two-tiered architecture is common, another design is starting to appear more frequently. To avoid embedding the application's logic at both the database side and the client side, a third software tier may be inserted. In three-tiered architectures, most of the business logic is frozen in the middle tier. In this architecture, when the business activity or business rules change, only the middleware must be modified. Figure 2-3 illustrates the three-tier architecture.

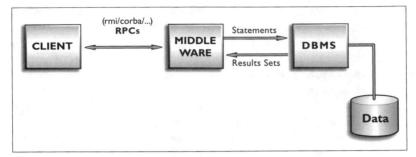

Figure 2-3: Three-tier architecture.

Database Standards

Database vendors are numerous, and, fortunately, industry standards exist. A group of companies or organizations often define these standards by consensus. It takes a long time before those creating the definitions agree on a common specification of functions. Standards bodies make sure these specifications match industry requirements. In some cases, though, developers do not wait for a standard to emerge. If they can invest in in-house–designed technology that will boost their productivity, they will develop it and use it. However, issues such as standard database connectivity and interoperability bring such benefits that the return on investment is worth waiting for.

SQL

SQL is not a complete programming language usable to build complex applications. It is commonly used within a host language that offers specific features for building complete applications. However, SQL is an industry standard to access databases. It enables data definition, manipulation and management, access protection, and transaction control. Its roots are in relational databases, and SQL handles many relational database objects, including tables, indexes, keys, rows, and columns. The American National Standards Institute (ANSI) standardized SQL in 1986 and defined it to be independent of any programming language and database management system.

The ANSI 1989 standard defines three programmatic interfaces to SQL:

◆ **Modules:** Separate compiled modules may define procedures and then call them from a traditional programming language.

◆ **Embedded SQL:** The specification defines embedded statements for a few traditional programming languages. It allows embedding static SQL statements within complete programs.

◆ **Direct invocation:** Access is implementation-defined.

While embedded SQL was the most popular choice a few years ago, it is not the best answer to the problem of querying databases in client-server environments. It is static in all senses of the term, and this limitation makes it unsuitable for newer software architectures.

SQL-92, the newer ANSI specification, addresses modern environment needs. It contains new features such as support for dynamic SQL and for an advanced technique to access result sets called scrollable cursors. While dynamic SQL is not as efficient as static SQL, it allows SQL statements to be prepared, to include parameters, and to be generated at run time. In the case of prepared statements, performance may be increased. In fact, dynamic SQL allows the database to prepare an access plan before the execution. This access plan is reused each time the statement is called.

SQL language is usable for a variety of purposes, including:

◆ Querying a database by entering SQL text directly

◆ Querying a database within a program

◆ Defining data organization

◆ Administering data

◆ Accessing multiple data servers

◆ Managing transactions

The SQL language supports a set of verbs used to define, store, manipulate, and retrieve data. The following are the basic SQL verbs used to build SQL clauses for such data manipulation:

To create a table:

```
CREATE TABLE table
(column type  [ NOT NULL | PRIMARY KEY |
UNIQUE | ... ]
[, column type        [ NOT NULL | PRIMARY KEY |
  UNIQUE | ... ]]*)
```

For example, to create a table of employees:

```
CREATE TABLE employees
(id          int PRIMARY KEY,
name         char(25) NOT NULL,
salary int)
```

To drop a table:

```
DROP TABLE table
```

For example:

```
DROP TABLE employees
```

To supply new record values:

```
INSERT INTO table    [ (column [, column ]*)]
VALUES (expr [, expr ]*)
```

For example, to add Jones as employee number one, with a salary of $60,000/year:

```
INSERT INTO employees
VALUES ("1", "JONES", 60000)
```

To delete rows:

```
DELETE FROM table
WHERE column [ < | > | = | <= | >= | <> | LIKE ] expr
[ AND | OR ... ]*]
```

For example, to delete all employees earning more than $150,000 a year:

```
DELETE FROM employees
WHERE salary > 150000
```

To retrieve data:

```
SELECT [ DISTINCT ] [table.]column [, [table.]column ]*
FROM table [= name] [, table [=name] ]*
[ WHERE [table.]column [ < | > | = | <= | >= | <> |
LIKE ] expr
[ AND | OR ... ]*]
[ ORDER BY [table.]column [ ASC | DESC ]
[, [table.]column [ ASC | DESC ]]]
[ HAVING ... ]
```

For example, to retrieve all employees earning more than $50,000, sorted by salary (higher first) and name:

```
SELECT * FROM employees
WHERE salary > 50000
ORDER BY salary DESC, name
```

To modify data:

```
UPDATE table SET column = expr [, column = expr ]*
WHERE [table.]column [ < | > | = | <= | >= | <> |
LIKE ] expr
[ AND | OR ... ]*
```

For example, to raise Jones' salary to $70,000 (Jones is employee number one):

```
UPDATE employees SET salary = 70000
WHERE id = 1
```

To create an index:

```
CREATE [ UNIQUE ] INDEX index
ON table (column [, column ]*)
```

For example, to create an index on the name field:

```
CREATE INDEX idx_employees
ON employees (name)
```

To create a stored procedure:

```
CREATE PROCEDURE procedure
[[(]@parameter type [= default ] [ IN | OUT | INOUT ]
[, @parameter type [= default ]
[ IN | OUT | INOUT ]]* [)]] [ WITH RECOMPILE ]
AS sqlstatement
```

For example, to create a stored procedure returning the highest salary via a parameter:

```
CREATE PROCEDURE maxsalary (@themax int OUT)
AS SELECT @themax = MAX(salary)
FROM employees
```

Book references are listed in the appendix for those who have not mastered SQL. DBMS reference books and online manuals may help while providing more details about specific implementations of SQL.

SAG-X/Open CLI

The X/Open and SQL Access Group defined the Call Level Interface (CLI). CLI is a library of function calls that support SQL statements. For example, Microsoft's ODBC (Open Database Connectivity) is a Call Level Interface. JDBC is also a Call

Level Interface. Most database vendors have optimized CLI implementations for their database management system products. ODBC and JDBC are less proprietary interfaces, though they intensively use these specific CLIs to access databases. The most important benefit for programmer's using the ODBC CLI or the JDBC CLI is interoperability — all clients adhere to a standard programming interface. CLI requires neither host variables nor other embedded SQL concepts that would make it less flexible from a programmer's perspective. It is still possible, however, to maintain and use specific functions of a database management system when accessing the database through a CLI.

An Industry Standard: ODBC

ODBC is Microsoft's implementation of a CLI. It allows the programmer to develop, compile, and deploy an application without targeting a specific DBMS. Modules called drivers link the application to the database of their choice. For this reason and because it is independent of the network layer protocols, ODBC permits maximum interoperability. The availability of specific drivers for almost all relational database management systems has determined its success. The JDBC mechanisms are very close to the ODBC, but are adapted for Java. In designing an appropriate interface for direct use from Java, issues such as security, implementation, robustness, and portability were addressed. The following section provides more details about ODBC.

THE ODBC INTERFACE

The ODBC interface defines a library of function calls that allow an application to connect to a DBMS, execute SQL statements, and retrieve results. Its syntax is based on the X/Open and SQL Access Group SQL CAE specification (1992), which defines a standard set of error codes, a standard way to initiate a connection, and a standard representation for data types. In addition to the core functions based on the X/Open and SQL Access Group Call Level Specification, it provides extended functions for handling scrollable cursors and asynchronous processing.

ODBC Components

The ODBC interface defines the possible interactions between the user application and the driver manager. Figure 2-4 shows the relationship between the four ODBC components.

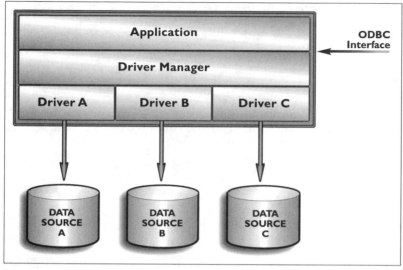

Figure 2-4: The four ODBC components.

APPLICATION

The user application calls ODBC functions to send SQL statements to the database and retrieve results. It performs these tasks:

- ◆ Requests a connection with a data source

- ◆ Sends SQL statements to the data source

- ◆ Defines storage areas and data types for the result sets

- ◆ Requests results

- ◆ Processes errors

- ◆ Controls transactions; requests commit or rollback operations

- ◆ Closes the connection

DRIVER MANAGER

Driver manager's primary purpose is to load specific drivers on behalf of the user application. It may also:

- ◆ Perform a lookup in an ODBC configuration file or system registry to map the ODBC Data Source Name (DSN) to a specific DBMS driver

- ◆ Process ODBC initialization calls

♦ Provide entry points to ODBC functions for each specific driver

♦ Perform parameter and sequence validation for ODBC calls

DRIVER

The driver processes ODBC function calls, sends SQL statements to a specific data source, and returns results back to the application. When necessary, the driver translates and/or optimizes requests so that the request conforms to the syntax supported by the specific DBMS. The driver:

♦ Establishes a connection to a data source

♦ Sends requests to the data source

♦ Performs translations when requested by the user application

♦ Returns results to the user application

♦ Formats errors in standard ODBC error codes

♦ Manipulates cursors if necessary

♦ Initiates transactions, if they are explicitly required

There are two types of ODBC drivers:

♦ Single-tier, which processes ODBC calls and SQL statements

♦ Multiple-tier, which processes ODBC calls and sends SQL statements to the data source

DATA SOURCE

The data source consists of the data the user application wants to access and its associated parameters — that is, the type of operating system, DBMS, and network layer (if any) used to access the DBMS.

Summary

This chapter discussed fundamental concepts such as relational databases, SQL, and database access programming interfaces.

The next chapter discusses the Java Database Connectivity API's role, components, and possible alternatives to it.

Chapter 3

Database Integration With JDBC

IN THIS CHAPTER

This chapter discusses how to integrate databases with Java using Java Database Connectivity (JDBC) and other techniques. This chapter includes:

◆ The role of JDBC

◆ The components of JDBC and their characteristics

◆ JDBC alternatives

JAVA DATABASE CONNECTIVITY CLASSES are Java classes that allow an application to send SQL statements to a database management system (DBMS) and retrieve the results. JDBC functions the same as Open Database Connectivity (ODBC). One of JDBC's strengths is interoperability – a developer can create JDBC applications without targeting a specific DBMS. Users can use specific JDBC drivers to target a specific database. Interoperability on the client side is also provided when using all Java solutions. Figure 3-1 shows Java clients running on different platforms.

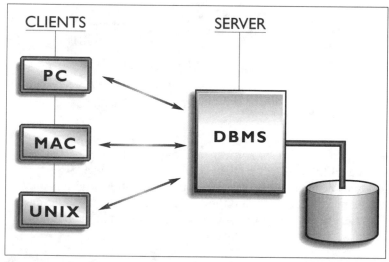

Figure 3-1: Java clients running on different platforms.

The Role of JDBC

The JDBC interface provides the application with a set of methods that enable database connections, queries, and result retrievals. It is the interface between specific database drivers and the Java user application, applet, or servlet.

The functions a user application can call are methods of connection, statements, or results object classes. Java is an object-oriented programming language, and the problems of impedance mismatch between Structured Query Language (SQL) and object-oriented programming (OOP) language have been minimized.

JDBC Characteristics

JDBC's characteristics are:

♦ JDBC is a "call-level" SQL interface for Java. This interface is totally independent of the available database management systems. It is a low-level application programming interface (API) that allows a Java program to issue SQL statements and retrieve their results. It also provides methods for error and warning messages management. As shown in Figure 3-2, JDBC is located at the client side.

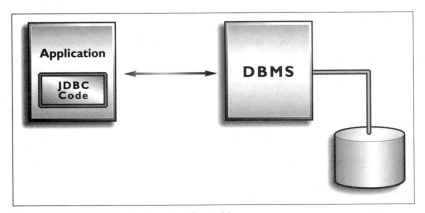

Figure 3-2: JDBC is located on the client side.

♦ SQL conformance: JDBC does not restrict the type of queries passed to an underlying DBMS driver. An application may use as much SQL functionality as desired. The underlying drivers are authorized to claim JDBC compliance on the condition they fully support ANSI SQL-92 Entry Level. SQL-2 Entry Level conformance is widely supported today and guarantees a wide level of portability.

◆ JDBC may be implemented on top of common SQL level APIs, in particular on top of ODBC.

◆ JDBC provides a Java interface that stays consistent with the rest of the Java system. There are no conflicts because of opposed philosophies expressed by the impedance mismatch between the object-oriented world (Java) and the tabular world (SQL).

◆ The JDBC mechanisms are simple to understand and use. This simplicity does not mean that functionality suffers.

◆ JDBC uses strong, static typing whenever possible. This approach allows for performing more error checking at compile time. It should not be a limitation to JDBC's usage, however.

◆ One functionality, one method: This concept has been adopted, as opposed to many other DBMS SQL level APIs, to keep it simple yet powerful for the beginner as well as the experienced developer.

JDBC Components

The following are JDBC components:

Application: The user application invokes JDBC methods to send SQL statements to the database and retrieve results. It performs these tasks:

◆ Requests a connection with a data source

◆ Sends SQL statements to the data source

◆ Defines storage areas and data types for the result sets

◆ Requests results

◆ Processes errors

◆ Controls transactions: requests commit or rollback operations

◆ Closes the connection

Driver Manager: Its primary purpose is to load specific drivers for the user application. It may also perform the following:

◆ Locate a driver for a particular database

◆ Process JDBC initialization calls

◆ Provide entry points to JDBC functions for each specific driver

◆ Perform parameter and sequence validation for JDBC calls

Driver: The driver processes JDBC methods invocations, sends SQL statements to a specific data source, and returns results back to the application. When necessary, the driver translates and/or optimizes requests so the request conforms to the syntax supported by the specific DBMS. It will:

♦ Establish a connection to a data source

♦ Send requests to the data source

♦ Perform translations when requested by the user application

♦ Return results to the user application

♦ Format errors in standard JDBC error codes

♦ Manipulate cursors if necessary

♦ Initiate transactions, if explicitly required

There are three types of JDBC drivers.

Proprietary Database Drivers: They process JDBC calls and send SQL statements to the data source. They may be "native-API partly-Java" or "native-protocol all-Java." A native-API driver forwards the calls to a locally installed library, usually developed in C and provided by the database vendor. It may be a Dynamic Link Library (DLL) or a .so shared library. Figure 3-3 shows native-API partly-Java drivers.

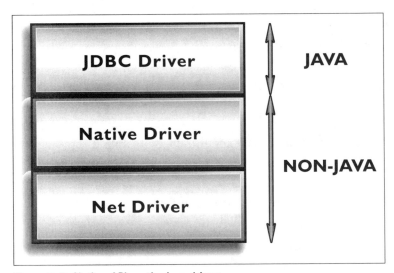

Figure 3-3: Native-API partly-Java drivers.

A native-protocol all-Java driver implements in Java all the layers necessary to communicate with the database. They are fully portable because they do not use local libraries or other native code. Figure 3-4 shows native-protocol all Java-drivers.

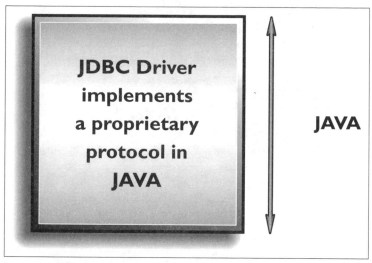

Figure 3-4: Native-protocol all Java-drivers.

Bridge Drivers: This driver creates a bridge between JDBC and another Call Level Interface (CLI). For example, the JDBC-ODBC Bridge is a bridge driver. It processes JDBC calls and, in turn, calls ODBC functions that will send SQL statements to the ODBC data source. Figure 3-5 shows the JDBC-ODBC Bridge driver.

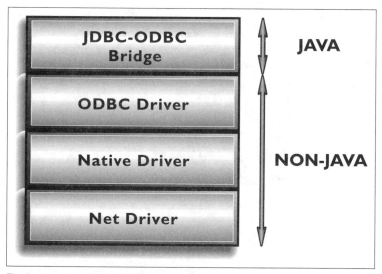

Figure 3-5: The JDBC-ODBC bridge driver.

DBMS-independent all-Java Net drivers: These drivers use a DBMS-independent published network protocol. They are very portable because they are 100 percent Java. Figure 3-6 shows the Net Driver.

Figure 3-6: The Net driver.

Data Source: The data source consists of the data the user application wants to access and its associated parameters — that is, the type of DBMS and network layer (if any) used to access the DBMS.

The JDBC interface defines the possible interactions between the user application and the driver manager. Figure 3-7 shows the relationship between the four JDBC components.

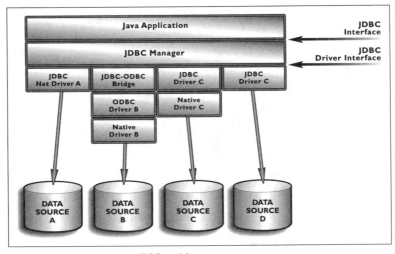

Figure 3-7: The complete JDBC architecture.

Integration Issues

Many applications call the ODBC interface or the native database drivers interfaces. In much the same way, if these applications were ported to Java, they would use the JDBC API to perform the same operations.

Consider these two questions when starting an integration project. First, will the future application, applet, or servlet be used in a trusted environment or on the Internet? Second, is it worth embedding all the application's logic into a separate tier as a hedge against the business rules evolving as fast as technology? The discussion of these issues in the following sections will help you decide which is the best architecture for your application's purpose.

Internet or Intranet?

If the application will be used within the intranet only, there is no need to worry about untrusted environments. Normally, every user that has access to the application will run a trusted system. According to today's security rules, this user can launch applications that connect to various hosts within various departments of the company to make a connection to applications and servers. Provided that these users run the usual desktop computer and operating system, they can use local file systems as well.

In contrast, if the application is deployed across the Internet to thousands or millions of unregistered users, it is mandatory to assume that these users run an untrusted environment. They are usually allowed to connect to your company's World Wide Web (WWW) server, browse pages, fill in forms, activate common gateway interfaces (CGIs), and download Java applets. These applets, while being real "applications" running on the client side, are usually not able to write to, or read from, local files. Unless the user specified otherwise, the user will not be able to open transmission control protocol (TCP) streams to arbitrary hosts on the Internet or within your company. In such a situation, it is not possible to rely on local resources such as parameters files, registry, or native libraries and drivers. On the contrary, everything must come from the network. In the case of a database application, these restrictions may impact the design of the application. For example, the location of the database server will not be looked up in a local file. No native database driver will be used. Chapter 4 discusses these issues. Also, the application usually connects to the host from which it came. This host is usually a WWW server. Depending on the architecture, this host may be running both the main WWW server and the DBMS server processes, or it may be running a smaller WWW server process that only delivers applets while also running the DBMS server. In this latter case, the main WWW server will present pages that refer to applets located at the uniform resource locator (URL) of the second dedicated WWW server.

It is possible, however, not to locate the DBMS on the WWW server. By using a third tier, for example, the DBMS may run on a dedicated machine with an enhanced input/output (I/O) subsystem. Again, it depends on the architecture, but from the software viewpoint, this middleware could provide specific services to the whole system.

The "Business Logic" of an Application

The business logic of an application is the way it operates according to the business rules. But what are these business rules? Are they standard colors? Standard screen layouts? Standard keyboard mappings? Generally, the business rules for the corporate data include:

◆ Standard formats

◆ Integrity rules

◆ Consistency rules

◆ Access control

For the operations allowed on the corporate data, the rules include:

◆ Creation/modification/replication/deletion of entities

◆ Execution of standard procedures

◆ Access control

Usually the actions are performed within the SQL language augmented with specifics of the underlying DBMS. These SQL statements are located on the client side and/or on the database side. For example, a SQL SELECT statement may be linked to a "PROCEED" button of the client graphical user interface (GUI), while other statements may be stored in the database as stored procedures. Whatever these statements will actually do, they will implicitly or explicitly use one or more business rules. What happens if the business rules change? It may be possible to modify the client code and the stored procedure that need modification according to the new rules. In the case of an application deployed to thousands of users, making such modifications may be problematic. There are some companies that need to adapt themselves to very frequent and important changes. Fortunately, there are solutions for such companies. Changing the stored procedures in one or more DBMSs is probably a lot easier than changing and deploying a thousand client applications. Because storing procedures in the DBMS offers a practical solution to well-known problems, the logic within stored procedures is usually kept in the

DBMS. That should not be true for the business logic inside client programs. Indeed, a third tier, best defined using an object paradigm, should embed most of the application's logic. In fact, applets solve the deployment problem because they are downloaded automatically each time they are requested, providing that the original versions are newer than those cached in the clients (if the clients support caching of applets).

Other Solutions

Many other solutions to the problem of modifying business rules have appeared since Java's early days. The problem concerned database application developers.

The CGI Approach

The CGI is usually implemented behind a World Wide Web server process on the same machine. While such CGIs may perform many tasks, such as sending e-mail or displaying the number of times a particular page was requested (hit count), they may also interact with a Database Management System and format hypertext markup language (HTML) pages "on the fly" for display in the user's browser. Figure 3-8 shows the CGI behind the Web server.

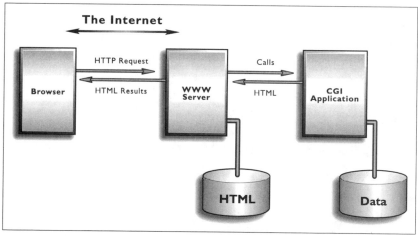

Figure 3-8: The CGI behind the WWW server.

Listing 3-1 is an example of an HTML form containing query fields. Submission of the form launches a CGI application on the Web server. This application opens a connection to a database and sends a SELECT query with the parameters passed as arguments. When the results are retrieved from the database, they are formatted and an HTML page is sent back to the client browser.

Listing 3-1: An HTML form.

```
<!DOCTYPE HTML PUBLIC "-//W3C//DTD HTML 3.2//EN">
<HTML>
<HEAD>
<TITLE>The CGI approach</TITLE>

</HEAD>
<BODY>
<H1>The CGI approach</H1>
<P>
<B>
/cgi-bin/emp_locator is a CGI which performs lookups in a database.
</B>
</P>
<P>
<HR>
<FORM METHOD="POST" ACTION="/cgi-bin/emp_locator">
<B>Employee Locator</B>
</P>
<P> Search on (multiple)
<SELECT NAME="LookFor" MULTIPLE>
<OPTION SELECTED>Name
<OPTION>Title
<OPTION>Department
<OPTION>Location
</SELECT>
</P>
<P>which
<SELECT NAME="How">
<OPTION SELECTED>starts with
<OPTION>contains
<OPTION>is exactly
<OPTION>sounds like
</SELECT>
</P>
<P>the following:
<INPUT TYPE="text" NAME="Match-pattern">
</P>
<P>
<INPUT TYPE="checkbox" NAME="Use-Case" VALUE="Yes">Case-sensitive
</P>
<P>
<INPUT TYPE="submit" VALUE="Submit">
</FORM>
<HR>
</P>
</BODY>
</HTML>
```

This HTML document displays the form in the browser window shown in Figure 3-9.

A Java applet that was downloaded from the network may perform some communication with the server from where it originated. Two kinds of mechanisms may be used to give an applet data that resides in a database.

In the first mechanism the applet connects itself to the server via the java.net.URL Connection class and asks the WWW server to initiate a common gateway interface that connects to the database, eventually sending it some parameters. This CGI application then forwards data to the applet as shown in Figure 3-10.

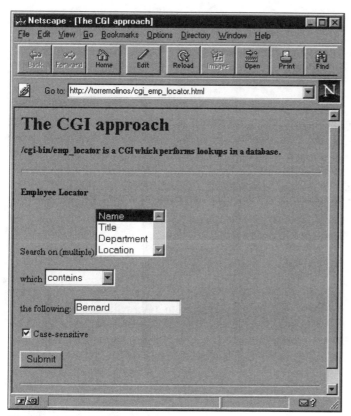

Figure 3-9: The CGI approach — HTML forms.

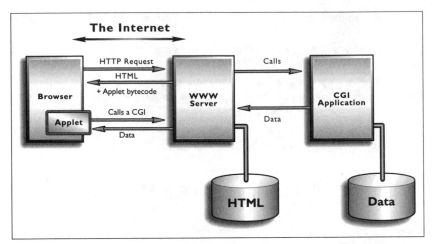

Figure 3-10: An applet using a proprietary protocol.

In this case, a Java applet sends the data used as input to the CGI application. As soon as the CGI retrieves the data from the database, it sends it back to the applet. This process is more interactive than the simple HTML form. Figure 3-11 shows such an applet.

There are two ways to send parameters to a CGI application: HTML GET form submission and HTML POST form submission. In the case studied here, the Java applet must mimic one of these ways. Here is an example of what must be sent along with the URL to perform a GET submission:

```
http://torremolinos/cgi-bin/emp_locator?LookFor=Name
&How=contains&pattern=Bernard
```

On the other hand, an HTML POST submission from Java will look like this:

```
POST /cgi-bin/emp_locator HTTP/1.0
Content-type: application/x-www-form-urlencoded
Content-length: 42
{your data goes here}
LookFor=Name&How=contains&pattern=Bernard
...
```

On behalf of data that was previously entered via HTML forms, the CGI application may build a custom HTML page containing an <APPLET> tag to tell the browser that an applet has to be downloaded. It can add <PARAMETERS> tags filled with data extracted from the database using the user's data that was previously entered through the HTML form, as shown in Figure 3-12.

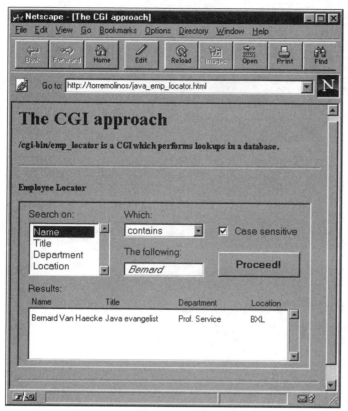

Figure 3-11: The Java applet approach.

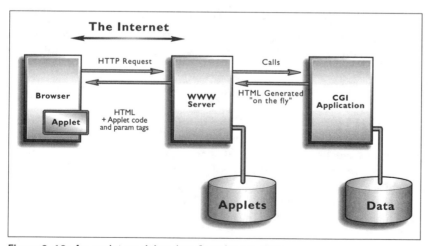

Figure 3-12: An applet receiving data from its parameters.

Listing 3-2 is an HTML form that is sent back to the client browser. It contains the applet tag and information passed as applet parameters. Such an HTML document is typically sent after a submission of values from an HTML form:

Listing 3-2: An HTML form.

```
<!DOCTYPE HTML PUBLIC "-//W3C//DTD HTML 3.2//EN">
<HTML>
<HEAD>
<TITLE>The CGI approach</TITLE>

</HEAD>
<BODY>
<H1>The CGI approach</H1>
<P>
<B>
/cgi-bin/emp_locator is a CGI which performs lookups in a database.
</B>
</P>
<P>
<HR>
<B>Employee Locator</B>
</P>
<APPLET CODE=myApplet width=600 height=500>
<PARAM NAME=name VALUE='Bernard Van Haecke'>
<PARAM NAME=title VALUE='Java evangelist'>
<PARAM NAME=location VALUE='BXL'>
</APPLET> <HR>
</P>
</BODY>
</HTML>
```

The first method to connect applets to a database is used when an interface is needed to build the query. The second connection method may be used only to process the results after an HTML POST or HTML GET submission.

While these approaches work, they have some inherent limitations. Because CGI applications add overhead to the WWW server, take care to avoid overloading the server.

Java Wrapper Classes

Java wrapper classes usually do not use JDBC classes to perform a database connection and send/retrieve data to and from the database. On the contrary, they often use native methods and libraries that are, by definition, not portable. They also offer a higher level of abstraction by mapping rows of data to Java objects data members, providing a solution to the impedance mismatch between SQL and Java.

Using JDBC with an ODBMS

While JDBC and JDBC drivers must support at least ANSI SQL-92 Entry Level, there are no limitations on the kind of statements that may be submitted to the Database Management System. An application query may be a specialized derivative of SQL. Many Object Database Management Systems (ODBMS) vendors have endorsed the JDBC specification. They will probably provide higher-level APIs to map directly stored objects to Java classes. The goal is to offer a persistent service for Java classes, without worrying about specific DBMS-API access issues that make programming more difficult and less efficient from a developer's point of view. Object databases are particularly well suited to store multimedia information. Among other kinds of data, they offer enhanced facilities to handle, store, retrieve, and query HTML documents, images, free text, video, audio, multidimensional graphics, and even Java objects. All these multimedia objects, if considered as persistent data members of an object-oriented programming language such as C++, Smalltalk, or Java, may then be manipulated very easily within such languages.

Using an Object/Relational DBMS Bridge

An Object/Relational DBMS bridge is a software tier that presents relational data in an object-oriented way and provides methods similar to those of ODBMSs. Like ODBMSs, such a bridge provides persistency to objects, but also integrates with a wide variety of relational DBMSs while exploiting their inherent specifications. An Object/Relational DBMS bridge may be used in conjunction with existing developments, thus preserving investments in resources such as relational DBMS engines, data they may contain, and physical resources associated with them. This software may be an alternative to using an Relational DBMS directly from JDBC.

Summary

This chapter discussed the integration of databases with Java using JDBC and other techniques, including:

- ◆ The role of JDBC
- ◆ The components of JDBC and their characteristics
- ◆ JDBC alternatives

The next chapter discusses the mechanisms, interfaces, and typical uses of JDBC.

Part II

Exploring JDBC

Part II presents JDBC in a comprehensive tutorial format — its architecture and components and all its features. You'll learn how to maximize its features and use the most advanced techniques.

After an introduction, you will study database connectivity using JDBC — step-by-step. You will then learn more advanced approaches to interact with a DBMS. Finally, you will study three-tiered architectures and DBMS integration, architecture, and design issues.

Chapter 4

Getting Started With JDBC

IN THIS CHAPTER
This chapter discusses the mechanisms used by JavaDatabase Conncectivity (JDBC), its programming interfaces, and some typical uses of JDBC.

JDBC is a set of programming interfaces. This chapter discusses which application programming interfaces (APIs) are of interest to the database application developer.

The JDBC Mechanisms

THE TWO MAJOR COMPONENTS of JDBC are the JDBC API and the JDBC Driver API. As Figure 4-1 shows, the JDBC API is a programming interface for database applications developers, while the JDBC Driver API is a lower level programming interface for developers of specific drivers. We focus on the JDBC API.

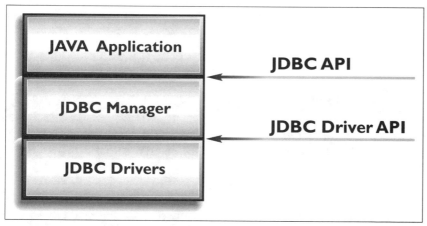

Figure 4–1: The JDBC APIs.

To write a successful database application with the Java Language Environment and JDBC, certain steps must be taken. These steps are very similar to those taken by C programmers using a Call Level Interface (CLI).

The first step is to create a method for connecting to the database, equivalent of a connection context, associated with a specific database driver. Eventually, parameters are provided to locate a specific database, to allow sign-on as a recognized user giving identification and authentication, and to target a specific database managed by the database management system (DBMS). Once a connection is established, various actions are allowed, including closing it, sending queries, updates, and everything that is called a SQL statement, including requests to execute a precompiled SQL statement and stored procedures. Of course, a mechanism to access the results sets is also provided. Figure 4-2 depicts the basic actions performed on the client and at the database side.

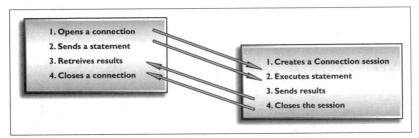

Figure 4-2: Actions performed on the client and at the DBMS sides.

A mechanism to handle errors is also provided. Exception management addresses this issue in Java by allowing the developer to call specific procedures after an error occurs.

The next section describes JDBC API interfaces in greater detail.

The JDBC Interfaces

The methods discussed in the prior section are expressed as Java interfaces that are implemented by specific database drivers. The JDBC interfaces that database application developers use are:

◆ **java.sql.DriverManager:** A class that provides methods to load drivers and to support the creation of database connections using methods expressed in the java.sql.Driver interface.

◆ **java.sql.Connection:** Represents a particular connection on which further actions will be allowed.

◆ **java.sql.Statement:** Associated to a connection, it allows SQL statements to be sent to the database.

◆ **java.sql.CallableStatement:** It has the same role as java.sql.Statement, but in the context of database stored procedures.

◆ **java.sql.PreparedStatement:** It also has the same role as java.sql.Statement, but in the context of precompiled SQL.

◆ **java.sql.ResultSet:** Allows access to the rows of a previously executed statement.

◆ **java.sql.ResultSetMetaData:** Gives information like type and properties of the columns in a result set.

◆ **java.sql.DatabaseMetaData:** Provides information about the database as a whole.

Figure 4-3 is a simplified view of the relationship between the driver manager and the connection, statement, and result set objects.

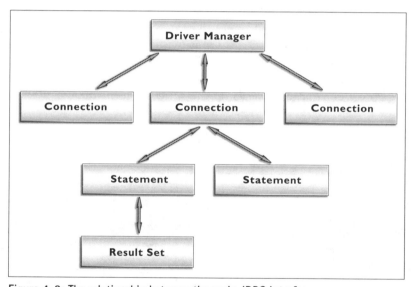

Figure 4-3: The relationship between the main JDBC interfaces.

Typical Use

Design choices between things that offer different qualities and drawbacks are made based on the targeted user community. To help evaluate the pros and cons of each choice, the next two sections explore different scenarios and show what is the best solution to address their problems.

Applications and Applets

Java's fame is mainly from its use of applets downloaded from the Internet. While the types of application are virtually unrestricted, there are still a few matters to consider.

The differences between untrusted applets and traditional applications are:

◆ An untrusted applet cannot access local files nor open arbitrary network connections to remote hosts. An application accesses the local file system according to the permissions granted the user.

◆ An untrusted applet cannot rely on specific facilities provided by the underlying operating system, such as a local registry, to locate a database. Applications often rely on such facilities; for example, Open Database Connectivity (ODBC) uses an .INI file or the registry, and most proprietary APIs use specific properties files.

◆ With an untrusted applet, response times may be arbitrary when traffic peaks arise on the Internet.

◆ Untrusted applets provide no way to estimate the maximum number of simultaneous users.

As Figure 4-4 shows, an applet is highly dependent on components that are not present in traditional scenarios — networks and application servers.

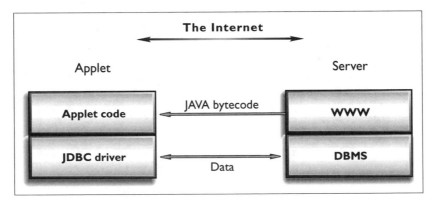

Figure 4-4: An applet communicating with a server.

These differences are not necessarily serious drawbacks. Indeed, it is neither necessary nor preferable for applets to look in specific files to locate a database. Complicated connection information may be provided, using parameters passed to the applet from within the HTML page, so the users will not have to remember long and cryptic URLs in order to open the JDBC connection.

Because this applet is trusted, for reasons such as it was signed with a cryptographic key or the user decided to trust applets from a specific host, does not mean that it will be allowed to behave in the same way as another application on the user's machine.

Another approach is the three-tier architecture, which is discussed in greater detail later. While some of its benefits were already explained, this approach solves what might be the applet's biggest problem. Eventually, the applet makes a connection to the third tier and requests or calls an action on a particular object. This request should trigger a conversation between the third tier and the database management system. In this case, connection information like database identification may be excluded from the applet's code. Figure 4-5 depicts such a three-tiered architecture.

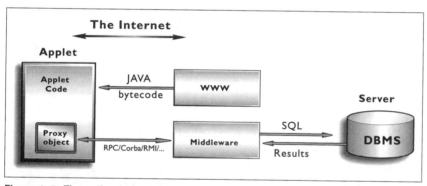

Figure 4-5: Three-tier design.

Java stand-alone applications are suitable within intranets and are deployable to specific users across the Internet, provided those users have access to some kind of parallel file transfer program. These applications run trusted code, are allowed to access the local file system, and open network connections to arbitrary hosts, just as normal applications do. Figure 4-6 represents the parts of a stand-alone application.

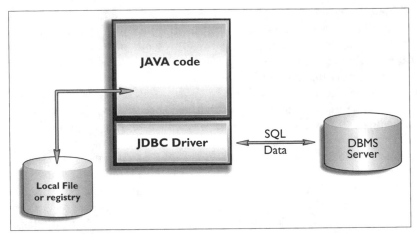

Figure 4-6: The parts of a stand-alone Java application.

ODBC Versus Specific Drivers as Subprotocol

ODBC is available on a wide variety of platforms, including Windows, Unix, and Macintosh environments. This wide use is not enough to make a Java-based project totally portable, but it is sufficient in many cases.

Using an ODBC leads to the same problem of deploying a non-Java underlying layer. It is very difficult to use such solutions on devices such as pure Network Terminals, but you may consider using an ODBC bridge or a native driver during development tests or within an environment known to be stable or not meant to evolve.

The reasons such solutions are difficult to use are:

◆ ODBC is a native component dependent on the platform

◆ ODBC uses a local registry or configuration file to look up data source names

◆ ODBC uses native drivers that are dependent on the platform

◆ ODBC is software that must be administered on each client platform separately

On the other hand, a full Java native-protocol driver, eventually using a third tier that does most of the job, offers these benefits:

♦ It is independent of the platform it is running on

♦ It uses a universal mechanism to name data sources — URLs

♦ It may be upgraded automatically

Summary

This chapter discussed the mechanisms used by JDBC, its programming interfaces, and some typical uses of JDBC.

The next chapter explains how to program with JDBC.

Chapter 5

Database Connectivity, Step by Step

IN THIS CHAPTER

This chapter discusses step-by-step programming with Java Database Connectivity (JDBC). This chapter includes:

◆ Initiating a database connection

◆ Sending simple SQL statements and retrieving results

◆ Error management

THIS CHAPTER EXPLAINS HOW to make a successful connection to a database, how to send SQL statements to this database, and how to retrieve the results. The procedure is very straightforward; typically, every database application developed using Java and JDBC uses it.

First Steps

JDBC is composed of a set of interfaces and classes that implement the functions needed to deal with a database management system (DBMS). We use these interfaces and classes in this chapter:

◆ java.sql.DriverManager

◆ java.sql.Driver

◆ java.sql.Connection

◆ java.sql.Statement

◆ java.sql.ResultSet

◆ java.sql.Date

◆ java.sql.Time

◆ java.sql.Timestamp

♦ java.sql.Types

♦ java.sql.DataTruncation

First, make sure that the JDBC Application Programming Interface (API) classes and specific drivers implementations are available on your system and reachable by following the `CLASSPATH` environment variable value. This environment variable should normally point to one or more directories where your Java classes are located. If necessary, update it or move the JDBC and drivers subdirectories to an appropriate location on your hard disk. When done, the Java class loader will be able to find these classes and will not try to download them from the network.

Typically, you should see a subtree resembling the following when scanning your `CLASSPATH` environment variable (`jdbc/odbc/…` was used for Listing 5-1; you may choose not to install it).

Listing 5-1: A typical class subtree.

```
classes/
+── java/
|  +── …/
|  |  |
|  +── sql/
|       +── CallableStatement.class
|       Connection.class
|       DatabaseMetaData.class
|       DataTruncation.class
|       Date.class
|       Driver.class
|       DriverInfo.class
|       DriverManager.class
|       DriverPropertyInfo.class
|       PreparedStatement.class
|       ResultSet.class
|       ResultSetMetaData.class
|       SQLException.class
|       SQLWarning.class
|       Statement.class
|       Time.class
|       Timestamp.class
|              Types.class
+──    jdbc/
+── odbc/
+──    JdbcOdbc.class
       JdbcOdbcBoundCol.class
       JdbcOdbcBoundParam.class
   …
   …
```

To make the JDBC classes available to the current class using the abbreviated name, use the import statement in source programs. The code will be more readable by not using the fully qualified names. So, the following line should be included at the top of the Java program, applet, or servlet:

```
import java.sql.*;
```

This statement is really useful for the programmer. Replace the star symbol with the relevant classes in the JDBC package.

Use the usual command line to compile your JDBC project:

```
% javac example.java
```

You may use the classpath parameter to specify additional Java classes that are not reachable through the CLASSPATH environment variable.

Database Connection

A connection must be initiated to access a database. The connection is a Java object containing Java methods to access the database. The connection class also holds information on the state of connections.. Various connection parameters are necessary, for example, to locate the database, to specify drivers and protocols, and to specify user account and password in the DBMS. The format of these parameters and how to set them is discussed later.

As shown in Figure 5-1, the first step is the establishment of a connection. The last step will, of course, be the termination ("closing") of the connection. Opening and closing the connection usually creates and releases user resources within the database management system and driver.

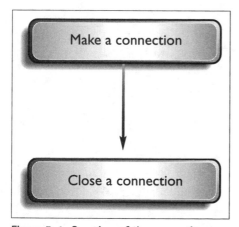

Figure 5-1: Overview of the connection.

To create an instance of a connection, it is necessary to understand the JDBC naming scheme.

JDBC's Database Naming

JDBC uses a particular syntax to name a database. The designers wanted to use a widely understood, appreciated, and supported convention: the Uniform Resource Locator (URL) syntax. In this case, the URL has the following form:

```
jdbc:<subprotocol>:<subname>
```

In this form, jdbc means that the protocol is JDBC, the subprotocol field is the name of the JDBC driver to be used, and the subname is a parameter string that is dependent on the subprotocol. Figure 5-2 illustrates the JDBC URL naming mechanism.

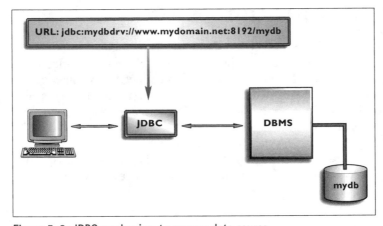

Figure 5-2: JDBC mechanism to name a data source.

These examples show some of the uses of database URLs:

```
jdbc:odbc:sampledb
```

A JDBC-Open Database Connectivity (ODBC) bridge will be used, and the ODBC DSN (data source name) is sampledb.

```
jdbc:odbc:sampledb;UID=javauser;PWD=hotjava
```

This URL is the same as the previous one, but adds a user-ID and password. Other attributes may also be added.

```
jdbc:mydbdrv://www.mydomain.net:8192/mydb
```

In this case, the subprotocol is called mydbdrv. The database engine is running on the www.mydomain.net host (the subname field), the Transmission Control

Protocol/Internet Protocol (TCP/IP) port that should be used is 8192, and `mydb` is the name of the database to be accessed. The significance of these parameters is somewhat arbitrary. For example, if the subprotocol (the driver) always uses the same port number, it is unnecessary to provide it in the URL. In this example, `mydb`, called a sub-subname, refers to a specific database instance. Other types of JDBC drivers may interpret the sub-subname as something else, other than a specific database instance name.

```
jdbc:dcenaming:employees
```

This URL suggests that a local Distributed Computing Environment (DCE) naming service should be used to locate the database named "employees." This service will resolve "employees" into a particular name more appropriate to locate the database engine. Another type of network naming protocol could be used, for example, NIS (Network Information System).

Note that the ODBC subprotocol URL should always conform to:

```
jdbc:odbc:<dsn>[;<attribute-name>=<attribute-value>]*
```

The JDBC URL syntax is flexible enough to allow specific drivers to interpret their own syntax.

JDBC Drivers

A specific database is usually reachable through one or more drivers. The Driver Manager and Driver objects provide methods to load a driver and handle driver properties. JDBC must have some knowledge about the available drivers. This knowledge comes from a jdbc.drivers system property. It can be set via the Java interpreter command line or via a property file.

Via the command line (which may be included in a shell script or batch file for greater convenience when invoking stand-alone programs):

```
% java -Djdbc.drivers=vendor1.driver1 example
```

Via a file, for example, when using the applet viewer or Sun's HotJava browser:

```
# On Unix, this file is ~/.hotjava/properties
jdbc.drivers=vendor1.driver1
```

While the database URL specifies a specific database and protocol to be used, it is sometimes preferable to let the JDBC choose between two or more drivers. In this case, it is possible to specify a driver list in the property called jdbc.drivers. The list of driver class names should be colon separated, for example:

```
'vendor1.dbdrv:vendor2.sql.foodriver:vendor3.db.connectdrv'
```

JDBC will try to use each of the drivers listed in jdbc.drivers until it finds one that can successfully connect to the given URL. Drivers that are untrusted code will be skipped. The driver will register itself with the driver manager to allow connections to be made.

In case the JDBC.driver system property is unavailable, there is a way to force a particular driver to be loaded. For example, the following line will load a JDBC-ODBC bridge driver:

```
Class.forName("sun.jdbc.odbc.JdbcOdbcDriver");
```

Another method is to use the following statements, but these statements will register the bridge driver class with the driver manager:

```
Driver myDriver = new sun.jdbc.odbc.JdbcOdbcDriver();
java.sql.DriverManager.registerDriver(myDriver);
```

INTERNALS

Methods are available to set or query driver and driver manager properties. They are used internally, and a programmer will usually not deal with them unless he or she wants to do some fine tuning. They are of interest for advanced programmers who need to discover and set specific properties.

For the moment, we will only see those dealing with JDBC message logging. Indeed, the driver manager and all drivers may issue logging and tracing information. A few methods are provided here to redirect these messages and to print specific messages in the log stream.

DriverManager

```
void setLogStream(java.io.PrintStream out);
java.io.PrintStream getLogStream();
void println(String logmessage);
```

Here is the explanation:

```
void setLogStream(java.io.PrintStream out);
```

The setLogStream() method sets the logging print stream that is used by the driver manager and by the drivers. It can be set to null to disable this facility.

```
java.io.PrintStream getLogStream();
```

The getLogStream() returns the print stream that is used for logging and tracing. It returns null when logging and tracing is disabled.

```
void println(String logmessage);
```

This method, shown in Listing 5-2, is used to send a message to the logging stream.

Listing 5-2: The log stream.

```
// setting the log stream
import java.sql.*;
class SimpleExample
{
  public static void main(String args[])
  {
  try {
  String url = "jdbc:odbc:mysource";
  Class.forName("sun.jdbc.odbc.JdbcOdbcDriver");
  DriverManager.setLogStream(java.lang.System.out);
  DriverManager.println("Driver registered with the DriverManager!");
  // ...
  } catch (java.lang.Exception ex) {}
  }
}
```

More advanced methods of driver manager are discussed in Chapter 6.

CREATING A CONNECTION

Before creating a connection, it is necessary to declare it. It is quite simple; just say that you need a connection object and name it:

```
Connection myConnection;
```

In this example, the connection object is named: `myConnection`.

To connect to the data source, the connection object must be made. The method that provides this functionality is:

```
java.sql.DriverManager.getConnection();
```

The following statement creates a connection object that will send statements to the database. The URL naming convention is used with the `getConnection()` method and is the way to specify the data source that is targeted.

```
String url = "jdbc:odbc:mysource";
Connection myConnection = DriverManager.getConnection(url,
  "javauser", "hotjava");
```

This example shows how to pass the URL string to the driver manager plus specific arguments to the driver itself. In this case:

- ◆ The protocol used is JDBC
- ◆ The driver is a JDBC-ODBC bridge

◆ The ODBC DSN is "mysource"

◆ A username is provided: "javauser"

◆ A password is provided: "hotjava"

The driver manager will try to find a registered JDBC driver that is allowed to reach the data source that is specified in the URL.

There are other methods that allow the user to get a connection to the database. They have the same name, but different parameters to differentiate these methods.

DriverManager

```
Connection getConnection(String url);
Connection getConnection(String url, String user, String password);
Connection getConnection(String url, java.util.Properties info);

Connection getConnection(String url);
```

The getConnection(String url) method does not use specific parameters to provide the user name and password. If necessary, and if allowed by the specific driver, these values may be passed within the URL string as shown in this example:

```
String url = "jdbc:odbc:mysource;UID=javauser;PWD=hotjava";
Connection myConnection = DriverManager.getConnection(url);

Connection getConnection(String url, String user, String password);
```

The getConnection(String url, String user, String password) method sends the second and third parameters to the driver and it usually interprets them as the user name and password to connect to the data source.

```
Connection getConnection(String url, java.util.Properties info);
```

In the case of the getConnection(String url, java.util.Properties info) method, the second parameter is a list of arbitrary string pairs such as "user" and its value, and "password" and its value. These two connection arguments should be included in the list. The list of such properties should be included in the driver's documentation. However, it is preferable to pass as much information as possible within the database URL.

What we learned so far allows us to begin our first Java stand-alone application. Listing 5-3 shows how to open a connection.

Listing 5-3: How to open a connection.

```
// opening a connection
import java.sql.*;
class SimpleExample
{
```

```
public static void main(String args[])
{
try {
String url = "jdbc:odbc:mysource";
Class.forName("sun.jdbc.odbc.JdbcOdbcDriver");
Connection myConnection =
     DriverManager.getConnection(url,
"javauser", "hotjava");
     // ...
     } catch (java.lang.Exception ex) {}
 }
}
```

CLOSING A CONNECTION

Because we learned how to open a connection, it seems reasonable to learn how to close it before going further.

Connection

```
void close();
boolean isClosed();
void setAutoClose(boolean autoclose);
boolean getAutoClose();
```

These methods all apply to a connection instance.

```
void close();
```

The close() method simply closes the current connection. Normally, a connection closes automatically when it is garbage-collected or when certain fatal errors occur. It may, however, be desirable to immediately close a connection under some circumstances.

```
boolean isClosed();
```

The isClosed returns true if the connection is closed, and false if it is open.

```
void setAutoClose(boolean autoclose);
```

A connection is normally in autoclose mode by default. Because other objects may depend on specific connections (for example, statements and result sets objects, which are discussed later), it may be necessary to keep a connection open after a transaction has been committed or rolled back (canceled). The setAutoClose() allows you to disable auto closing.

```
boolean getAutoClose();
```

This method returns true in case the connection is in autoclose state, and false in the opposite case. Listing 5-4 shows how to close a connection.

Listing 5-4: Closing a connection.

```
// closing a connection
import java.sql.*;
class SimpleExample
{
  public static void main(String args[])
  {
      try {
      // ...
      String url = "jdbc:odbc:mysource";
      Class.forName("sun.jdbc.odbc.JdbcOdbcDriver");
      Connection myConnection =
      DriverManager.getConnection(url,
            "javauser", "hotjava");
      // ...
  if (!myConnection.isClosed())
     myConnection.close();
      // ...
      } catch (java.lang.Exception ex) {}
  }
}
```

Adjusting Properties

It is possible to set and query connection properties that affect the general behavior of commands to be performed within the connection.

CONNECTION BEHAVIOR

The methods available to set and query the connection object are listed below.

Connection

```
void setReadOnly(boolean readonly);
boolean isReadOnly();
void setCatalog(String catalog);
String getCatalog();


void setReadOnly(boolean readonly);
```

It may be necessary to put a connection in read-only mode. By default, it is not set as read-only. Setting it in read-only mode may sometimes be practical and may enable database optimizations where the connection will not be used for database updates.

```
boolean isReadOnly();
```

The return is true if the connection has been set in read-only mode. Use
isReadOnly to test the connection mode.

```
void setCatalog(String catalog);
```

A catalog is a database subspace containing the database objects affected by the
operations performed within the connection. Some DBMSs manage multiple databases at the same time. It is possible to restrict the subspace to one or another database using the setCatalog() method. Where the DBMS or the driver associated
with the connection does not support catalogs, this method will silently ignore all
calls to it.

```
String getCatalog();
```

The getCatalog() method will give the catalog name that is currently in use or
a null value. Listing 5-5 shows how to adjust connection properties.

Listing 5–5: Adjusting connection properties.

```
// adjusting connection properties
import java.sql.*;
class SimpleExample
{
  public static void main(String args[])
  {
  try {
      // ...
      String url = "jdbc:odbc:mysource";
      Class.forName("sun.jdbc.odbc.JdbcOdbcDriver");
      Connection myConnection =
      DriverManager.getConnection(url,
            "javauser", "hotjava");
      if (myConnection.isReadOnly())
      System.out.println("Connection is read only");
      myConnection.setReadOnly(true);
      System.out.println("Default catalog: " +
      myConnection.getCatalog());
      // use the pubs2 database
myConnection.setCatalog("pubs2");
      // ...
      if (!myConnection.isClosed())
      myConnection.close();
      // ...
      } catch (java.lang.Exception ex) {}
  }
}
```

PUTTING IT ALL TOGETHER

The essential steps in every Java project that uses JDBC to obtain and terminate a connection to a DBMS are:

- ◆ Import java.sql.* to avoid long member names

- ◆ Build a JDBC URL

- ◆ Load one or more specific JDBC driver with class.forName()

- ◆ If necessary, set the JDBC log stream with setLogStream()

- ◆ If necessary, adjust the connection properties

- ◆ Open a connection with getConnection()

- ◆ Terminate the connection with close()

A DO-NOTHING CLIENT

The example in Listing 5-6 does nothing but open a connection and close it. The JDBC log stream is set to the standard output to trace everything that happens.

Listing 5-6: A do-nothing client.

```
// a do-nothing client
import java.sql.*;
class SimpleExample
{
 public static void main(String args[])
 {
 String url = "jdbc:odbc:mysource";
      try
      {
      Class.forName("sun.jdbc.odbc.JdbcOdbcDriver");
      DriverManager.setLogStream(
            java.lang.System.out);
            Connection myConnection =
            DriverManager.getConnection(url,
                 "javauser", "hotjava");
            myConnection.close();
      }
      catch(java.lang.Exception ex)
      {
            ex.printStackTrace();
      }
 }
}
```

Note that code to catch java.lang.Exception is explicitly included. We will see later what this means. For the moment, just note that the compiler would complain if we do not catch it.

```
2 errors
compiling: ex.java
ex.java(13): Exception java.lang.ClassNotFoundException must be
  caught, or it must be declared in the throws clause of this method.
Class.forName("sun.jdbc.odbc.JdbcOdbcDriver");
  ^
ex.java(15): Exception java.sql.SQLException must be caught, or it
  must be declared in the throws clause of this method.
DriverManager.getConnection(url,
  ^
```

What happens? The following lines are printed to the JDBC log stream shown in Listing 5-7 during the execution of this small Java program:

Listing 5-7: JDBC log stream.

```
DriverManager.getConnection("jdbc:odbc:mysource")
trying
  driver[className=sun.jdbc.odbc.JdbcOdbcDriver,context=null,jdbc.odb
  c.JdbcOdbcDriver@1393878]
*Driver.connect (jdbc:odbc:mysource)
JDBC to ODBC Bridge: Checking security
No SecurityManager present, assuming trusted application/applet
JDBC to ODBC Bridge 1.0
Current Date/Time: Wed Aug 07 19:42:19 1996
Loading JdbcOdbc library
Allocating Environment handle (SQLAllocEnv)
hEnv=5308508
Allocating Connection handle (SQLAllocConnect)
hDbc=5310680
Connecting (SQLDriverConnect), hDbc=5310680,
  szConnStrIn=DSN=mysource;UID=javauser;PWD=hotjava
RETCODE = 1
getConnection returning
  driver[className=sun.jdbc.odbc.JdbcOdbcDriver,context=null,sun.jdbc
  .odbc.JdbcOdbcDriver@1393878]
*Connection.close
Disconnecting (SQLDisconnect), hDbc=5310680
Closing connection (SQLFreeConnect), hDbc=5310680
Closing environment (SQLFreeEnv), hEnv=5308508
```

The JDBC log is quite long, and we actually did nothing but open and close a connection. It is interesting to see all the silently performed actions.

Sending SQL Statements

The connection object will send SQL statements to the database engine. There are different methods to perform this, depending on the kind of operation needed. In this chapter, we focus on sending normal SQL statements. Unlike prepared statements or calls to stored procedures that are discussed later, normal SQL statements are usually constructed, sent, and executed only once. This is, for example, the case within an interactive query tool where the user builds his or her own queries. Normal statements include both statements to query data from the database and statements to update its data.

BUILDING STATEMENTS

The step that directly follows the creation of the connection is the creation of a SQL statement. This does not mean that it is forbidden to build a SQL query string before opening the connection. You are free to do this. The exact meaning is that a JDBC statement is an object associated to a connection and it will be used later to request an execution of a SQL string within this connection environment space in the DBMS.

As shown in Figure 5-3, the step order is very simple.

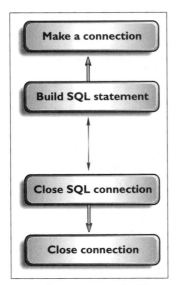

Figure 5-3: Overview: Building a SQL statement.

Closing the SQL statement releases all the data associated with the statement. Here is the method to build a statement object.

Connection

```
Statement createStatement();
Statement createStatement();
```

The statement object is obtained by calling this method on the connection instance, as shown in Listing 5-8.

Listing 5-8: How to create a statement.

```
...
...
Connection myConnection = DriverManager.getConnection(url,
                "javauser", "hotjava");
Statement myStatement = myConnection.createStatement();
myConnection.close();
...
...
```

SENDING STATEMENTS

The SQL statement is sent to the DBMS where it is parsed, optimized, and executed. But we have not yet built the statement text. Indeed, the SQL string passes to the database when the call for execution of the statement is issued, as shown in Figure 5-4.

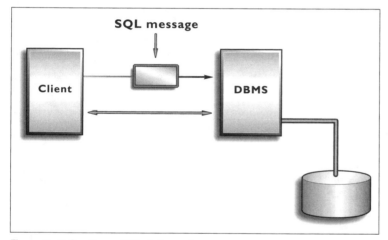

Figure 5-4: Sending a SQL statement.

The driver converts this SQL string into the DBMS native SQL grammar. It is possible to see the converted string without sending it to the database. Usually, you will not use this facility, but sometimes it is necessary to know what the native translation of a query is prior to sending it.

Connection

```
String nativeSQL(String sql);
```
The method applies on the connection object because it is DBMS-dependent. Indeed, a connection is associated to one and only one DBMS through its driver.

```
String nativeSQL(String sql);
```

The string passed as an argument is the "user" SQL statement; `nativeSQL()` returns the native form of this statement. Listing 5-9 shows the language to obtain the native SQL translation.

Listing 5-9: Native SQL translation.

```
. . .
. . .
Connection myConnection = DriverManager.getConnection(url,
            "javauser", "hotjava");
Statement myStatement = myConnection.createStatement();
String myQuery("SELECT * FROM employees ORDER BY salary
 DESCENDING");
System.out.println("This query: " + myQuery);
System.out.println("is sent to the DBMS as: " +
 myConnection.nativeSQL(myQuery));
myConnection.close();
. . .
. . .
```

All the previous steps, opening a connection and creating a statement, are necessary before executing a query. None of them can be skipped. Figure 5-5, while still somewhat simple, shows the current action sequence.

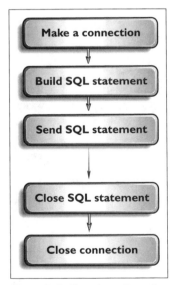

Figure 5-5: Overview of sending
a SQL statement.

The method chosen to send a SQL statement to the database depends on the type of statement and type of data it returns.

Statement

```
ResultSet executeQuery(String sql);
int executeUpdate(String sql);
boolean execute(String sql);

ResultSet executeQuery(String sql);
```

If the query returns normal rows of data, then the executeQuery() should be used. In this case, the query is typically a static SQL SELECT statement. The SQL text is simply passed as a string argument. It does not have to be translated to the native form with nativeSQL(). This method returns a result set object that is discussed in the next section of this chapter.

```
int executeUpdate(String sql);
```

If the SQL statement returns nothing [returning nothing is different than returning zero (0) rows] or returns an integer value, as is the case with SQL INSERT, UPDATE, or DELETE clauses, executeUpdate should be used. The call returns the integer value or 0 (zero) for statements that return nothing.

```
boolean execute(String sql);
```

When a SQL statement returns more than one result, execute() has to be used to request execution of the statement. The section on multiple result sets discusses this issue in detail. Listing 5-10 shows how to execute a query.

Listing 5-10: How to execute a query.

```
// how to execute a query
import java.sql.*;
class SimpleExample
{
 public static void main(String args[])
  {
  String url = "jdbc:odbc:mysource";
      try
      {
      Class.forName("sun.jdbc.odbc.JdbcOdbcDriver");
      DriverManager.setLogStream(
            java.lang.System.out);
            Connection myConnection =
                  DriverManager.getConnection(url,
                        "javauser", "hotjava");
            Statement myStatement =
                  myConnection.createStatement();
            ResultSet rs = myStatement.executeQuery(
"SELECT name, id, salary FROM employees ORDER BY" +
"salary DESC");
            myConnection.close();
```

```
        }
        catch(java.lang.Exception ex)
        {
                ex.printStackTrace();
        }
   }
}
```

The example in Listing 5-11 illustrates the executeUpdate() method:

Listing 5-11: How to perform an update.

```
// how to execute an update
import java.sql.*;
class SimpleExample
{
  public static void main(String args[])
  {
  String url = "jdbc:odbc:mysource";
      try
      {
      Class.forName("sun.jdbc.odbc.JdbcOdbcDriver");
      DriverManager.setLogStream(
                 java.lang.System.out);
            Connection myConnection =
                 DriverManager.getConnection(url,
            "javauser", "hotjava");
            Statement myStatement =
                 myConnection.createStatement();
            int res = myStatement.executeUpdate("UPDATE" +
  employees SET salary = salary*1.1 WHERE id = 1");
            myConnection.close();
      }
      catch(java.lang.Exception ex)
      {
                ex.printStackTrace();
      }
   }
}
```

CLOSING A STATEMENT

It is often necessary to close explicitly a statement after the DBMS executes it. Indeed, database context and JDBC statement resources stay open until the connection is closed or the statement is garbage-collected. It is not desirable to consume resources when there is no reason to do so. Closing the statement also closes the returned result set.

   STATEMENT

```
void close();
```

```
void close();
```

The close() method is simply called on a statement object and takes no arguments.

SENDING BLOBS

It is sometimes necessary to send and retrieve pictures, sound, or other multimedia files to a database. This kind of object is called a Binary Large Object (BLOB). While it has absolutely nothing to do with Java objects [nor C++ or other object-oriented programming (OOP) language object], BLOB is not restricted to images, sound, and multimedia content. For example, a multikilobyte or multimegabyte text is also a BLOB. BLOBs do not have to be ASCII or Unicode; they may be pure binary.

Insertion, update, or retrieval of very large values is usually done by passing the values in small chunks of data. This approach is often more convenient for programmers. JDBC, however, uses data streams. JDBC provides three kinds of streams: ASCII streams, Unicode streams, and binary streams.

Because there is no way to send streams within a simple SQL statement, the streams pass as parameters. Refer to the dynamic SQL section to learn how to send BLOBs to the database.

ADJUSTING PROPERTIES

Properties that change the default behavior of JDBC or of the driver exist. They can be set before sending the SQL statement to the database.

DATA TRUNCATION WHEN SENDING DATA   Data truncation happens when inserting or updating data in the database. This truncation is dependent on the DBMS and driver that fixes the maximum size for data types. An error usually happens if the truncation occurs during a database write. JDBC provides a method to limit the size of a field to a maximum value; if the limit is exceeded, JDBC raises a SQLException.

Statement

```
void setMaxFieldSize(int max);
int getMaxFieldSize();

void setMaxFieldSize(int max);
```

The method setMaxFieldSize() allows the programmer to set a maximum field size that will be valid on the current statement. The parameter is the number of bytes allowed.

```
int getMaxFieldSize();
```

The method getMaxFieldSize() returns the maximum size allowed for the current statement. Listing 5-12 shows data truncation on write.

Listing 5-12: Data truncation on write.

```
// data truncation on write
import java.sql.*;
class SimpleExample
{
 public static void main(String args[])
 {
 String url = "jdbc:odbc:mysource";
     try
     {
...
...
Connection myConnection =
 DriverManager.getConnection(url, "javauser", "hotjava");
Statement myStatement = myConnection.createStatement();
myStatement.setMaxFieldSize(12);
int res = myStatement.executeUpdate("UPDATE
 employees SET comment = 'The quick br...' WHERE name='jones'");
...
...
     }
     catch(java.lang.Exception ex)
     {
          ex.printStackTrace();
     }
  }
}
```

TIME-OUTS

The execution of a statement may be delayed for one of several reasons. A mechanism called time-out exists so programmers have a way to handle such situations. The query time-out is the time the JDBC driver will wait for a statement to execute. If the limit is exceeded, the driver raises an exception. This exception may be caught, and one or more retries initiated.

Statement

```
void setQueryTimeout(int seconds);
int getQueryTimeout();

void setQueryTimeout(int seconds);
```

This is the method used to set a limit to the time-out mechanism. The parameter is the number of seconds it will wait before raising the SQLException. A zero value means no limit.

```
int getQueryTimeout();
```

The method `getQueryTimeout()` returns the number of seconds corresponding to the time-out limit. A zero value also means there is no limit and that the driver can wait forever if necessary. Listing 5-13 shows time-outs.

Listing 5-13: Time-outs.

```
// time-outs
...
...
Connection myConnection =
  DriverManager.getConnection(url, "javauser", "hotjava");
Statement myStatement = myConnection.createStatement();
// we do not want to wait forever
myStatement.setQueryTimeout(10);
int res = myStatement.executeUpdate("UPDATE
  employees SET salary = 1000000 WHERE name='jones'");
...
...
```

Another property may prove useful when sending data to the database: the setting for the escape sequence.

Statement

```
void setEscapeProcessing(boolean enable);
```
This statement enables or disables escape substitution by the driver. Escape substitution is the default behavior and occurs before sending the SQL statement to the database. When enabled, the driver translates escape syntax strings to native SQL (see Chapter 6 on SQL Escape Syntax).

What We Have Done So Far

This section reviews what has been covered thus far.

◆ Import java.sql.* to avoid having to write long member names

◆ Build a JDBC URL

◆ Load one or more specific JDBC driver with `class.forName()`

◆ If necessary, set the JDBC log stream with `setLogStream()`

◆ If necessary, adjust the connection properties

◆ Open a connection with `getConnection()`

◆ Create a statement object

◆ Build a SQL statement

◆ Execute the SQL statement

◆ Close the statement

◆ Terminate the connection with close()

Example

Here is an example for executing a statement. It sends a SQL query to a database with a time-out value of 180 seconds. Listing 5-14 shows the code for executing a statement.

Listing 5-14: Executing a statement.

```
// executing a statement
import java.sql.*;
class SimpleExample
{
  public static void main(String args[])
  {
  String url = "jdbc:odbc:mysource";
      try
      {
      Class.forName("sun.jdbc.odbc.JdbcOdbcDriver");
      DriverManager.setLogStream(
            java.lang.System.out);
            Connection myConnection =
            DriverManager.getConnection(url,
                  "javauser", "hotjava");
      Statement myStatement =
                  myConnection.createStatement();
      myStatement.setQueryTimeout(180);
      ResultSet rs = myStatement.executeQuery(
            "SELECT * FROM employees");
      myStatement.close();
            myConnection.close();
      }
      catch(java.lang.Exception ex)
      {
            ex.printStackTrace();
      }
  }
}
```

Handling Results

A DBMS usually returns results after executing a statement. The results are of different types. The `executeQuery()` method returns a result set object, and the `executeUpdate()` returns an integer. Of course, because the result of the `executeQuery()` method will always be used within the program, it would be useless to discard the result of a SQL query. In the case of an update, the result should also be used, at least to verify that everything happened as expected and to discover how many rows of data were affected by the update.

Fetchable Result Types

The SQL clauses listed in Table 5-1 return known result types: rows of data and/or integer value.

TABLE 5-1 DIFFERENT STATEMENTS RETURN DIFFERENT RESULT TYPES

Type of SQL statement	Type returned
CREATE TABLE employees (...)	nothing
SELECT * FROM employees	rows and integer
SELECT MAX(salary) FROM employees	rows and integer
UPDATE employees SET salary = 70000	
WHERE name = "Jones"	integer
INSERT INTO employees VALUES (...)	integer
DELETE FROM employees	
WHERE salary > 150000	integer

In summary, there are two possible result set return types: an integer or a result set composed of rows of table data. Of course, there are different methods for handling such results, and there is even a way to discover the result type of an unknown SQL query.

GETTING THE RESULT SET

SQL statements that return an integer such as DELETE, UPDATE, and INSERT do not need additional processing. The method to send them returns an integer and is usually interpreted as a counter. Other SQL statements do not return rows of data or a counter.

This is not the case with queries that return normal rows of data. The result set will be composed of zero or more rows coming from the database. The following step scans this result set, row by row, until all rows have been fetched. This operation is done within a loop, as shown in Figure 5-6. We will see later how to analyze the data that compose rows.

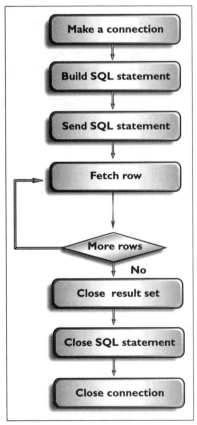

Figure 5-6: Overview of getting the result set.

The result set object is created when sending the statement to the DBMS. It is created by executing the statement object. Closing the result set releases all data associated with the result set.

RETRIEVING ROWS

Result sets are composed of rows. The `ResultSet.next()` method is used in the loop to access these rows.

ResultSet

```
boolean next();
```

Figure 5-7 illustrates the mechanism used to scan the rows in the result set.

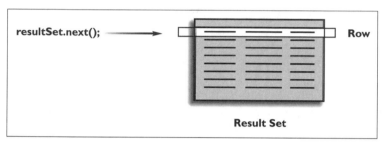

resultSet.next();   Row

Result Set

Figure 5-7: The `next()` method is used to scan a result set.

```
boolean next();
```

It is important to position the cursor before the first row of the result set. The method `next()` needs to be called first to access the first row. After the first call, the first row becomes the current row, and it is ready to be processed. Successive calls to `next()` will make the next rows current, row by row, of course. Listing 5-15 shows how to scan a result set.

Listing 5-15: How to scan a result set.

```
...
Connection myConnection = DriverManager.getConnection(url,
                "javauser", "hotjava");
Statement myStatement = myConnection.createStatement();
ResultSet rs = myStatement.executeQuery(sqlQuery);
while (rs.next())
{
  // we got a row
}
myStatement.close();
myConnection.close();
...
...
```

GETTING THE NUMBER AND LABEL OF COLUMNS

A row is usually composed of table data that may be organized in different columns of different types. It may be important to discover the properties of the result set's rows, the number of columns, and the type of data in each column. We will see later how to get such information about result sets. Only the column number and column labels will be used now.

ResultSet

```
int getMetaData().getColumnCount();
String getMetaData().getColumnLabel(int i);
```

The `getMetaData()` method returns a `ResultSetMetaData` object that is explained later because it is quite complex. Calling `getColumnCount()` on this object returns the expected value.

```
int getMetaData().getColumnCount();
```

The return type is integer and is the number of columns in the rows composing this result set.

```
String getMetaData().getColumnLabel(int i);
```

The parameter is the column index where a value of 1 indicates the first column. The method obviously returns the label for the column at this index.

It may be more efficient to store the `ResultSetMetaData` object once instead of calling the method to create it each time it is necessary to access a property. The driver may provide caching, but it is often preferable not to abuse such features when not really needed. Listing 5-16 shows how to call these methods.

Listing 5-16: Getting the number and label of columns.

```
...
Connection myConnection = DriverManager.getConnection(url,
                "javauser", "hotjava");
Statement myStatement = myConnection.createStatement();
ResultSet rs = myStatement.executeQuery(sqlQuery);
int maxColumns = rs.getMetaData().getColumnCount();
for (int i = 1; i <= maxColumns; i++)
{
  if (i > 1) System.out.print(", ");
  System.out.print(rs.getMetaData().getColumnLabel(i));
}
System.out.println("====================================");
while (rs.next())
{
  // we got a row
}
```

```
myStatement.close();
myConnection.close();
...
...
```

ACCESSING COLUMNS

As shown in Figure 5-8, columns must be fetched one by one, in left-to-right order. Fetching may be done in a loop using the column indexes or column names discovered by the ResultSetMetaData object.

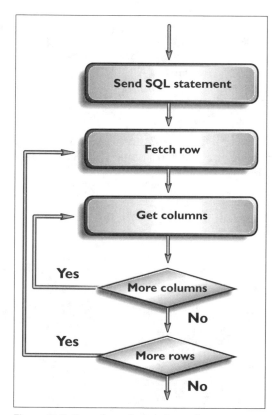

Figure 5-8: Overview of accessing columns.

The row's contents are accessible via "getXXX()" methods that allow the extraction of the various values of the columns of rows in the result set.

There are two ways of accessing columns: by column index or by column name. Accessing a column by name is more convenient, but less efficient because it internally needs many comparisons of strings before finding the column. Certain SQL statements return tables without column names or with multiple identical column names. It is absolutely necessary to use column numbers in these cases. Figure 5-9 illustrates the access to a row's columns.

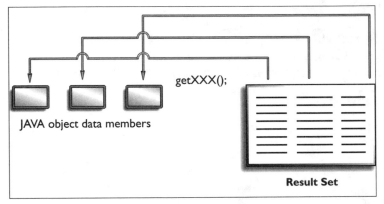

Figure 5-9: Accessing columns with getXXX().

All columns within a row must be read in left-to-right order, and each column must only be read once. This rule may not be true with some DBMSs, but it is preferable to observe it to ensure maximum portability.

BY COLUMN INDEXES
Below is the list of "getXXX()" methods available to fetch columns in a row:

Result Set

```
String getString(int columnIndex);
boolean getBoolean(int columnIndex);
byte getByte(int columnIndex);
short getShort(int columnIndex);
int getInt(int columnIndex);
long getLong(int columnIndex);
float getFloat(int columnIndex);
double getDouble(int columnIndex);
java.math.BigDecimal getBigDecimal(int columnIndex, int scale);
byte[] getBytes(int columnIndex);
java.sql.Date getDate(int columnIndex);
java.sql.Time getTime(int columnIndex);
java.sql.Timestamp getTimestamp(int columnIndex);
java.io.InputStream getAsciiStream(int columnIndex);
java.io.InputStream getUnicodeStream(int columnIndex);
java.io.InputStream getBinaryStream(int columnIndex);
Object getObject(int columnIndex);
```

```
return_type getXXX(int columnIndex);
```

All these methods return the column value in the current row. Column indexes are integers.

This example shows how to execute a SQL statement and retrieve the results using column indexes. Note that the rows are always read from left-to-right and that columns are only read once. Listing 5-17 shows the statement using column indexes.

Listing 5-17. Using column indexes.

```
...
java.sql.Statement myStatement = myConnection.createStatement();
ResultSet rs = myStatement.executeQuery("SELECT name, title, salary
                    FROM employees");
while (rs.next()) {
 // print the columns of the row that was retrieved
 String empName = rs.getString(1);
 String empTitle = rs.getString(2);
 long empSalary = rs.getLong(3);
 System.out.println("Employee " + empName + " is " + empTitle + "
                    and earns $" + empSalary);
}
...
...
```

BY COLUMN NAMES
Column names may be more convenient to use. Here are the "getXXX()" methods supporting column names:

ResultSet

```
String getString(String columnName);
boolean getBoolean(String columnName);
byte getByte(String columnName);
short getShort(String columnName);
int getInt(String columnName);
long getLong(String columnName);
float getFloat(String columnName);
double getDouble(String columnName);
java.math.BigDecimal getBigDecimal(String columnName, int scale);
byte[] getBytes(String columnName);
java.sql.Date getDate(String columnName);
java.sql.Time getTime(String columnName);
java.sql.Timestamp getTimestamp(String columnName);
java.io.InputStream getAsciiStream(String columnName);
java.io.InputStream getUnicodeStream(String columnName);
java.io.InputStream getBinaryStream(String columnName);
Object getObject(String columnName);


return_type getXXX(String columnName);
```

The parameter should match exactly with the row's column name that needs to be accessed.

The same example using column names is shown in Listing 5-18.

Listing 5-18: Using column names.

```
...
java.sql.Statement myStatement =
                          myConnection.createStatement();
ResultSet rs = myStatement.executeQuery("SELECT name, title, salary
  FROM employees");
while (rs.next()) {
// print the columns of the row that was retrieved
String empName = rs.getString("name");
String empTitle = rs.getString("title");
long empSalary = rs.getLong("salary");
System.out.println("Employee " + empName + " is " + empTitle + " and
  earns $" + empSalary);
}
...
...
```

Managing multiple result types

As discussed earlier, the methods that send SQL queries and SQL updates are different. SQL queries return result sets; SQL updates return a count of the rows updated. SQL statements will normally execute using query and update methods. However, under some circumstances, it may be difficult to estimate the type of result. An application may not know whether a given SQL statement will return a result set or a counter until the statement executes, as, for example, in the case of an interactive query tool or when calling an unknown stored procedure.

A mechanism is provided to accommodate these needs. It allows an application to execute statements and then process an arbitrary collection of sets of rows and single update counts. Figure 5-10 gives an idea of the steps performed in this scenario.

How is it possible to distinguish the difference between return types? The following methods give the answer.

Statement:

```
boolean execute(String sql);
ResultSet getResultSet();
int getUpdateCount();
boolean getMoreResults();

boolean execute(String sql);
```

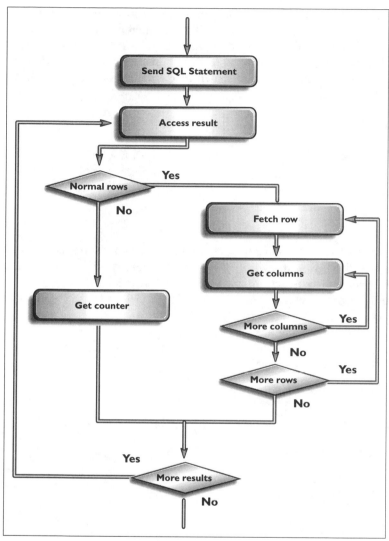

Figure 5-10: Overview of managing multiple result types.

The SQL string passed as parameter to this method is a statement that may return multiple results or a statement whose return type is unknown in advance, programmatically speaking. It gives an indication on the form of the result or of the first result, in case multiple results are returned. It will return true if a result set is available or false if it is an integer such as an update count.

```
ResultSet getResultSet();
```

The method `getResultSet()` returns the current result as a `ResultSet`. It may only be called once per result. The result set is then scanned by the usual method. This method may also be used to verify that the current result is a result set, in which case it does not return null. A null return means that there are no more results or the result is an update count, in which case it should be fetched with the `getUpdateCount()` method.

```
int getUpdateCount();
```

The method `getUpdateCount()` returns the current result, which should be an integer value, or -1 if it is a result set or if there are no more results. It should be called only once per result.

```
boolean getMoreResults();
```

This method moves to a statement's next result. In case it is a result set, it returns true. It returns false if it is an integer or there are no more results. This method implicitly closes a current result set obtained with `getResultSet()`.

There are no more results when (`!getMoreResults() && (getUpdateCount() == -1)`).

Listing 5-19 best illustrates the mechanism.

Listing 5-19: How to discover the result type.

```
...
Connection myConnection = DriverManager.getConnection(url,
              "javauser", "hotjava");
Statement myStatement = myConnection.createStatement();
ResultSet rs;
if (myStatement.execute(sqlStatement))
{
 // we have a ResultSet
 rs = myStatement.getResultSet();
 while (rs.next())
 {
     // process the rows
 }
}
else
{
 // we have an update count
 System.out.println(myStatement.getUpdateCount());
}
myStatement.close();
myConnection.close();
...
...
```

The example in Listing 5-20 is adapted to process the results of a statement that returns multiple results — both result sets and update counts in arbitrary order.

Listing 5-20: How to handle multiple result types.

```
...
...
Connection myConnection = DriverManager.getConnection(url,
            "javauser", "hotjava");
Statement myStatement = myConnection.createStatement();
boolean resultSetIsAvailable;
boolean moreResultsAvailable;
int i = 0;
int res=0;
resultSetIsAvailable = myStatement.execute(sqlText);
ResultSet rs = null;
for (moreResultsAvailable = true; moreResultsAvailable; )
{
  if (resultSetIsAvailable)
  {
      if ((rs = myStatement.getResultSet()) != null)
      {
            // we have a resultset
            ResultSetMetaData rsmd = rs.getMetaData();
            int numCols = rsmd.getColumnCount();
            // display column headers
            for (i = 1; i <= numCols; i++)
            {
                  if (i > 1) System.out.print(", ");
                  System.out.print(
                              rsmd.getColumnLabel(i));
            }
            System.out.println("");
            // step through the rows
            while (rs.next())
            {
                  // process the columns
                  for (i = 1; i <= numCols; i++)
                  {
                        if (i > 1)
                              System.out.print(", ");
            System.out.print(
                              rs.getString(i));
                  }
                  System.out.println("");
            }
      }
  }
  else
  {
      if ((res = curStmt.getUpdateCount()) != -1)
      {
```

```
                     // we have an updatecount
                     System.out.println(res + " row(s) affected.");
              }
              // else no more results
              else
              {
                     moreResultsAvailable = false;
              }
       }
   if (moreResultsAvailable)
   {
          resultSetIsAvailable = myStatement.getMoreResults();
   }
}
if (rs != null) rs.close();
myStatement.close();
...
...
```

Canceling unwanted results

It may happen that a statement's result is no longer needed for one or another reason. In this case, closing the result set will usually be sufficient (see the close() method). However, a cancel() method exists and may be called on the statement object. It may be called from a thread to cancel a statement being executed within another thread.

Statement:

```
void cancel();
```

```
void cancel();
```

This method, shown in Listing 5-21, cancels a statement being executed.

Listing 5-21: Canceling unwanted results.

```
...
java.sql.Statement myStatement =
                            myConnection.createStatement();
ResultSet rs = myStatement.executeQuery("SELECT name, title, salary
 FROM employees");
int i = 0;
while (rs.next()) {
 // increment the counter
 i++;
 // print the columns of the row that was retrieved
 String empName = rs.getString("name");
 String empTitle = rs.getString("title");
 long empSalary = rs.getLong("salary");
 System.out.println("Employee " + empName + " is " + empTitle + "
                    and earns $" + empSalary);
```

```
// cancel all results if 100 rows of data were already
// retrieved
if (i >= 100) myStatement.cancel();
}
...
...
```

Closing the result

As in the case with statements and connections, result sets must be closed when no longer needed.

ResultSet:

```
void close();
```

```
void close();
```

This method closes the result set and releases database and JDBC resources associated with it. When a statement object is closed, re-executed, or used to retrieve the next result of multiple result sets, its result set is automatically closed.

TYPE CONVERSION

Depending on the situation, it may be necessary to perform automatic conversions between SQL types used in a specific result set column and Java types. For example, it is allowed to use getString() to access an element of SQL type DATE. The short example in Listing 5-22 shows how to force a conversion of SQL type DATE to Java String.

Listing 5-22. Type conversion.

```
...
java.sql.Statement myStatement = myConnection.createStatement();
ResultSet rs = myStatement.executeQuery("SELECT name, datehired,
  salary FROM employees");
while (rs.next()) {
  // print the values of the row that was retrieved
  String empName = rs.getString("name");
  String empDateHired = rs.getString("datehired");
  long empSalary = rs.getLong("salary");
  System.out.println("Employee " + empName + " was hired on the " +
            empDateHired + " and earns $" + empSalary);
}
...
...
```

Table 5-2 shows the supported conversions via the getXXX() methods. Unsupported conversions will usually raise a SQLException when attempted.

TABLE 5-2 JAVA TO SQL TYPES CONVERSIONS

	TINYINT	SMALLINT	INTEGER	BIGINT	REAL	FLOAT
getByte()	☻	☺	☺	☺	☺	☺
getShort()	☺	☻	☺	☺	☺	☺
getInt()	☺	☺	☻	☺	☺	☺
getLong()	☺	☺	☺	☻	☺	☺
getFloat()	☺	☺	☺	☺	☻	☺
getDouble()	☺	☺	☺	☺	☺	☻
getBigDecimal()	☺	☺	☺	☺	☺	☺
getBoolean()	☺	☺	☺	☺	☺	☺
getString()	☺	☺	☺	☺	☺	☺
getBytes()						
getDate()						
getTime()						
getTimestamp()						
getAsciiStream()						
getUnicodeStream()						
getBinaryStream()						
getObject()	☺	☺	☺	☺	☺	☺

	DOUBLE	DECIMAL	NUMERIC	BIT	CHAR	VARCHAR
getByte()	☺	☺	☺	☺	☺	☺
getShort()	☺	☺	☺	☺	☺	☺
getInt()	☺	☺	☺	☺	☺	☺
getLong()	☺	☺	☺	☺	☺	☺
getFloat()	☺	☺	☺	☺	☺	☺
getDouble()	☻	☺	☺	☺	☺	☺
getBigDecimal()	☺	☻	☻	☺	☺	☺
getBoolean()	☺	☺	☺	☻	☺	☺

	DOUBLE	DECIMAL	NUMERIC	BIT	CHAR	VARCHAR
getString()	☺	☺	☺	☺	☻	☻
getBytes()						
getDate()					☺	☺
getTime()					☺	☺
getTimestamp()					☺	☺
getAsciiStream()					☺	☺
getUnicodeStream()					☺	☺
getBinaryStream()						
getObject()	☺	☺	☺	☺	☺	☺

	LONGVARCHAR	BINARY	VARBINARY	LONGVARBINARY
getByte()	☺			
getShort()	☺			
getInt()	☺			
getLong()	☺			
getFloat()	☺			
getDouble()	☺			
getBigDecimal()	☺			
getBoolean()	☺			
getString()	☺	☺	☺	☺
getBytes()		☻	☻	☺
getDate()	☺			
getTime()	☺			
getTimestamp()	☺			
getAsciiStream()	☻	☺	☺	☺
getUnicodeStream()	☻	☺	☺	☺
getBinaryStream()		☺	☺	☻
getObject()	☺	☺	☺	☺

(continued)

TABLE 5-2 *(Continued)*

	DATE	TIME	TIME STAMP
getByte()			
getShort()			
getInt()			
getLong()			
getFloat()			
getDouble()			
getBigDecimal()			
getBoolean()			
getString()	☺	☺	☺
getBytes()			
getDate()	☺		☺
getTime()		☺	☺
getTimestamp()	☺		☺
getAsciiStream()			
getUnicodeStream()			
getBinaryStream()			
getObject()	☺	☺	☺

A ☺ means the corresponding method is recommended. A ☺ means the corresponding get method can be used.

Note that it may be convenient to convert all SQL types to string when retrieving data to display it in tabular format. The getString() method accepts any type and will always do the implicit conversion to a Java string. Chapter 6 provides more information on SQL data types and Java types.

RECEIVING BLOBS

Retrieving pictures, sounds, and movies from a database is an expected JDBC function. It makes sense in the context of applets delivered via Web pages, but because Java has a fair set of multimedia facilities, it makes sense in stand-alone Java applications as well.

As for sending such binary large objects, Java streams are used to retrieve LONGVARBINARY or LONGVARCHAR data. However, the possibility exists to retrieve the data in fixed-size chunks. The limits are imposed by the `Statement.getMaxFieldSize()` value. Another limitation due to underlying implementation constraints is that each stream must be accessed immediately after the get method. Indeed, they will be closed on successive get calls on the result set.

Three separate methods support the retrieval of streams:

- getBinaryStream(), which does not perform any conversion

- getAsciiStream(), which returns a stream providing one-byte wide ASCII characters

- getUnicodeStream(), which returns a stream providing two-byte wide Unicode characters

These methods were listed in the earlier section describing how to scan the row's columns of a result set. Listing 5-23 shows how to retrieve binary large objects from a database. The fields containing a BLOB are emp_pict and emp_welcome.

Listing 5-23: How to retrieve BLOBs.

```
...
java.sql.Statement myStatement = myConnection.createStatement();
ResultSet rs = myStatement.executeQuery("SELECT name, emp_pict,
 emp_welcome FROM employees");
// we retrieve in 4K chunks
byte[] buffer = new byte[4096];
int size;
while (rs.next()) {
 // fetch employee's name
 String empName = rs.getString("name");
 // fetch employee's picture
 java.io.InputStream strin =
      rs.getBinaryStream("emp_pict");
 for (;;)
 {
     size = strin.read(buffer);
     if (size == 0)
     {
          break;
          }
     // Send the buffer to some output stream
     output.write(buffer, 0, size);
 }
// fetch employee's voicemail welcome message
java.io.InputStream strin2 =
     rs.getBinaryStream("emp_welcome");
 for (;;)
 {
     size = strin2.read(buffer);
```

```
        if (size == 0)
        {
                break;
        }
        // Send the buffer to some output stream
        output.write(buffer, 0, size);
    }
}
...
...
```

Adjusting properties

Properties that affect result sets may be set or queried through various methods. Always verify that the settings are as independent of the data source as possible.

Data truncation on reads: Data truncation may happen when reading data from a database. How it is handled depends on the circumstances. Normally, data truncation results in a warning. However, if the maximum field size is set to a certain value, and if the application attempts to read a field larger than the limit, the data will be silently truncated to the maximum limit. As a reminder, the setMaxFieldSize() and getMaxFieldSize() were explained in the section on sending SQL statements. Listing 5-24 shows data truncation on reads.

Statement:

```
void setMaxFieldSize(int max);
int getMaxFieldSize();
```

Listing 5-24: Data truncation on reads.

```
...
java.sql.Statement myStatement =
                          myConnection.createStatement();
ResultSet rs = myStatement.executeQuery("SELECT name, title, salary
  FROM employees");
myStatement.setMaxFieldSize(128);
while (rs.next()) {
  // print the columns of the row that was retrieved
  String empName = rs.getString("name");
  String empTitle = rs.getString("title");
  long empSalary = rs.getLong("salary");
  System.out.println("Employee " + empName + " is " +
            empTitle + " and earns $" + empSalary);
}
...
...
```

Limiting the number of rows: Under some circumstances, it may not be useful or preferable to retrieve millions of rows of data. One such circumstance is, for example, if the data destination is the user's screen. While you should always build and send queries that make sense to be able to exploit their result, it may happen that the number of returned rows is unpredictable. In this case, it is possible to set a limit.

Statement:
```
void setMaxRows(int max);
int getMaxRows();
```

```
void setMaxRows(int max);
```

This code sets the maximum limit to max. In other words, max is the maximum number of rows that a result set may contain. If the limit is exceeded, the excess rows will be silently dropped from the result set.

```
int getMaxRows();
```

This code returns the current value of the limit. A value of zero means no limit at all. Listing 5-25 shows how to limit the number of rows returned by a query.

Listing 5-25: Limiting the number of rows returned by a query.
```
. . .
. . .
java.sql.Statement myStatement =
                        myConnection.createStatement();
ResultSet rs = myStatement.executeQuery("SELECT name, title, salary
  FROM employees");
// we do not want more than 1000 rows of data retrieved
myStatement.setMaxRows(1000);
while (rs.next()) {
// print the columns of the row that was retrieved
  String empName = rs.getString("name");
  String empTitle = rs.getString("title");
  long empSalary = rs.getLong("salary");
  System.out.println("Employee " + empName + " is " +
          empTitle + " and earns $" + empSalary);
}
. . .
. . .
```

Examining the results: The next two methods are useful for examining and navigating through a resulting row of data.

ResultSet:
```
boolean wasNull();
int findColumn(String columnName);
```

```
boolean wasNull();
```

In case a column has the value of SQL NULL, this method returns true. Note that it should be called after calling the getXXX() method to access the column.

```
int findColumn(String columnName);
```

This method attempts to find the index of the column name passed in a parameter. It returns the column index as an integer. Listing 5-26 shows how to examine the columns of a result set.

Listing 5-26: Examining the columns of a result set.

```
...
...
java.sql.Statement myStatement =
                        myConnection.createStatement();
ResultSet rs = myStatement.executeQuery("SELECT name, title, salary
 FROM employees");
while (rs.next()) {
 // print the columns of the row that was retrieved
 String empName = rs.getString("name");
     if rs.wasNull() System.out.println("Ooops, column " +
          rs.findColumn("name") + " is NULL!");
 String empTitle = rs.getString("title");
 if rs.wasNull() System.out.println("Ooops, column " +
     rs.findColumn("title") + " is NULL!");
 long empSalary = rs.getLong("salary");
 if rs.wasNull() System.out.println("Ooops, column " +
     rs.findColumn("salary") + " is NULL!");
 System.out.println("Employee " + empName + " is " +
          empTitle + " and earns $" + empSalary);
}
...
...
```

SQL cursor

Cursors are often used when programming database applications. They offer a practical way of scanning the result sets and perform positioned delete and updates.

Result Set:

```
String getCursorName();
```



```
String getCursorName();
```

When a result table is retrieved, a named cursor is created. This cursor is used when stepping through the result set rows and may be used to update or delete data pointed to by the cursor. It is called positioned update/positioned delete. JDBC supports this feature by giving the name of the SQL cursor used by a result set. Note that if positioned update/delete is not supported by the DBMS, a SQLException will be thrown.

PUTTING IT ALL TOGETHER AGAIN

Figure 5-11 summarizes all the steps we studied in this chapter. They are the essential steps for communicating with a database, sending queries and updates, and retrieving the results from Java. Listing 5-27 also summarizes this chapter.

Listing 5–27: Retrieving results.

```
// retrieving results
// the SQL statement is taken from the standard input
import java.sql.*;
import java.io.*;
class SimpleExample
{
 public static void main(String argv[])
 {
 String url = "jdbc:odbc:mysource";
 try
 {
     Class.forName("sun.jdbc.odbc.JdbcOdbcDriver");
     DriverManager.setLogStream(java.lang.System.out);
     Connection myConnection =
     DriverManager.getConnection(url, "javauser", "hotjava");
     Statement myStatement = myConnection.createStatement();
     boolean resultSetIsAvailable;
     boolean moreResultsAvailable;
     int i = 0;
     int res=0;
     String sqlText = (new DataInputStream(System.in)).readLine();
     resultSetIsAvailable = myStatement.execute(sqlText);
     ResultSet rs = null;
     for (moreResultsAvailable = true; moreResultsAvailable; )
     {
             if (resultSetIsAvailable)
             {
                     if ((rs = myStatement.getResultSet()) != null)
                     {
                             // we have a resultset
                             ResultSetMetaData rsmd =
                              rs.getMetaData();
                             int numCols = rsmd.getColumnCount();
                             // display column headers
                             for (i = 1; i <= numCols; i++)
                             {
```

```
                                        if (i > 1) System.out.print(",
                                         ");
                                        System.out.print(
                                          rsmd.getColumnLabel(i));
                                }
                                System.out.println("");
                                // step through the rows
                                while (rs.next())
                                {
                                        // process the columns
                                        for (i = 1; i <= numCols; i++)
                                        {
                                        if (i > 1)
                                                System.out.print(", ");
                                            System.out.print(
                                              rs.getString(i));
                                        }
                                        System.out.println("");
                                }
                        }
                else
                {
                        if ((res = myStatement.getUpdateCount()) != -1)
                        {
                                // we have an updatecount
                                System.out.println(res +
                                                        " row(s)
affected.");
                        }
                        // else no more results
                        else
                        {
                                moreResultsAvailable = false;
                        }
                }if
                (moreResultsAvailable)
                {
                        resultSetIsAvailable =
                                myStatement.getMoreResults();
                }
        }
    if (rs != null) rs.close();
    myStatement.close();
    myConnection.close();
}
catch(java.lang.Exception ex)
{
    ex.printStackTrace();
}
}
```

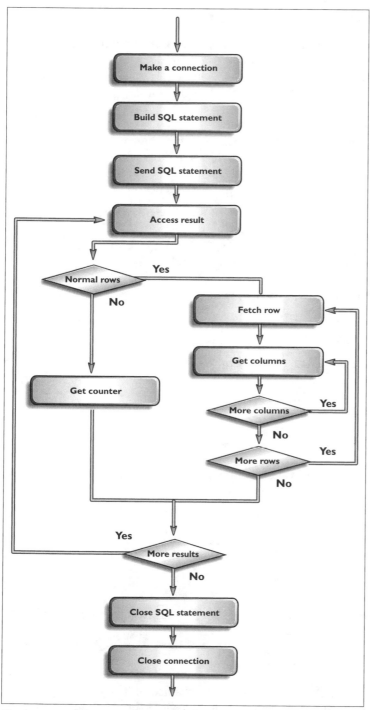

Figure 5-11: Overview of all the steps for communicating with a database.

Error and Warning Management

JDBC uses the exception mechanism to pass error or warning information to programs. This mechanism signals an abnormal condition that may be handled to prevent a program termination. The exception mechanism is used when a recoverable error occurs and it must be caught to correct the situation.

SQLEXCEPTION

When a database access error occurs, a SQLException is thrown that provides information on the error. Each SQLException provides several kinds of information:

◆ A description of the error, used as the Java Exception message

◆ A SQLstate string conforms to the XOPEN SQLstate conventions

◆ A vendor-specific error code, usually the actual DBMS error code

◆ A chain to a next exception, if any

The following methods may be used within a program on a SQLException object.

SQLException

```
String getMessage();
String getSQLState();
int getErrorCode();
SQLException getNextException();
```

```
String getMessage();
```

The message is used as the Java exception message, is available via this method, and is returned as string.

```
String getSQLState();
```

The code getSQLstate conforms to the XOPEN SQLstate definition.

```
int getErrorCode();
```

This code returns the vendor specific exception code. You should refer to the documentation for more information.

```
SQLException getNextException();
```

This method is used to get the SQLException chained to this one.

In all our examples, we were able to catch SQLExceptions without doing anything special once we caught them. The next example, Listing 5-28, shows how to use exception information. Because exceptions signal an abnormal condition, you use the provided information to try to continue the program execution.

Listing 5-28: Catching SQLExceptions.

```
// catching SQLExceptions
import java.sql.*;
class SimpleExample
{
 public static void main(String args[])
 {
 String url = "jdbc:odbc:mysource";
      try
      {
      Class.forName("sun.jdbc.odbc.JdbcOdbcDriver");
      DriverManager.setLogStream(
             java.lang.System.out);
             Connection myConnection =
             DriverManager.getConnection(url,
                    "javauser", "hotjava");
      Statement myStatement =
                    myConnection.createStatement();
      ResultSet rs = myStatement.executeQuery(
             "SELECT * FROM employees");
      // ...
      myStatement.close();
             myConnection.close();
      }
      catch(SQLException ex)
      {
             // there may be multiple error objects
             // chained together
             System.out.println("\n*** SQLException caught ***\n");
             while (ex != null)
             {
                    System.out.println("SQLState: " +
                           ex.getSQLState());
                    System.out.println("Message: " +
                           ex.getMessage());
                    System.out.println("Vendor Code: " +
                           ex.getErrorCode());
                    System.out.println("");
                           ex.getNextException();
             }
      }
      catch(java.lang.Exception ex)
      {
             ex.printStackTrace();
      }
 }
}
```

SQLWARNING

This class provides information on database access warnings. Such warnings are silently chained to the class instance whose method caused it to be reported until they are fetched with the following method.

Connection, statement, or result set

```
SQLWarning getWarnings();
```

```
SQLWarning getWarnings();
```

This method returns a SQLWarning object or null if no warning occurred. The SQLWarning class, that extends SQLException, provides:

SQLWarning

```
String getMessage();
String getSQLState();
int getErrorCode();
SQLWarning getNextWarning();
```

```
String getMessage();
```

The warning message is available via this method, returned as string.

```
String getSQLState();
```

The code getSQLstate conforms to the XOPEN SQLstate definition.

```
int getErrorCode();
```

This code returns the vendor-specific warning code. Refer to the vendor's documentation for more information.

```
SQLException getNextWarning();
```

This method is used to get the SQLWarning chained to this one.

The following example, Listing 5-29, shows how to check for warnings. We explicitly call the getWarnings() method on the Connection, statement, and result set objects. The code for checkWarnings() is a generic method to handle all warnings that may occur during the program execution.

Listing 5-29: Checking SQLWarnings.

```java
// checking SQLWarnings
import java.sql.*;
class SimpleExample
{
 public static void main(String args[])
 {
 String url = "jdbc:odbc:mysource";
      try
      {
      Class.forName("sun.jdbc.odbc.JdbcOdbcDriver");
      DriverManager.setLogStream(
              java.lang.System.out);
              Connection myConnection =
              DriverManager.getConnection(url,
                  "javauser", "hotjava");
      checkWarnings(myConnection.getWarnings());
      Statement myStatement =
                  myConnection.createStatement();
      checkWarnings(myStatement.getWarnings());
      ResultSet rs = myStatement.executeQuery(
              "SELECT * FROM employees");
      checkWarnings(rs.getWarnings());
      // ...
      myStatement.close();
              myConnection.close();
      }
      catch(SQLException ex)
      {
              // there may be multiple error objects
              // chained together
              System.out.println("\n*** SQLException caught ***\n");
              while (ex != null)
              {
                      System.out.println("SQLState: " +
                          ex.getSQLState());
                      System.out.println("Message: " +
                          ex.getMessage());
                      System.out.println("Vendor Code: " +
                          ex.getErrorCode());
                      System.out.println("");
                      ex.getNextException();
              }
      }
      catch(java.lang.Exception ex)
      {
              ex.printStackTrace();
      }
 }
 private static void checkWarnings(SQLWarning warn)
                            throws SQLException
 {
```

```
        if (warn != null)
        {
        // there may be multiple warnings chained
                // together
                System.out.println("\n*** SQLWarning caught ***\n");
                while (warn != null)
                {
                        System.out.println("SQLState: " +
                                warn.getSQLState());
                        System.out.println("Message: " +
                                warn.getMessage());
                        System.out.println("Vendor Code: " +
                                warn.getErrorCode());
                        System.out.println("");
                        warn.getNextWarning();
                }
        }
    }
}
```

DATA TRUNCATION

When JDBC unexpectedly truncates data on a read, a data truncation warning is reported. When it occurs on a write, a data truncation exception is thrown. In both cases, the SQLstate is set to "01004."

A set of methods is available to discover what happened.

DataTruncation

```
int getDataSize();
int getTransferSize();
int getIndex();
boolean getParameter();
boolean getRead();
```

```
int getDataSize();
```

This method returns the number of bytes that should have been transferred. It returns -1 if the size is unknown. The size may be an approximation if data conversions occurred.

```
int getTransferSize();
```

This method returns the number of bytes actually transferred. A -1 means that the size is unknown.

```
int getIndex();
```

This method gets the index of the column or parameter that was truncated. A -1 means that the index is unknown, in which case the next two methods should be ignored.

```
boolean getParameter();
```

This returns true if the value truncated was passed through a statement's parameter. It returns false if it was returned by a column.

```
boolean getRead();
```

This returns true if the data truncation occurred on a database read. It returns false if the data was truncated on a write. Listing 5-30 shows how to catch a data truncation exception.

Listing 5–30: How to catch a data truncation exception.

```
. . .
. . .
 {
      try
      {
            // initiate a connection,
            // then execute a statement
            // ...
      }
      catch(DataTruncation ex)
      {
            System.out.println("\n*** DataTruncationexception
             caught ***\n");
                  int idx = ex.getIndex();
            System.out.print("Index: " + idx);
            if (idx != -1)
            {
                  if (ex.getParameter())
                  {
                        // the truncation happened
                        // in a parameter
                        System.out.print(" of the set
                              of parameters");
                  }
                  else
                  {
                        // the truncation happened
                        // on a resultset column
                        System.out.print(" in the resultset");
                  }
            }
            if (ex.getRead())
            {
```

```
                        // the truncation happened
                        // on a read
                        System.out.println(" was truncated on a read");
                }
                else
                {
                        // the truncation happened
                        // on a write
                        System.out.println(" was truncated on a write");
                }
                System.out.println("It was: " +
                        ex.getDataSize() + " bytes long");
                System.out.println("Actual size: " +
                        ex.getTransferSize() +
                        " bytes transferred");
                System.out.println("");
        }
  // ...
  }
  ...
  ...
```

Summary

In this chapter, you learned how to:

- Import java.sql.* to avoid long member names

- Build a JDBC URL

- Load one or more specific JDBC driver with `class.forName()`

- If necessary, set the JDBC log stream with `setLogStream()`

- If necessary, adjust the connection properties

- Open a connection with `getConnection()`

- Create a statement object

- Build a SQL statement

- Execute the SQL statement

- Manage multiple result sets

- Fetch rows of data in cases of result set of rows

- Fetch columns of rows by column name or column index

- ◆ Fetch integer results

- ◆ Check for warnings

- ◆ Manage data truncation errors

- ◆ Close the result set

- ◆ Close the statement

- ◆ Terminate the connection with `close()`

- ◆ Catch exceptions

The next chapter discusses data type conversions, how to use the SQL escape syntax, what a database transaction is, some theory, and provides exercises on SQL cursors.

Chapter 6

Fine Tuning JDBC Queries and Updates

IN THIS CHAPTER
This chapter discusses the essential techniques for fine-tuning database queries and updates from JDBC, including:

◆ Dealing with data type conversion

◆ The SQL escape syntax

◆ Database transactions

◆ Handling SQL cursors

Driver and DriverManager Internals

It is possible to obtain detailed information from the Driver and the DriverManager through a set of methods. They are advanced functions, and a programmer usually will not use Driver or DriveManager unless the programmer wants to discover or set specific JDBC behaviors. Only those functions that are of the most interest to an application developer are listed below, the others being more useful for JDBC driver developers.

DriverManager:

```
void setLoginTimeout(int seconds);
int getLoginTimeout();
void setLogStream(java.io.PrintStream out);
java.io.PrintStream getLogStream();
void println(String logmessage);

void setLoginTimeout(int seconds);
```

This method sets the maximum time allowed when attempting to log in to a database. All registered JDBC drivers use the timeout value, expressed in seconds. It may be useful to modify this parameter in the case of the Internet scenario. An exception occurs whenever the timer expires.

```
int getLoginTimeout();
```

The method `getLoginTimeout()` returns the current timeout value.

```
void setLogStream(java.io.PrintStream out);
```

The JDBC logging facility was used in previous examples. It allows the tracing of all JDBC activity during program execution by providing a PrintStream. Once the log stream has been set, the tracing facility can be disabled by providing a null parameter to the same method.

```
java.io.PrintStream getLogStream();
```

The method `getLogStream()` returns the current JDBC logging PrintStream, or null if logging is disabled.

```
void println(String logmessage);
```

This method is used on the DriverManager object to print a message on the current JDBC log stream. The DriverManager is very talkative, and this facility may be useful for inserting your own messages in the log stream, as, for example, before all critical sections of a program to facilitate debugging.

Driver:

```
boolean acceptsURL(String url);
int getMajorVersion();
int getMinorVersion();
boolean jdbcCompliant();
DriverPropertyInfo[] getPropertyInfo(String url,
  java.util.Properties info);
```

```
boolean acceptsURL(String url);
```

In some cases, it may be of interest to know if a particular driver is able to connect to the given Uniform Resource Locator (URL). This method will return true if the driver is able to understand the subprotocol specified in the URL.

```
int getMajorVersion();
```

This method returns the driver's major version number.

```
int getMinorVersion();
```

This method returns the driver's minor version number.

```
boolean jdbcCompliant();
```

In case the driver fully supports the JDBC API and SQL 92 Entry Level, this method returns true. It is a good way to verify that a driver is JDBC compliant.

```
// getting driver info
import java.sql.*;
class SimpleExample
{
  public static void main(String args[])
  {
      try
      {
              Driver myDriver = new jdbc.foobar.MyDriver();
              DriverManager.registerDriver(myDriver);
              DriverManager.setLogStream(
                      java.lang.System.out);
              System.out.println("Connection to" +
  "jdbc:mydriver://javabank.com/ possible? " +
myDriver.acceptsURL ("jdbc:mydriver://javabank.com/"));
              System.out.println("Major Version: " +
myDriver.getMajorVersion());
              System.out.println("Minor Version: " +
myDriver.getMinorVersion());
              System.out.println("JDBC COMPLIANT driver? "
 + myDriver.jdbcCompliant());
      }
      catch(java.lang.Exception ex)
      {
              ex.printStackTrace();
              }
  }
}
```

```
DriverPropertyInfo[] getPropertyInfo(String url,
 java.util.Properties info);
```

This method returns an array of `DriverPropertyInfo` objects describing the driver's possible properties. It takes the URL as an argument as well as a proposed list of property name/value pairs that will be sent to open the connection. An empty array is returned when no properties are required.

The `getPropertyInfo()` method is used to discover what properties should be provided to make a connection to a database. It could, for example, be used within a generic graphical user interface (GUI) tool that has no prior knowledge about the properties it should prompt a user for to get the connection. The `DriverPropertyInfo` objects should be analyzed to discover the possible properties, both those that are required and those that are optional. It may be necessary to iterate through several calls to the `getPropertyInfo()` method because additional property values may become necessary, as soon as the values are supplied.

The `DriverPropertyInfo` class is composed of these members:

DriverPropertyInfo:

```
String DriverPropertyInfo.name;
String DriverPropertyInfo.description;
boolean DriverPropertyInfo.required;
String DriverPropertyInfo.value;
String[] DriverPropertyInfo.choices;
```

```
String DriverPropertyInfo.name;
```

This is the name of the property.

```
String DriverPropertyInfo.description;
```

This gives a description of the property. It may be null.

```
boolean DriverPropertyInfo.required;
```

This result is set to true if a value must be supplied to the property during a `Driver.connect()`. False means that the property is optional.

```
String DriverPropertyInfo.value;
```

This field is the current value of the property, or null if no value is known.

```
String[] DriverPropertyInfo.choices;
```

If the property may be chosen from a set of values, this array contains the possible choices.

SQL Data Type Conversions

The Java data types are not exactly isomorphic to the SQL data types. However, mapping SQL data types into Java allows users to store and retrieve data without losing information.

Mapping Data Types to Java

When types are known at compile time, the following mappings are used. Note that JDBC also provides a mechanism to fully support dynamically typed data access when result and parameter types are not known at compile time (see the Dynamic Database Access section).

CHARACTER STRINGS

There are three SQL data types for SQL strings:

- ◆ CHAR

- ◆ VARCHAR

- ◆ LONGVARCHAR

In Java, we have `String` and `char[]` types to hold these SQL data types. `String` is used as the default mapping, knowing that it is possible to convert a `String` to a `char[]` and a `char[]` to a `String`. Thus, reading and writing data may be achieved without knowing the exact data type expected.

Space padding is automatically done whenever dealing with fixed length types such as SQL CHAR(n). Spaces are added to the end of a string to set its length to "n" when a SQL CHAR(n) must be sent to the database. When a SQL CHAR(n) field is retrieved, additional padding is done to get a string of length "n."

Note that a LONGVARCHAR may overflow a string when retrieved using `ResultSet.getString()`. In this case, it is advised to retrieve the LONGVARCHAR field in small chunks using a Java input stream. This may occur when retrieving BLOBs (Binary Long Objects) from the database.

NUMBERS

SQL integer types allow for 1-(TINYINT), 2-(SMALLINT), 4-(INTEGER), and 8 byte-wide values (BIGINT). They can, therefore, be mapped to Java types such as Java byte, short, int, and long respectively.

Fixed point numbers may be expressed as SQL DECIMAL and SQL NUMERIC, where absolute precision is preserved. They can be mapped to `java.math.BigDecimal` without losing precision. This type may be used to perform addition, subtraction, multiplication, and division. Note that these SQL types may also be accessed as Java strings, although it is difficult to perform math on strings.

Floating point numbers are mapped as follows: SQL REAL, which requires 7 digits of mantissa precision, to Java float, SQL FLOAT, and SQL DOUBLE, which require 15 digits of mantissa precision, to Java double.

BINARY TYPES

SQL types BINARY, VARBINARY, and LONGVARBINARY may be expressed as byte arrays in Java. As for LONGVARCHAR fields, LONGVARBINARY fields may be retrieved using Java streams for multimegabyte data values.

The SQL BIT data type may be mapped to the Java boolean type.

TIME-RELATED TYPES

The SQL DATE, TIME, and TIMESTAMP data types are time-related types. They can be expressed as `java.sql.Date` (yyyy-mm-dd), `java.sql.Time` (hh:mm:ss), and `java.sql.Timestamp` (yyyy-mm-dd hh:mm:ss.nanosecond), respectively.

Note that `java.sql.Date`, `java.sql.Time`, and `java.sql.Timestamp` are three subclasses of `java.util.date`. Depending on which one is in use, different `java.util.date` members are affected. These subclasses include:

- `java.sql.Date` sets the java.util.date.hour, .minute, .second, and .milliseconds fields to zero

- `java.sql.Time` sets the java.util.date.year, .month, and .day fields according to 1970, January 1st

- `java.sql.Timestamp` has a similar behavior but also sets a nanosecond field

Type Mapping Tables

Table 6-1 shows the standard mapping from SQL data types to Java types. Although they are common SQL data types, some databases may not support them.

TABLE 6-1 MAPPING TABLE FROM SQL TYPES TO JAVA TYPES

SQL type	Java type
CHAR	String
VARCHAR	String
LONGVARCHAR	String
NUMERIC	java.math.BigDecimal
DECIMAL	java.math.BigDecimal

SQL type	Java type
BIT	boolean
TINYINT	byte
SMALLINT	short
INTEGER	int
BIGINT	long
REAL	float
FLOAT	double

SQL type	Java type
DOUBLE	double
BINARY	`byte[]`
VARBINARY	`byte[]`
LONGVARBINARY	`byte[]`
DATE	`java.sql.Date`
TIME	`java.sql.Time`
TIMESTAMP	`java.sql.Timestamp`

Table 6-2 shows the default mapping from Java types to SQL data types. The mapping from String is normally VARCHAR. Where the String length exceeds the drivers limit on VARCHAR values, it becomes LONGVARCHAR. The same occurs with `byte[]` and VARBINARY and LONGVARBINARY.

TABLE 6-2 MAPPING TABLE FROM JAVA TYPES TO SQL TYPES

Java type	SQL type
String	VARCHAR or LONGVARCHAR
java.math.BigDecimal	NUMERIC
boolean	BIT
byte	TINYINT

(continued)

TABLE 6-2 *(Continued)*

short	SMALLINT
int	INTEGER
long	BIGINT
float	REAL
double	DOUBLE
byte[]	VARBINARY or LONGVARBINARY
java.sql.Date	DATE
java.sql.Time	TIME
java.sql.Timestamp	TIMESTAMP

SQL Escape Syntax

To be JDBC-compliant, a database driver must support both SQL-2 entry level and semantics for some parts of the ANSI SQL-2 transitional level. Because the syntax used for this level is often different across DBMSs, JDBC provides an escape syntax for these semantics. The JDBC drivers convert the escape syntax into a DBMS-specific syntax, allowing portability of programs that require these features.

Escape Syntax

The escape syntax is the same as the escape syntax of Open Database Connectivity (ODBC). The escape syntax may not be the same as the ANSI syntax. Its form is:

```
{keyword parameters}
```

FOR STORED PROCEDURES

The following escape syntax is adopted to call stored procedures. The "?=" may be dropped when the stored procedure does not return a result. The procedure parameters may be IN and/or OUT parameters or simple literals.

```
{[?=] call stored_procedure_name [param1[, param2 ...]]}
```

For example, a stored procedure that returns a value and takes two parameters would be called as shown here:

```
{?= call proc_purge_employees employees, emp_messages}
```

FOR TIME/DATE

JDBC supports ISO standard formats for date, time, and timestamp. They must be escaped as shown here to be interpreted as expected:

```
{d 'yyyy-mm-dd'}                            to specify a date
{t 'hh:mm:ss'}                              to specify a time literal
{ts 'yyyy-mm-dd hh:mm:ss.f...'} or {ts 'yyyy-mm-dd hh:mm:ss'}
 to specify a timestamp
{fn function(args, ...)}            for scalar functions
```

Scalar functions and their arguments must be escaped and preceded by the "fn" keyword. In JDBC, the following scalar functions, if supported by the driver, are translated into the DBMS's specific syntax for these functions:

System Functions

```
{fn database()}
{fn user()}
```

Numeric Functions

```
{fn abs(number)}
{fn acos(float)}
{fn asin(float)}
{fn atan(float)}
{fn atan2(float1, float2)}
{fn ceiling(number)}
{fn cos(float)}
{fn cot(float)}
{fn degrees(number)}
{fn exp(float)}
{fn floor(number)}
{fn log(float)}
{fn log10(float)}
{fn mod(int1, int2)}
{fn pi()}
{fn power(number, power)}
{fn radians(number)}
{fn rand(int)}
{fn round(number, places)}
{fn sign(number)}
{fn sin(float)}
{fn sqrt(float)}
```

```
{fn tan(float)}
{fn trauncate(number, places)}
```

String Functions

```
{fn ascii(string)}
{fn char(code)}
{fn concat(str1, str2)}
{fn difference(str1, str2)}
{fn insert(str1, start, len, str2)}
{fn lcase(string)}
{fn left(string, count)}
{fn length(string)}
{fn locate(str1, str2, start)}
{fn ltrim(string)}
{fn repeat(string, count)}
{fn replace(str1, str2, str3)}
{fn right(string, count)}
{fn rtrim(string)}
{fn soundex(string)}
{fn space(count)}
{fn substring(string, start, len)}
{fn ucase(string)}
```

Date and Time Functions

```
{fn curdate()}
{fn curtime()}
{fn dayname(date)}
{fn dayofmonth(date)}
{fn dayofweek(date)}
{fn dayofyear(date)}
{fn hour(time)}
{fn minute(time)}
{fn month(date)}
{fn monthname(date)}
{fn now()}
{fn quarter(date)}
{fn second(time)}
{fn timestampadd(interval, count, timestamp)}
{fn timestampdiff(interval, tstp1, tstp2)}
{fn week(date)}
{fn year(date)}
```

Other Functions

```
{fn ifnull(expr, value)}
{fn convert(value, type)}    type may be any SQL datatype
```

FOR CHARACTERS THAT HAVE A SPECIAL MEANING

Special characters used for character matching, such as "%" and "_" in LIKE clauses, must be escaped with an escape character to be interpreted literally. This escape character must be declared as:

```
{escape 'escapechar'}
```

This declaration must be included at the end of any SQL text where these characters have to be interpreted literally. In the example that follows, the qualification clause matches any value of field_n that begins with an underscore character:

```
SELECT * FROM table WHERE field_n LIKE '\_%' {escape '\'}
```

FOR OUTER JOINS

Grammar for outer joins is database-dependent. The JDBC escape syntax for outer joins is:

```
{oj outerjoin}
```

where outerjoin respects:

```
table LEFT OUTER JOIN {table | outerjoin} ON searchcondition
```

For example, the next query may be used to list all employees and their pending messages (0 or more). Even employees who do not have message entries will be returned by the query:

```
SELECT employees.name, emp_messages.message
FROM {oj employees LEFT OUTER JOIN emp_messages
ON employees.emp_id = emp_messages.emp_id}
```

This SQL string would translate to this (using a Sybase System 11):

```
SELECT employees.name, emp_messages.message
FROM employees, emp_messages
WHERE employees.emp_id *= emp_messages.emp_id
```

Other DBMSs would translate the code into their specific dialect. Remember that the Connection.nativeSQL (String anySqlString) may be used to discover the translation of all escaped syntaxes for your own DBMS.

Transaction Management

JDBC supports database transaction management. Transactions provide a way to group SQL statements so they are treated as a whole — either all statements in the group are executed or no statements are executed. All statements within a transaction are treated as a work unit. Transactions are thus useful to guarantee, among other things, data consistency.

Completing a transaction is called committing the transaction, while aborting it is called rolling back the transaction. A rollback undoes the whole transaction. A transaction's boundaries are the beginning of its block and the commit or rollback. Once a commit has been issued, the transaction cannot be rolled back. Note that some DBMSs support nested transactions as well as intermediate markers within a transaction to indicate a point to which it can be rolled back.

Transaction Modes

Two transaction modes are usually supported by commercial DBMSs: the unchained mode and the ANSI-compatible chained mode. Check your DBMS's documentation to determine which is the default.

◆ The unchained mode requires explicit statements to identify the beginning of a transaction block and its end, which will always be a commit or rollback statement. The transaction block may be composed of any SQL statements.

◆ The chained mode does not require explicit statements to delimit the transaction statements because it implicitly begins a transaction before any SQL statement that retrieves or modifies data. The transaction must still be explicitly ended with a transaction commit or rollback.

Be aware that stored procedures that use the unchained transaction mode may be incompatible with other chained mode transactions.

Transaction Isolation Levels

ANSI defines three standard levels of transaction isolation. Transaction isolation makes sense when concurrent transactions execute simultaneously. The ANSI specification defines restrictions on the kinds of action permitted in concurrent transactions so as to prevent dirty reads, nonrepeatable reads, and phantoms.

◆ Level 1: No dirty reads. Dirty reads occur when a transaction updates a row, then a second transaction reads that row before the first transaction commits. If the first transaction rolls back the change, the information read by the second transaction becomes invalid.

◆ **Level 2:** No nonrepeatable reads. Nonrepeatable reads occur when a transaction reads a row and then another transaction updates the same row. If the second transaction commits, subsequent reads by the first transaction get different values than the original read.

◆ **Level 3:** No phantoms. Phantoms occur when a transaction reads a set of rows that satisfy a search condition and then another transaction updates, inserts, or deletes one or more rows that satisfy the first transaction's search condition. In this case, if the first transaction performs subsequent reads with the same search condition, it reads a different set of rows.

The higher levels include restrictions imposed by all the lower levels. In practice, compatibility with all the transaction isolation levels is achieved using locking techniques. Check your database documentation for information on these techniques and see how they can affect performances in a multiuser environment. As a general rule, the higher the transaction isolation level, the longer locks are held.

Managing Transactions with JDBC

JDBC always opens connections in autocommit mode. This opening mode means that each statement is executed as a separate transaction without needing to supply commit or rollback commands. In this default mode, it is not possible to perform rollbacks.

JDBC provides methods to turn off autocommit mode, to set the transaction isolation level, and to commit or rollback transactions. JDBC transactions begin as soon as the autocommit mode is disabled. In this case, an implicit transaction is associated with the connection, and it is completed or aborted with commit and rollback methods. The commit or rollback starts a new implicit transaction. The commit and rollback make JDBC close all PreparedStatements, CallableStatements, and ResultSets opened during the transaction. Simple statement objects stay open. This is the default behavior and it may be disabled.

The JDBC methods to manage transactions are these:

Connection

```
void setTransactionIsolation(int isolationlevel);
int getTransactionIsolation();
void setAutoCommit(boolean autocommit);
boolean getAutoCommit();
void commit();
void rollback();
void setAutoClose(boolean autoClose);
boolean getAutoClose();
```

```
void setTransactionIsolation(int isolationlevel);
```

This method sets the transaction isolation level. The possible JDBC transaction isolation levels are the following:

`TRANSACTION_READ_UNCOMMITTED`:   Dirty reads are allowed.

`TRANSACTION_READ_COMMITTED`:   Reads on a row are blocked until the transaction is committed.

`TRANSACTION_REPEATABLE_READ`:   Repeated reads on a row will return the originally read data, regardless of any updates by other users prior to commitment of the transaction.

`TRANSACTION_SERIALIZABLE`:   All reads are disallowed until the transaction is committed.

`TRANSACTION_NONE`:   Transactions are not supported. This method cannot be called while in the middle of a transaction.

`int getTransactionIsolation();`   It returns the current transaction isolation levels. A value of zero means that transactions are not supported.

`void` **`setAutoCommit`**`(boolean autocommit);`   The method setAutoCommit(false) implicitly begins a new transaction. Either commit() or rollback() must be used to terminate the transaction.

`boolean getAutoCommit();`   This method returns the current autocommit state. False means that user transactions are in use.

`void` **`commit`**`();`   This method completes the transaction. All changes made since the previous transaction termination (committed or rolled back) are made permanent and all transaction locks are released.

`void` **`rollback`**`();`   All changes made since the previous transaction termination (committed or rolled back) are dropped. This method undoes the current transaction statements and all transaction locks are released.

`void` **`setAutoClose`**`(boolean autoClose);`   When the connection is in auto-close mode, all its PreparedStatements, Callable Statement, and ResultSets are closed when the transaction is committed or rolled back. This is the default behavior, but it can be disabled by passing false as parameter. Some databases allow these objects to remain open across commits, whereas other databases close them.

`boolean` **`getAutoClose`**`();`   This method returns the current autoclose state for this connection.

EXAMPLE

```
// transactions
import java.sql.*;
class SimpleExample
{
  public static void main(String args[])
  {
    String url = "jdbc:odbc:mysource";
    try
  {
  Class.forName("sun.jdbc.odbc.JdbcOdbcDriver");
          Connection myConnection =
                DriverManager.getConnection(url,
                    "javauser", "hotjava");
          Statement firstStmt =
                myConnection.createStatement();
          Statement secondStmt =
                myConnection.createStatement();
          myConnection.setTransactionIsolation(
                Connection.TRANSACTION_SERIALIZABLE);
          myConnection.setAutoCommit(false);
          firstStmt.executeUpdate(
          "DELETE emp_messages WHERE id IN
                (SELECT id FROM employees WHERE name =
                  'Jones')");
          firstStmt.close();
          secondStmt.executeUpdate(
          "DELETE employees WHERE name = 'Jones'");
          secondStmt.close();
          myConnection.commit();
          myConnection.setTransactionIsolation(
                Connection.TRANSACTION_NONE);
          myConnection.close();
      }
      catch(java.lang.Exception ex)
      {
          ex.printStackTrace();
      }
  }
}
```

Cursors

Cursors are used to access a set of rows returned by a SQL SELECT statement. They are associated with query statements and have a symbolic name that may be used to access individual rows of data. Associated with cursors are cursor result sets and

cursor positions. Note that some DBMSs do not support cursors.
Thus, a cursor:

◆ Is associated with a SELECT statement

◆ Has a name

◆ Has a position

◆ May affect ResultSets by positioned update/delete statements using the cursor name

Figure 6-1 illustrates the cursor mechanism.

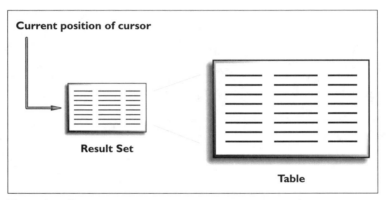

Figure 6-1: Cursor components.

Operation Theory

JDBC supports simple cursors that can be used in positioned update or positioned delete statements. They remain valid until the ResultSets or their parent Statements are closed.

Statement

```
void ResultSet.setCursorName(String name);
String ResultSet.getCursorName();
boolean DatabaseMetaData.supportsPositionedDelete();
boolean DatabaseMetaData.supportsPositionedUpdate();
```

```
void ResultSet.setCursorName(String name);
```

This method is used to give a statement a specific cursor name. Cursor names should be unique. A cursor name is automatically provided by default, which is often sufficient.

```
String ResultSet.getCursorName();
```

This method returns the current ResultSet's cursor name. This cursor name may be used later for positioned updates and positioned deletes.

```
boolean DatabaseMetaData.supportsPositionedDelete();
```

This `DatabaseMetaData` method returns true when the database supports positioned deletes.

```
boolean DatabaseMetaData.supportsPositionedUpdate();
```

This method returns true when the database supports positioned updates.

Practical Examples

The following examples are somewhat simplified. They illustrate the cursor mechanism for positioned updates and positioned deletes. In a real-world application, the SELECT statement would have a WHERE clause to limit the cursor scope. The condition that is tested before doing the positioned delete or positioned update is usually more elaborate.

```
// cursors: positioned delete
import java.sql.*;
class SimpleExample
{
 public static void main(String args[])
 {
      String url = "jdbc:odbc:mysource";
      try
      {
 Class.forName("sun.jdbc.odbc.JdbcOdbcDriver");
      Connection myConnection =
            DriverManager.getConnection(url,
                  "javauser", "hotjava");
      Statement firstStmt =
            myConnection.createStatement();
      Statement secondStmt =
            myConnection.createStatement();
      ResultSet rs = firstStmt.executeQuery(
      "SELECT * FROM employees FOR UPDATE");
      String csr = rs.getCursorName();
      int temp;
      // we scan the resultset, row by row
```

```
        while (rs.next())
        {
                temp = rs.getInt("salary");
                // activate positioned delete
                if (temp >= 100000)
                {
                        secondStmt.executeUpdate(
        "DELETE employees WHERE CURRENT OF " + csr);
                }
        }
        rs.close();
        firstStmt.close();
        secondStmt.close();
        myConnection.close();
      }

        catch(java.lang.Exception ex)
      {
        ex.printStackTrace();
      }
   }
}
```

The same remarks are valid for the positioned update example shown here:

```
// cursors: positioned update
import java.sql.*;
class SimpleExample
{
  public static void main(String args[])
  {
      String url = "jdbc:odbc:mysource";
      try
      {
      Class.forName("sun.jdbc.odbc.JdbcOdbcDriver");
            Connection myConnection =
                    DriverManager.getConnection(url,
                        "javauser", "hotjava");
            Statement firstStmt =
                    myConnection.createStatement();
            Statement secondStmt =
                    myConnection.createStatement();
            ResultSet rs = firstStmt.executeQuery(
            "SELECT * FROM employees FOR UPDATE");
            String csr = rs.getCursorName();
            int temp;
            // we scan the resultset, row by row
            while (rs.next())
            {
                    temp = rs.getInt("salary");
                    // activate positioned update
                    if (temp >= 100000)
                    {
                            secondStmt.executeUpdate(
```

```
                  "UPDATE employees SET salary=salary*1.1
                                WHERE CURRENT OF " + csr);
                      }
              }
              rs.close();
              firstStmt.close();
              secondStmt.close();
              myConnection.close();
        }
    catch(java.lang.Exception ex)
    {
              ex.printStackTrace();
        }
  }
}
```

Summary

This chapter discussed some essential techniques for fine-tuning database queries and updates from JDBC:

◆   Dealing with data type conversion

◆   The SQL escape syntax

◆   Database transactions

◆   Handling SQL cursors

The next chapter discusses more advanced techniques such as callable statements, dynamic SQL, and the metadata interfaces of JDBC.

Chapter 7:

Advanced Techniques

IN THIS CHAPTER
This chapter introduces and shows how to deal with advanced techniques of
Structured Query Language (SQL) and Java Database Connectivity (JDBC) that add
a professional touch to applications:

◆ Handling stored procedures from JDBC

◆ Dynamic SQL

◆ Fetching database metadata

◆ Dynamic data access

THIS CHAPTER DISCUSSES ADVANCED techniques supported by JDBC. These techniques may prove to be very powerful when developing professional applications
or applets. Some database management system (DBMS) and JDBC drivers may not
support all these techniques.

Callable Statements

Callable statements are SQL statements that invoke stored procedures, which are
also called database Remote Procedure Calls (RPCs). The RPC is popular in the Unix
system programming world. It is used here in the sense of invoking remote code
that is stored in the database — stored procedures. Such procedures, when supported by the DBMS, allow storing of user statements containing SQL text in the
database. These procedures are usually stored for reuse from user session to user
session. They are useful for embedding application logic at the database side.
Figure 7-1 illustrates the invocation mechanism for stored procedures.

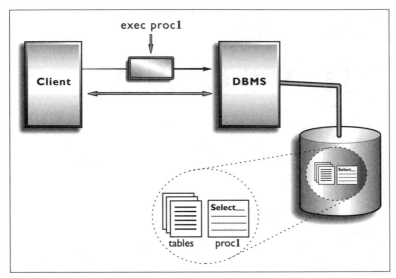

Figure 7-1: Invoking a stored procedure.

Statements that invoke stored procedures should use the JDBC CallableStatement class. A dedicated method must be called to prepare the callable statement. The usual methods are then used to execute the statement.

Connection

```
CallableStatement prepareCall(String sql);
```

where the argument is of the form:

```
"{? =call stored_procedure_name ?, ?, ....}"
```

```
CallableStatement prepareCall(String sql);
```

This method prepares a callable statement. It returns a CallableStatement object. Why something more elaborate than a simple Statement object is needed is discussed later.

Stored procedures may return multiple result types because they may be composed of SQL statements that return diverse result types: result sets and update counts. The usual methods are used to retrieve these results. However, when a procedure returns both multiple results and OUT parameter values, the OUT parameters should be retrieved last. Stored procedures may be called with parameters. They provide maximum flexibility by allowing values to be passed from and to the user's application. There are two types of such parameters: IN and OUT. IN parameters pass data to the stored procedure, and OUT parameters are values returned by the procedure code. Special JDBC methods exist to set and access these parameters. As

Figure 7-2 shows, setting IN values and registering OUT parameters must be done before the callable statement is executed. Figure 7-2 illustrates how to handle the parameters of callable statements.

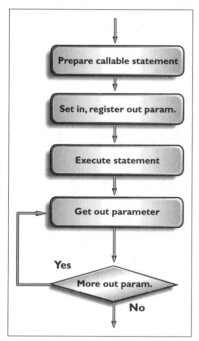

Figure 7-2: Overview of dealing with parameters.

Once the statement has been executed, all its OUT parameters may be explored, one by one, in left-to-right order. Note that Figure 7-2 illustrates the processing that must be done for a stored procedure that does **not** return ResultSets. If it returns a ResultSet, we would simply add a loop to fetch the result set **before** accessing the OUT parameters.

Setting Parameters

IN and OUT parameters must be set or registered prior to executing a callable statement.

IN PARAMETERS
IN parameters receive a value from the user's application. They are set via setXXX() methods that take two arguments: the parameter index, beginning at 1, and the value to set. The following methods are used to set values corresponding to their parameter's specific type.

CallableStatement

```
void setNull(int parameterIndex, int sqlType);
void setBoolean(int parameterIndex, boolean x);
void setByte(int parameterIndex, byte x);
void setShort(int parameterIndex, short x);
void setInt(int parameterIndex, int x);
void setLong(int parameterIndex, long x);
void setFloat(int parameterIndex, float x);
void setDouble(int parameterIndex, double x);
void set BigDecimal(int parameterIndex, java.math.BigDecimal x);
void setString(int parameterIndex, String x);
void setBytes(int parameterIndex, byte x[]);
void setDate(int parameterIndex, java.sql.Date x);
void setTime(int parameterIndex, java.sql.Time x);
void setTimestamp(int parameterIndex, java.sql.Timestamp x);
void setAsciiStream(int parameterIndex, java.io.InputStream x, int
  length);
void setUnicodeStream(int parameterIndex, java.io.InputStream x, int
  length);
void setBinaryStream(int parameterIndex, java.io.InputStream x, int
  length);
void setObject(int parameterIndex, Object x);
void setObject(int parameterIndex, Object x, int targetSqlType);
void setObject(int parameterIndex, Object x, int targetSqlType, int
  scale);
void clearParameters();
```

```
void setObject(...);
```

The setObject() methods belong to advanced JDBC features. They allow given Java objects to be stored in the database. However, they are converted to the database target SQL data type before they are actually sent to the database. Note that it is possible to pass database specific abstract data types by using a driver specific Java type and using a targetSqlType of java.sql.types.OTHER with the setObject(int parameterIndex, Object x, int targetSqlType) and the setObject(int parameterIndex, Object x, int targetSqlType, int scale) methods.

```
void clearParameters();
```

Normally, parameter values remain unaffected for repeated use of a statement. When invoked, this method immediately releases the resources used by the current parameters, and their values are cleared.

OUT PARAMETERS

OUT parameters must be registered prior to executing the callable statement. This registration is the way to specify their type. The following methods are available to register OUT parameters:

CallableStatement

```
void registerOutParameter(int parameterIndex, int sqlType);
void registerOutParameter(int parameterIndex, int sqlType, int
  scale);
```

```
void registerOutParameter(int parameterIndex, int sqlType);
```

The first argument is the parameter index, beginning at 1. The type argument must be defined in `java.sql.Types`.

```
void registerOutParameter(int parameterIndex, int sqlType, int
  scale);
```

This method is used to register OUT parameters of type SQL numeric or decimal. The scale argument represents the desired number of digits to the right of the decimal point.

Accessing Parameters

It is necessary to access parameters in left-to-right order and with the method that matches their type. These methods are provided for this purpose:

CallableStatement

```
boolean wasNull();
String getString(int parameterIndex);
boolean getBoolean(int parameterIndex);
byte getByte(int parameterIndex);
short getShort(int parameterIndex);
int getInt(int parameterIndex);
long getLong(int parameterIndex);
float getFloat(int parameterIndex);
double getDouble(int parameterIndex);
java.math.BigDecimal getBigDecimal(int parameterIndex, int scale);
byte[] getBytes(int parameterIndex);
java.sql.Date getDate(int parameterIndex);
java.sql.Time getTime(int parameterIndex);
java.sql.Timestamp getTimestamp(int parameterIndex);
Object getObject(int parameterIndex);
```

```
boolean wasNull();
```

When an OUT parameter has a null value, this method returns true. Note that you must call the corresponding `getXXX()` method **before** calling `wasNull()`.

Example

Listing 7-1 illustrates how to prepare a callable statement, how to set IN parameters, how to register OUT parameters, how to execute the statement, and how to access the OUT parameters. In this example, the first parameter is an IN parameter used to pass a value to the stored procedure. The second one is an OUT parameter used to retrieve a value after the execution of the stored procedure.

Listing 7-1: Dealing with stored procedure parameters.

```
. . .
. . .
Connection myConnection = DriverManager.getConnection(url,
        "javauser", "hotjava");
CallableStatement myStmt = myConnection.prepareCall(
  "{call my_stored_procedure ?, ?}");
myStmt.setString(1, "Hotjava");
myStmt.registerOutParameter(2, java.sql.Types.VARCHAR);
int res = myStmt.executeUpdate();
String outParam = myStmt.getString(2);
myStmt.close();
myConnection.close();
. . .
. . .
```

Dynamic SQL

A prepared statement is a SQL statement that is sent to the database prior to its execution. Unlike stored procedures, prepared statements will not remain in the database after the resources associated with it are freed. They may be called a number of times with different parameter values. Figures 7-3 and 7-4 illustrate some differences between the execution of simple SQL statements and the execution of prepared statements.

In Figure 7-3, the SQL text is sent to the database along with specific values and literals. This example illustrates an INSERT.

When executing a prepared statement (Figure 7-4), the SQL statement is already at the database side. Only parameter values are passed.

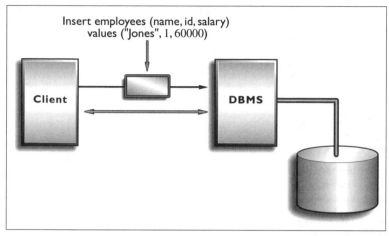

Figure 7-3: Sending a static statement.

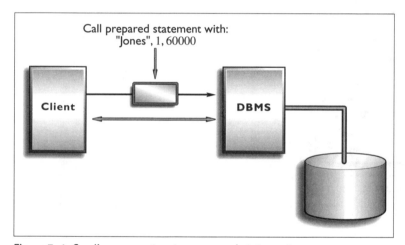

Figure 7-4: Sending parameters to a prepared statement.

As Figure 7-5 shows, five steps must be followed to use prepared statements with JDBC:

1. Prepare the SQL statement

2. Set IN parameters

3. Execute the statement

4. Get the results, if any

5. If necessary, set new IN parameter values and reexecute the statement

The last step is optional, but in many cases prepared statements are used for this facility.

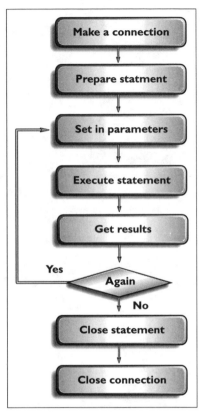

Figure 7-5: Overview of prepared statements.

Connection

```
PreparedStatement prepareStatement(String sql);


PreparedStatement prepareStatement(String sql);
```

This method is used to get a PreparedStatement object for later execution. Parameters are symbolized by "?" characters.

Passing IN Parameters

As for callable statements, prepared statement IN parameters must be set one by one. These methods are available for this purpose:

PreparedStatement

```
void setNull(int parameterIndex, int sqlType);
void setBoolean(int parameterIndex, boolean x);
void setByte(int parameterIndex, byte x);
void setShort(int parameterIndex, short x);
void setInt(int parameterIndex, int x);
void setLong(int parameterIndex, long x);
void setFloat(int parameterIndex, float x);
void setDouble(int parameterIndex, double x);
void setBigDecimal(int parameterIndex, java.math.BigDecimal x);
void setString(int parameterIndex, String x);
void setBytes(int parameterIndex, byte x[]);
void setDate(int parameterIndex, java.sql.Date x);
void setTime(int parameterIndex, java.sql.Time x);
void setTimestamp(int parameterIndex, java.sql.Timestamp x);
void setAsciiStream(int parameterIndex, java.io.InputStream x, int
  length);
void setUnicodeStream(int parameterIndex, java.io.InputStream x, int
  length);
void setBinaryStream(int parameterIndex, java.io.InputStream x, int
  length);
void setObject(int parameterIndex, Object x);
void setObject(int parameterIndex, Object x, int targetSqlType);
void setObject(int parameterIndex, Object x, int targetSqlType, int
  scale);
void clearParameters();
```

Note that the setObject() and clearParameters() methods have the same meaning as for callable statements.

Executing the Query and Retrieving Results

Once all IN parameters are set, the execution of a prepared statement is performed as for normal statements. A prepared statement may return a count value as well as a ResultSet. Listing 7-2 shows all these steps put together.

Listing 7-2: Dealing with prepared statement parameters.

```
...
...
Connection myConnection = DriverManager.getConnection(url,
            "javauser", "hotjava");
PreparedStatement myStmt = myConnection.prepareStatement(
  "UPDATE employees SET salary = ? WHERE department = ?");
myStmt.setInt(1, 100000);
```

```
myStmt.setString(2, "Systems and Networking");
int res = myStmt.executeUpdate();
myStmt.setInt(1, 200000);
myStmt.setString(2, "Engineering");
res = myStmt.executeUpdate();
myStmt.setInt(1, 300000);
myStmt.setString(2, "Management");
res = myStmt.executeUpdate();
myStmt.close();
myConnection.close();
...
...
```

Dealing with BLOBs

There was no way to send Binary Large Objects (BLOBs) to a database using normal SQL statements. This feature is simply not supported within normal SQL statements. Because prepared statements support the `setAsciiStream()`, `setUnicode-Stream()`, and `setBinaryStream()` methods of setting IN parameters, it is possible to send multikilobyte and multimegabyte values to the database.

SENDING BLOBS

Very large binary data will be sent using input/output (I/O) streams and `setBinaryStream()`. It is unnecessary to send the data in small chunks as is required for receiving BLOBs because the JDBC driver will make repeated calls on the I/O stream to read its content and send it to the database as the actual parameter data. Listing 7-3 illustrates an insertion of BLOBs using input streams.

Listing 7-3: Sending very large parameters to the database.

```
...
...
Connection myConnection = DriverManager.getConnection(url,
            "javauser", "hotjava");
java.io.File pictFile = new java.io.File("jones.jpeg");
java.io.File audioFile = new java.io.File("jones.au");
int pictFileLen = (int) pictFile.length();
int audioFileLen = (int) audioFile.length();
java.io.InputStream fPict =
  new java.io.FileInputStream(pictFile);
java.io.InputStream fAudio =
  new java.io.FileInputStream(audioFile);
PreparedStatement myStmt = myConnection.prepareStatement(
  "UPDATE employees SET emp_pict = ?, emp_welcome = ?
    WHERE id = ?");
myStmt.setBinaryStream(1, fPict, pictFileLen);
myStmt.setBinaryStream(2, fAudio, audioFileLen);
myStmt.setInt(3, 1);
int res = myStmt.executeUpdate();
```

```
myStmt.close();
myConnection.close();
...
...
```

Metadata Interfaces

Metadata interfaces are useful to query a database or a ResultSet for meta information. A programmer normally will not use the DatabaseMetaData interface; however, it provides many interesting methods for discovering database behaviors, default values, supported functions, and so forth. The ResultSetMetaData interface will probably be used more often, because it provides information on ResultSets that are, indeed, results of user queries.

Information on Database Objects

The scope of database metadata is very broad. One of its most interesting uses is to obtain information on the database objects themselves.

Connection
```
DatabaseMetaData getMetaData();

DatabaseMetaData getMetaData();
```

   A database can provide information on its objects, such as tables, stored procedures, SQL grammar, and various properties. All this information is obtainable through methods that apply to a `DatabaseMetaData` object. The code `getMetaData()` returns such an object.

The DatabaseMetaData Interface

The DatabaseMetaData interface provides a number of methods to access database metadata. The methods fit into different categories, such as minor information on the database itself, information on what kind of features it supports, on its limitations, and on all database objects it contains. Most of them return string, boolean, or integer values, but a number of them return ResultSets. How to deal with ResultSets is discussed later.

Miscellaneous Database Information

The DatabaseMetaData interface is a rich interface. It provides many methods useful to discover the specifics of the database.

DatabaseMetaData

```
boolean allProceduresAreCallable();
boolean allTableAreSelectable();
String getURL();
String getUserName();
boolean isReadOnly();
boolean nullsAreSortedHigh();
boolean nullsAreSortedLow();
boolean nullsAreSortedAtStart();
boolean nullsAreSortedAtEnd();
String getDatabaseProductName();
String getDatabaseProductVersion();
String getDriverName();
String getDriverVersion();
int getDriverMajorVersion();
int getDriverMinorVersion();
boolean usesLocalFiles();
boolean usesLocalFilePerTable();
boolean supportsMixedCaseIdentifiers();
boolean storesUpperCaseIdentifiers();
boolean storesLowerCaseIdentifiers();
boolean storesMixedCaseIdentifiers();
boolean supportsMixedCaseQuotedIdentifiers();
boolean storesUpperCaseQuotedIdentifiers();
boolean storesLowerCaseQuotedIdentifiers();
boolean storesMixedCaseQuotedIdentifiers();
String getIdentifierQuoteString();
String getSQLKeywords();
String getNumericFunctions();
String getStringFunctions();
String getSystemFunctions();
String getTimeDateFunctions();
String getSearchStringExcape();
String getExtraNameCharacters();
```

Listing 7-4 illustrates how to get various kinds of information using some of the DatabaseMetaData object methods.

Listing 7-4: DatabaseMetaData

```
// databasemetadata
import java.sql.*;
class SimpleExample
{
  public static void main(String args[])
  {
      String url = "jdbc:odbc:mysource";
      try
      {
  Class.forName("sun.jdbc.odbc.JdbcOdbcDriver");
              Connection myConnection =
              DriverManager.getConnection(url,
                  "javauser", "hotjava");
```

```
                    DatabaseMetaData mtdt =
                            myConnection.getMetaData();
                    System.out.println("URL in use: " +
                            mtdt.getURL());
                    System.out.println("User name: " +
                            mtdt.getUserName());
                    System.out.println("DBMS name: " +
                            mtdt.getDatabaseProductName());
                    System.out.println("DBMS version: " +
                            mtdt.getDatabaseProductVersion());
                    System.out.println("Driver name: " +
                            mtdt.getDriverName());
                    System.out.println("Driver version: " +
                            mtdt.getDriverVersion());
                    System.out.println("supp. SQL Keywords: " +
                            mtdt.getSQLKeywords());
                    myConnection.close();
            }
        catch(java.lang.Exception ex)
        {
                    ex.printStackTrace();
            }
    }
}
```

The example's output may be similar to the following code, which is particular to Sybase System 11.

```
URL in use: jdbc:odbc:mysource
User name: javauser
DBMS name: SQL Server
DBMS version: SQL Server/11.0/P/Sun_svr4/OS 5.4/1/OPT/Thu Dec 7
 23:58:01 PST 1995
Driver name: JDBC-ODBC Bridge (SYSYB95.DLL)
Driver version: 1.0101 (02.12.0000)
supp. SQL Keywords:
 arith_overflow,break,browse,bulk,char_convert,checkpoint,clustered,
 commit,compute,confirm,controlrow,data_pgs,database,dbcc,disk,dummy
 ,dump,endtran,errlvl,errorexit,exit,fillfactor,holdlock,identity_in
 sert,if,kill,lineno,load,mirror,mirrorexit,noholdlock,nonclustered,
 numeric_truncation,offsets,once,over,perm,permanent,plan,print,proc
 ,processexit,raiserror,read,readtext,reconfigure,replace,reserved_p
 gs,return,role,rowcnt,rowcount,rule,save,setuser,shared,shutdown,so
 me,statistics,stripe,syb_identity,syb_restree,syb_terminate,temp,te
 xtsize,tran,trigger,truncate,tsequal,used_pgs,user_option,waitfor,w
 hile,writetext
```

Features Supported

The DatabaseMetaData interface is a rich interface that provides many methods for discovering the features supported by the database.

DatabaseMetaData

```
boolean supportsAlterTableWithAddColumn();
boolean supportsAlterTableWithDropColumn();
boolean supportsColumnAliasing();
boolean nullPlusNonNullIsNull();
boolean supportsConvert();
boolean supportsConvert(int fromType, int toType);
boolean supportsTableCorrelationNames();
boolean supportsDifferentTableCorrelationNames();
boolean supportsExpressionsInOrderBy();
boolean supportsOrderByUnrelated();
boolean supportsGroupBy();
boolean supportsGroupByUnrelated();
boolean supportsGroupByBeyondSelect();
boolean supportsLikeEscapeClause();
boolean supportsMultipleResultSets();
boolean supportsMultipleTransactions();
boolean supportsNonNullableColumns();
boolean supportsMinimumSQLGrammar();
boolean supportsCoreSQLGrammar();
boolean supportsExtendedSQLGrammar();
boolean supportsANSI92EntryLevelSQL();
boolean supportsANSI92IntermediateSQL();
boolean supportsANSI92FullSQL();
boolean supportsIntegrityEnhancementFacility();
boolean supportsOuterJoins();
boolean supportsFullOuterJoins();
boolean supportsLimitedOuterJoins();
String getSchemaTerm();
String getProcedureTerm();
String getCatalogTerm();
boolean isCatalogAtStart();
String getCatalogSeparator();
boolean supportsSchemasInDataManipulation();
boolean supportsSchemasInProcedureCalls();
boolean supportsSchemasInTableDefinitions();
boolean supportsSchemasInIndexDefinitions();
boolean supportsSchemaInPriviledDefinitions();
boolean supportsCatalogsInDataManipulation();
boolean supportsCatalogsInProcedureCalls();
boolean supportsCatalogsInTableDefinitions();
boolean supportsCatalogsInIndexDefinitions();
boolean supportsCatalogsInPrivilegeDefinitions();
boolean supportsPositionedDelete();
boolean supportsPositionedUpdate();
boolean supportsSelectForUpdate();
boolean supportsStoredProcedures();
boolean supportsSubqueriesInComparisons();
boolean supportsSubqueriesInExists();
boolean supportsSubqueriesInIns();
```

```
boolean supportsSubqueriesInQuantifieds();
boolean supportsCorrelatedSubqueries();
boolean supportsUnion();
boolean supportsUnionAll();
boolean supportsOpenCursorAcrossCommit();
boolean supportsOpenCursorAcrossRollback();
boolean supportsOpenStatementAcrossCommit();
boolean supportsOpenStatementAcrossRollback();
```

Various Database Limitations

The DatabaseMetaData interface also provides many methods for discovering the database's limitations.

DatabaseMetaData

```
int getMaxBinaryLiteralLength();
int getMaxCharLiteralLength();
int getMaxColumnNameLength();
int getMaxColumnsInGroupBy();
int getMaxColumnsInIndex();
int getMaxColumnsInOrderBy();
int getMaxColumnsInSelect();
int getMaxColumnsInTable();
int getMaxConnections();
int getMaxCursorNameLength();
int getMaxIndexLength();
int getMaxSchemaNameLength();
int getMaxProcedureNameLength();
int getMaxCatalogNameLength();
int getMaxRowSize();
boolean doesMaxRowSizeIncludeBlobs();
int getMaxStatementLength();
int getMaxStatements();
int getMaxTableNameLength();
int getMaxTablesInSelect();
int getMaxUserNameLength();
int getDefaultTransactionIsolation();
boolean supportsTransactions();
boolean supportsTransactionIsolationLevel(int level);
boolean supportsDataDefinitionAndDataManipulationTransactions();
boolean supportsDataManipulationTransactionsOnly();
boolean dataDefinitionCausesTransactionCommit();
boolean dataDefinitionIgnoredInTransactions();
```

Listing 7-5 illustrates a metadata method for discovering the database's ANSI compliance level.

Listing 7-5: Metadata method for discovering ANSI compliance level.

```java
// discovering ANSI compliance
import java.sql.*;
class SimpleExample
{
 public static void main(String args[])
 {
      String url = "jdbc:odbc:mysource";
      try
 {
 Class.forName("sun.jdbc.odbc.JdbcOdbcDriver");
          Connection myConnection =
               DriverManager.getConnection(url,
                    "javauser", "hotjava");
          DatabaseMetaData mtdt =
               myConnection.getMetaData();
          System.out.println("ANSI92 Entry Level: " +
               mtdt.supportsANSI92EntryLevelSQL());
          System.out.println("ANSI92 Intermediate: " +
               mtdt.supportsANSI92IntermediateSQL());
          System.out.println("ANSI92 Full SQL: " +
               mtdt.supportsANSI92FullSQL());
          System.out.println("Minimum SQL Grammar: " +
               mtdt.supportsMinimumSQLGrammar());
          System.out.println("Core SQL Grammar: " +
               mtdt.supportsCoreSQLGrammar());
      System.out.println("Extended SQL Grammar: "
           + mtdt.supportsExtendedSQLGrammar());
      myConnection.close();
      }
      catch(java.lang.Exception ex)
      {
          ex.printStackTrace ();
      }
  }
}
```

INFORMATION ON DATABASE OBJECTS

The DatabaseMetaData interface also provides many methods for discovering the database's contents.

DatabaseMetaData

```
ResultSet getProcedures(String catalog, String schemaPattern, String
  procedureNamePattern);
ResultSet getProcedureColumns(String catalog, String schemaPattern,
  String procedureNamePattern, String columnNamePattern);
ResultSet getTables(String catalog, String schemaPattern, String
  tableNamePattern, String types[]);
getschemas();
ResultSet getCatalogs();
ResultSet getTableTypes();
ResultSet getColumns(String catalog, String schemaPattern, String
  tableNamePattern, String columnNamePattern);
ResultSet getColumnPrivileges(String catalog, String schema, String
  table, String columnNamePattern);
ResultSet getTablePrivileges(String catalog, String schemaPattern,
  String tableNamePattern);
ResultSet getBestRowIdentifier(String catalog, String schema, String
  table, int scope, boolean nullable);
ResultSet getVersionColumns(String catalog, String schema, String
  table);
ResultSet getPrimaryKeys(String catalog, String schema, String
  table);
ResultSet getImportedKeys(String catalog, String schema, String
  table);
ResultSet getExportedKeys(String catalog, String schema, String
  table);
ResultSet getCrossReference(String primaryCatalog, String
  primarySchema, String primaryTable, String foreignCatalog, String
  foreignSchema, String foreignTable);
ResultSet getTypeInfo();
ResultSet getIndexInfo(String catalog, String schema, String table,
  boolean unique, boolean approximate);
```

Most of these methods need arguments such as catalog name, schema name, procedure, table, and column name. All the parameters named xxxPattern do not have to match a particular database object name. If necessary, they may be composed of the "%" and "_" matching characters. The "%" matches zero or more characters, while "_" matches any one character.

All these methods return ResultSets. Indeed, they usually return multiple values, which means providing results through ResultSets is very convenient. As Figure 7-6 shows, the usual method is used to scan those result sets.

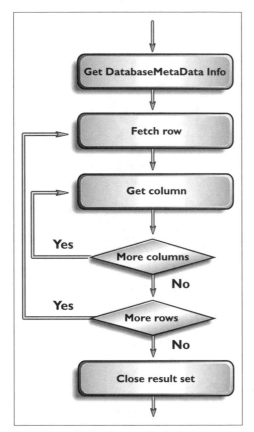

Figure 7-6: Processing methods that return a
ResultSet.

Listing 7-6 includes some database metadata calls that show how to query metadata information using these last methods.

Listing 7-6: Metadata on database objects.

```
// retrieving results
import java.sql.*;
class SimpleExample
{
 public static void main(String args[])
  {
      String url = "jdbc:odbc:mysource";
      try
      {
            Class.forName("sun.jdbc.odbc.JdbcOdbcDriver");
            Connection myConnection =
                  DriverManager.getConnection(url,
                        "javauser", "hotjava");
```

```
            DatabaseMetaData dmtd = myConnection.getMetaData();
            // list catalogs managed by this dbms
            scanRS("Info on " + dmtd.getCatalogTerm() + "(s):",
                  dmtd.getCatalogs());
            // list all tables in current catalog, belonging
            // to all schemas, of all types
            scanRS("Info on tables:",
                  dmtd.getTables(myConnection.getCatalog(), "%",
                        "%", null));
            // list all procedures in current catalog,
            // belonging to all schemas
            scanRS("Info on " + dmtd.getProcedureTerm() + "(s):",
                  dmtd.getProcedures(myConnection.getCatalog(),
                        "%", "%"));
            myConnection.close();
      }
      catch(java.lang.Exception ex)
      {
            ex.printStackTrace();
      }
}
private static void scanRS(String info, ResultSet rs)
                        throws SQLException
{
      System.out.println(info);
      System.out.println();
      if (rs != null)
      {
            int i;
            // we have a ResultSet

            ResultSetMetaData rsmd = rs.getMetaData();
            int numCols = rsmd.getColumnCount();
            // display column headers
            for (i = 1; i <= numCols; i++)
            {
                  if (i > 1) System.out.print(", ");
                  System.out.print(rsmd.getColumnLabel(i));
            }
            System.out.println("");
            // step through the rows
            while (rs.next())
            {
                  // process the columns
                  for (i = 1; i <= numCols; i++)
                  {
                        if (i > 1) System.out.print(", ");
                        System.out.print(rs.getString(i));
                  }
            System.out.println("");
            }
      }
      else
```

```
        {
                System.out.println("no data returned...");
        }
        System.out.println ();
    }
}
```

The Listing 7-6 example prints information similar to the following listing. The data returned here came from a Sybase System 11 server. The user's current catalog is the default sample database provided by Sybase.

Info on database(s)

```
TABLE_QUALIFIER
master
model
pubs2
sybsecurity
sybsyntax
sybsystemprocs
tempdb
test
testdb2
userdb
```

Info on tables

```
TABLE_QUALIFIER, TABLE_OWNER, TABLE_NAME, TABLE_TYPE, REMARKS
pubs2, dbo, sysalternates, SYSTEM TABLE, null
pubs2, dbo, syscolumns, SYSTEM TABLE, null
pubs2, dbo, syscomments, SYSTEM TABLE, null
pubs2, dbo, sysconstraints, SYSTEM TABLE, null
pubs2, dbo, sysdepends, SYSTEM TABLE, null
pubs2, dbo, sysindexes, SYSTEM TABLE, null
pubs2, dbo, syskeys, SYSTEM TABLE, null
pubs2, dbo, syslogs, SYSTEM TABLE, null
pubs2, dbo, sysobjects, SYSTEM TABLE, null
pubs2, dbo, sysprocedures, SYSTEM TABLE, null
pubs2, dbo, sysprotects, SYSTEM TABLE, null
pubs2, dbo, sysreferences, SYSTEM TABLE, null
pubs2, dbo, syssegments, SYSTEM TABLE, null
pubs2, dbo, systypes, SYSTEM TABLE, null
pubs2, dbo, sysusermessages, SYSTEM TABLE, null
pubs2, dbo, sysusers, SYSTEM TABLE, null
pubs2, dbo, au_pix, TABLE, null
pubs2, dbo, authors, TABLE, null
pubs2, dbo, blurbs, TABLE, null
pubs2, dbo, discounts, TABLE, null
pubs2, dbo, publishers, TABLE, null
pubs2, dbo, roysched, TABLE, null
pubs2, dbo, sales, TABLE, null
```

```
pubs2, dbo, salesdetail, TABLE, null
pubs2, dbo, stores, TABLE, null
pubs2, dbo, titleauthor, TABLE, null
pubs2, dbo, titles, TABLE, null
```

Info on Stored Procedure(s)

```
PROCEDURE_QUALIFIER, PROCEDURE_OWNER, PROCEDURE_NAME,
  NUM_INPUT_PARAMS, NUM_OUTPUT_PARAMS, NUM_RESULT_SETS, REMARKS,
  PROCEDURE_TYPE
pubs2, dbo, byroyalty, null, null, null, null, 1
pubs2, dbo, discount_proc, null, null, null, null, 1
pubs2, dbo, history_proc, null, null, null, null, 1
pubs2, dbo, insert_sales_proc, null, null, null, null, 1
pubs2, dbo, insert_salesdetail_proc, null, null, null, null, 1
pubs2, dbo, storeid_proc, null, null, null, null, 1
pubs2, dbo, storename_proc, null, null, null, null, 1
pubs2, dbo, title_proc, null, null, null, null, 1
pubs2, dbo, titleid_proc, null, null, null, null, 1
pubs2, guest, testproc, null, null, null, null, 1
```

The ResultSetMetaData Interface

Once a ResultSet has been returned by the database, it is possible to get all kinds of information concerning the ResultSet, such as the columns it contains and its type and label. The ResultSetMetaData interface offers the following methods for finding out about a result set's metadata. These methods also work on ResultSets returned by some of the DatabaseMetaData class because those ResultSets are just ResultSets.

Information on ResultSet Columns

The ResultSetMetaData interface is a rich interface providing many methods for obtaining information about the columns of a result set.

ResultSetMetaData

```
int getColumnCount();
int getColumnDisplaySize(int column);
String getColumnLabel(int column);
String getColumnName(int column);
String getSchemaName(int column);
int getPrecision(int column);
int getScale(int column);
String getTableName(int column);
String getCatalogName(int column);
```

```
int getColumnType(int column);
String getColumnTypeName(int column);
```

Column Properties

The ResultSetMetaData interface provides many methods for obtaining information about the properties of the columns of a result set.

ResultSetMetaData

```
boolean isAutoIncrement(int column);
boolean isCaseSensitive(int column);
boolean isSearchable(int column);
boolean isCurrency(int column);
int isNullable(int column);
boolean isSigned(int column);
boolean isReadOnly(int column);
boolean isWritable(int column);
boolean isDefinitelyWritable(int column);
```

Note that there is no way to get information on rows of data or their numbers. Such information is only available on columns. The method in Listing 7-7 gets the number and label of each column.

Listing 7-7: ResultSetMetaData.

```
...
...
                int i;
                // we have a ResultSet

                ResultSetMetaData rsmd = rs.getMetaData();
                int numCols = rsmd.getColumnCount();
                // display column headers
                for (i = 1; i <= numCols; i++)
                {
                        if (i > 1) System.out.print(", ");
                        System.out.print(rsmd.getColumnLabel(i));
                }
                System.out.println("");
...
...
```

Dynamic Data Access

While the DatabaseMetaData and ResultSetMetaData interfaces provide numerous methods to access a database without knowing its schema, other methods exist to support generic data access. These methods allow data to be accessed dynamically through generic Java objects. They are of the form getObject() and setObject() to retrieve and to set data, respectively, in a table or result set's columns.

The usual methods to send and retrieve data allow you to map one or more SQL data types to specific Java types. The methods explained here allow you to use Java objects, regardless of what type SQL data is accessed. Precise mapping rules are used. Indeed, specific SQL data types must correspond to specific Java types, and specific Java types must correspond to specific SQL types.

Dynamically Typed Data Retrieval

Dynamically typed data retrieval is performed using ResultSet.getObject() to access columns, or CallableStatement.getObject() to access OUT parameters of stored procedures. Table 7-1 shows the default mapping from SQL types to Java types that are subtypes of Object. No mapping to Java streams is provided.

TABLE 7-1 DEFAULT MAPPING FROM SQL TYPES TO JAVA OBJECT TYPES

SQL type	Java object type
CHAR	String
VARCHAR	String
LONGVARCHAR	String
NUMERIC	java.math.BigDecimal
DECIMAL	java.math.BigDecimal
BIT	Boolean
TINYINT	Integer
SMALLINT	Integer
INTEGER	Integer
BIGINT	Long
REAL	Float
FLOAT	Double
DOUBLE	Double
BINARY	byte[]
VARBINARY	byte[]

(continued)

TABLE 7-1 *(Continued)*

LONGVARBINARY	byte[]
DATE	java.sql.Date
TIME	java.sql.Time
TIMESTAMP	java.sql.Timestamp

ResultSet

```
Object getObject(int columnIndex);
Object getObject(String columnName);
```

The getObject() method is used like other getXXX() methods but returns a Java object whose type may be discovered using Table 7-1. It corresponds to the SQL data type of the accessed result set column.

CallableStatement

```
void registerOutParameter(int parameterIndex, int sqlType);
void registerOutParameter(int parameterIndex, int sqlType, int
  scale);
Object getObject(int parameterIndex);
```

As seen earlier with callable statements, it is necessary to register OUT parameters before executing the call and accessing them. A Java object type corresponding to the SQL data type passed as parameter is returned.

Dynamically Typed Data Insertion/Update

Dynamically typed data insertion or update may only be performed through IN parameters of stored procedures or prepared statements. Specific SQL data types may be explicitly targeted in accordance with Table 7-2.

TABLE 7-2 CONVERSIONS BETWEEN JAVA OBJECT TYPES AND TARGET SQL TYPES

	TINYINT	SMALLINT	INTEGER	BIGINT	REAL	FLOAT
String	☺	☺	☺	☺	☺	☺
BigDecimal	☺	☺	☺	☺	☺	☺
Boolean	☺	☺	☺	☺	☺	☺
Integer	☺	☺	☺	☺	☺	☺
Long	☺	☺	☺	☺	☺	☺
Float	☺	☺	☺	☺	☺	☺
Double	☺	☺	☺	☺	☺	☺
byte[]						
java.sql.Date						
java.sql.Time						
java.sql.Timestamp						

	DOUBLE	DECIMAL	NUMERIC	BIT	CHAR	VARCHAR
String	☺	☺	☺	☺	☺	☺
BigDecimal	☺	☺	☺	☺	☺	☺
Boolean	☺	☺	☺	☺	☺	☺
Integer	☺	☺	☺	☺	☺	☺
Long	☺	☺	☺	☺	☺	☺
Float	☺	☺	☺	☺	☺	☺
Double	☺	☺	☺	☺	☺	☺
byte[]						
java.sql.Date					☺	☺
java.sql.Time					☺	☺
java.sql.Timestamp					☺	☺

(continued)

TABLE 7-2 *(Continued)*

	LONGVARCHAR	BINARY	VARBINARY	LONGVARBINARY
String	☺	☺	☺	☺
BigDecimal	☺			
Boolean	☺			
Integer	☺			
Long	☺			
Float	☺			
Double	☺			
byte[]		☺	☺	☺
java.sql.Date	☺			
java.sql.Time	☺			
java.sql.Timestamp	☺			

	DATE	TIME	TIMESTAMP
String	☺	☺	☺
BigDecimal			
Boolean			
Integer			
Long			
Float			
Double			
byte[]			
java.sql.Date	☺		☺
java.sql.Time		☺	
java.sql.Timestamp	☺	☺	☺

A ☺ means the conversion can be done. No support for Java streams is provided.

CallableStatement or PreparedStatement

```
void setObject(int parameterIndex, Object x);
void setObject(int parameterIndex, Object x, int targetSqlType);
void setObject(int parameterIndex, Object x, int targetSqlType, int
 scale);
```

When no target SQL type is specified to the setObject() method, the Java object is directly converted according to the default mapping as shown in Table 7-3. If a target SQL type is provided, the Java object is first mapped to its default corresponding type and then converted to the specified SQL type (see Table 7-2).

TABLE 7-3 DEFAULT MAPPING FROM JAVA OBJECT TYPES TO SQL TYPES

Java object type	SQL type
String	VARCHAR or LONGVARCHAR
java.math.BigDecimal	NUMERIC
Boolean	BIT
Integer	INTEGER
Long	BIGINT
Float	REAL
Double	DOUBLE
byte[]	VARBINARY or LONGVARBINARY
java.sql.Date	DATE
java.sql.Time	TIME
java.sql.Timestamp	TIMESTAMP

Multithreading

JDBC is multithread safe. Several threads can call the same java.sql object simultaneously and perform operations asynchronously. For example, multiple statements can be executed concurrently within the same connection. It does not mean that all JDBC drivers are able to manage concurrent executions asynchronously, but even in this case, the developer can assume fully concurrent executions. Indeed, fully

JDBC-compliant drivers will serialize calls automatically, even if they do not support asynchronous executions (i.e., where they are not multithread safe themselves). Such behavior is totally transparent to the programmer, even if the driver provides some form of synchronization. In this case, the application threads will run concurrently (a reduced concurrency).

Multithread support is exploitable to execute multiple statements on the same connection and to allow more control over a running execution. Indeed, it is possible to cancel a long running statement in one thread using the `Statement.cancel()` method of another thread.

Summary

This chapter discussed advanced techniques of SQL and JDBC that add a professional touch to applications, including:

- ◆ Handling stored procedures from JDBC
- ◆ Dynamic SQL
- ◆ Fetching database metadata
- ◆ Dynamic data access

The next part of this book contains many working examples, from simple to complex, that cover most of the theory discussed in previous chapters.

Chapter 8

The Three-Tier Approach for Using Distributed Objects

IN THIS CHAPTER

This chapter discusses an alternative to the two-tier model. The Java Remote Method Invocation allows distribution of objects across software tiers while providing an ideal place for the application logic. The areas discussed in this chapter include:

◆ An introduction to software partitioning

◆ Object persistency

◆ Java Remote Method Invocation

◆ CORBA

THE FIRST CHAPTERS OF this book mentioned the next wave of client-server architectures. This wave presents a philosophy with a great impact on software design. Indeed, it changes the commonly accepted rules of implementing data access and processing both at the client and the database sides. The following paragraphs discuss these issues, but try to keep things simple while providing possible solutions in Java.

Recall the basics of traditional client-server architecture involving a relational database. As Figure 8-1 shows, Java Database Connectivity (JDBC) is located on the client side. Most of the code that accesses and processes data uses JDBC intensively and is also located on the client side. The code embeds the application logic— for example, Structured Query Language (SQL) queries, information on data type conversions, and information on data structures. There is, however, a part of the code located on the database side. Indeed, stored procedures also hold information on data or contain SQL expressions to be executed by the database engine.

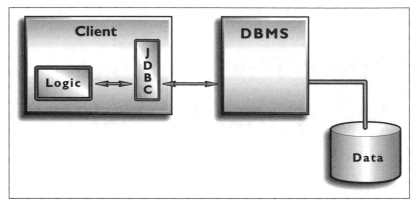

Figure 8-1: Two-tier architecture with JDBC on the client side.

It is very difficult to modify the code on both sides as often as the rules change. All clients that connect to the database must be modified to reflect the new rules. Programmers know that it is annoying to maintain different pieces of software that basically access the same data. The code of one program may barely import into another program even when developed with the same programming language and tools. Approaches such as standard in-house developed libraries address the problem but too often, do not totally solve it.

The idea of three-tier architecture involves moving most of the code that accesses and processes data into a third tier. This tier basically holds all of the business logic necessary to run the clients, if not the business itself.

How does it work? Let's begin with the easiest part: Almost nothing changes on the database side. It still maintains data and holds the most important stored procedures or those that consume the most CPU cycles. It keeps its role of providing concurrent accesses, integrity, recovery, and ease of data administration.

Clients no longer hold any bytecode that accesses data using SQL. They will never see rows of data. They will never map these rows of data to local variables or object data members. Because the clients are written in Java and there are only objects in Java, the clients will keep manipulating data as Java objects and will eventually call the appropriate methods on these objects.

The remaining part is the most sensitive one: the third tier. This tier is a client of the database and, in a sense, a server for the client applications. This tier holds the code to access data and SQL queries, using JDBC to perform its operations. This is where rows of data are mapped into Java objects. For example, a query returning a list of employees would return a set of Java objects called employee, and a method called raiseSalary could be invoked on individual employee objects or a set of objects.

The client application uses employee objects and knows the raiseSalary method but they are not implemented within its code. Shared objects are called proxy objects on the client side. They are implemented in the middleware and whenever a client invokes the raiseSalary method, the raiseSalary method is triggered within the middleware, executing an SQL update that will update the employee's salary in the database. The object implementation is called the nonvisible object — the implementation is not visible from the clients.

Figure 8-2 clearly illustrates the architecture. JDBC is located within the middleware.

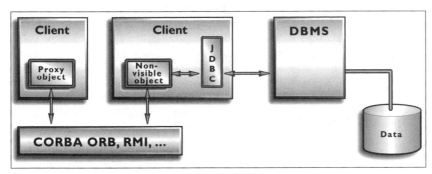

Figure 8-2: The three-tier architecture with JDBC in the middleware.

Let's discuss the software bus that ties proxy objects and nonvisible objects (NVOs) together. Actually, a big part of the real implementation of three-tier architectures is dependent on this software bus. There are numerous possibilities but the most common in Java are RMI and CORBA. RMI stands for Remote Method Invocation while CORBA stands for Common Object Request Broker Architecture. These concepts are described later.

The rows of data must be mapped into Java object data members within the middleware. This hard work is necessary because of the impedance mismatch between all object-oriented programming languages and SQL. By definition, the data that is stored in database tables is persistent. All first-generation client-server clients were used to access persistent data in tabular format through SQL, but now we want them only to manipulate objects.

Object Persistency

Usual Java objects or class instances are transient, unless they are serialized to a file. This simply means that they do not persist outside of the application that instantiated them. Values fill data members at run time, and these data members are garbage-collected and cleared when no longer used. Exiting the program destroys the objects.

If you use a proper object-oriented programming language such as Java, you may think that there should be a way to avoid constructing essential objects each time you need them. Indeed, why should you need to perform the same operations to build objects each time the program executes? There must be some way to avoid this rebuilding.

Object persistency is the solution. It allows you to keep objects data members alive, even when the application is not running. There are many ways to make objects persistent (to *persistify* objects), and database management systems seem well suited for this purpose. They offer many data-oriented services, plus a common query language. While SQL is used within the scope of relational databases, an object query language (OQL) queries objects stored within object database management systems (DBMS).

The most common DBMS is relational, not object-oriented; but it does not matter. It is easy to write methods to perform the most basic tasks related to persistency. Here are a few of them:

◆ Creation of a new object

◆ Deletion

◆ Update

◆ Query that returns one object or a set of objects

◆ Duplication of objects (object cloning)

There is no need to define a custom query language to perform lookups on persistified objects; a single querySQLWhere() method whose arguments are vectors of data member names and values is a good start.

A word about mapping Java objects to tabular data in tables is necessary. Java classes may or may not extend (inherit from) another class. We can simply map the data members of a class to corresponding fields of a table if the class is not extending another. In this case, each record of the table represents an instance of the class. We call them *persistified* objects. A design choice which is left to the developer is made when a class extends another class. Either an instance of this class is mapped to a row in two different tables (one table per class) or it is mapped to only one table. In the latter case, the table's rows contain all the fields of the base class plus those of the inherited class. This second approach can be more efficient because it does not require joining multiple tables when trying to access the *persistified* objects. Figure 8-3 shows how to map simple objects to a table.

Figure 8-3 illustrates the parts of a persistified object:

◆ The client side only sees data members and methods of persistified objects

◆ The database only stores data members in its tables

◆ The middleware provides basic methods to handle persistified objects; it does the mapping and provides application-logic related methods

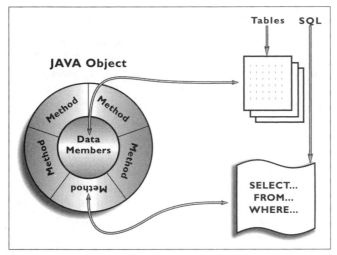

Figure 8-3: Mapping of Java object versus traditional DBMS object.

To summarize, persistification occurs in the middleware and provides a longer lifetime to application-essential objects. Now it is time to discover a few ways to have transparent access to persistified Java objects.

Java Remote Method Invocation

Java RMI is a Java-to-Java remote object technology similar to remote procedure calls (RPC). It allows you to create distributed applications in which the methods of Java objects may be invoked from programs running on other virtual machines, at other locations of the network.

RMI may solve the issue of accessing middleware object instances from clients. It is light, reliable, and works over TCP/IP (Transmission Control Protocol/Internet Protocol) and the Internet.

How can it be implemented in our three-tier architecture? Java clients must obtain a reference to the remote object that resides in the middleware. RMI provides a bootstrap naming service mechanism for that purpose, which is Uniform Resource Locator (URL)-based. Clients obtain references to registered remote objects and then invoke methods on these objects. Parameters pass as method arguments, as is usual with any method. Using Javasoft's object serialization technique, the RMI protocol does the marshaling and unmarshaling to convert Java types to a stream of bytes and this stream of bytes back to Java types. The RMI wire protocol transmits this stream of bytes on networks. Simple, isn't it? An example of a Java application using RMI is found in Chapter 10.

Other Techniques

Other techniques are usable as a reliable software bus between clients and middleware. CORBA (Common Object Request Broker Architecture), defined by the Object Management Group (OMG), is a complete architecture for distributing objects. It is the most serious, consistent, and robust approach to distributed computing available.

Many vendors already have CORBA-compliant products ranging from mainframe-class to PC-class. Products that comply with the CORBA 2.0 standard are interoperable, which means that they may be used in mixed environments. They can use a large number of network transport protocols including TCP/IP, which is used on the Internet. (IIOP, which stands for Internet Inter-ORB Protocol, is an implementation of GIOP, the Generic Inter-ORB Protocol, and works with TCP/IP.) State-of-the-art administration, integration, and development tools are usually bundled with CORBA software, as is the case with SunSoft Solaris NEO.

JOE

Joe is Sun's solution to enable Java applications and applets to connect to CORBA environments such as Solaris NEO. It includes a Java Object Request Broker (an ORB), which connects applets to remote NEO objects running on any machine across the Internet. Networked objects may then be used from applets and applications.

OMG's Interface Definition Language (IDL) can generate Java class stubs. IDL files are standard CORBA object interface files and provide language independence. The distributed objects may be implemented in a variety of languages such as C and C++, but Java is used because the database access is through JDBC on the middle tier.

Summary

This chapter discussed an alternative to the two-tier model. Using the Java Remote Method Invocation, it is possible to distribute objects across software tiers while providing an ideal place for the application logic. The topics discussed were:

- An introduction to software partitioning
- Object persistency
- Java Remote Method Invocation
- CORBA

The next chapter discusses design issues for the Internet and intranet, as well as possible implementation choices.

Chapter 9

Design Issues

IN THIS CHAPTER
This chapter discusses design issues for the Internet and intranet, as well as implementation and platform choices. The issues discussed include:

♦ Intranet/Internet

♦ 100 percent Java or non-100 percent Java

♦ Choosing a database management system (DBMS)

ALTHOUGH THERE ARE MANY issues that may be discussed regarding real-world applications for the Internet or the intranet, this chapter focuses on those that are likely to be the most important ones for your current and future projects.

Intranet/Internet

There are many differences between the Internet and an intranet. The main differences are:

♦ The Internet is "wild." There are millions of "netizens" on the Internet, all with different interests. Millions of users also means a heavy load on the Internet.

♦ Many different services are provided on the Internet, each using a dedicated protocol. In some cases, different implementations of the same service are not fully interoperable.

♦ Content, location, and free access are subject to change on the Internet, especially on the World Wide Web (WWW).

♦ The number of users within an intranet is usually stable and known. This environment is a trusted environment.

♦ Services provided on the intranet are clearly identified, documented, allowed or denied, and cached for performance. The most reliable protocols are used and they never conflict.

♦ Data content, information sources, authors, access, and privileges are better defined on the intranet.

153

As the foregoing shows, the intranet is a secure environment. The Internet, the network of networks, is not a secure environment. This lack of security engenders a number of problems that may affect Internet services using Java Database Connectivity (JDBC) to connect to corporate databases.

The Number of Simultaneous Users

While the number of simultaneous intranet users is somewhat predictable, it is not possible to determine the number of simultaneous users of a service on the Internet. Some sites record millions of hits a day on their Web pages and their hit-rate changes day after day. Consider an order-entry application used exclusively within an intranet and an online stock exchange information system on the Internet. It is very difficult to estimate the number of visitors interested in watching stock quotes, while it is very easy to locate the employees who will need to access the order-entry system. Among other problems, the following problems may appear on a system not entirely designed for the Internet:

◆ With too many users logged in at the same time, the database management system is unable to handle more sessions.

◆ With too many users simultaneously performing heavy queries, the response time is unacceptable.

◆ Users log in on a per-user basis, are assigned a new nickname, and choose a personal password. There is one database user-identifier per new user. The database may not be able to handle millions of log-in entries in its system tables.

There are solutions to these problems, but they may not be best suited for your purposes. One solution is to replicate the databases.

Replication

Replication allows more users to log in at the same time, while spreading the load on different servers. In such an architecture, multiple sites replicate the data. A Java application can try to connect to one of these replication servers. If it does not succeed, it can try to connect to the next one, continuing until it connects. From a programming viewpoint, the Java application can be implemented using successive try-catch blocks, each passing a different JDBC Uniform Resource Locator (URL) using the `DriverManager getConnection()` method. Consider these four URLs:

```
jdbc:dbdrv://www.mydomain.com:8192/db1
jdbc:dbdrv://www2.mydomain.com:8192/db2
jdbc:dbdrv://relay1.mydomain.sf.ca.us/db3
jdbc:dbdrv://relay2.mydomain.sf.ca.us/db4
```

Assume your enterprise has a fast backbone linking the different sites and database replication occurs real-time. If the successive try-catch blocks are used to try to connect to a data source, there is a greater chance the user will connect to a database and the application will behave independently of the actual data source. It may not work with applets. Some Web browsers do not allow an applet to connect to another server other than the server it came from.

Latency

The Internet is quite crowded today. Even upgrading a provider's lines every day will not increase its throughput significantly until gigabit backbones become available. As a result, the response time to obtain a connection to a server may be long. The data transfer rate may also be very slow. Like many other Internet services, database servers suffer from this inherent and unpredictable latency. Indeed, the connection context consumes a fair amount of database resources, and the more waiting users on a system, the more load on the database server.

There is only one solution to this problem: keep the database transactions as short as possible. Do not keep an unnecessary connection open. Many users function in a stateless manner, and most of them will probably interrupt their connection by simply switching to another WWW site.

ONE LOGIN PER TYPE OF APPLICATION

Even for services that are customer-customized, it may not be a good idea to assign a different database user ID for each user. A better approach is to assign specific database IDs per group of users or, if possible, a unique database login for the whole application. In other words, it may be feasible to handle as many different user profiles as possible using a few or even a single database login. In the latter case, the application would be responsible for storing in dedicated tables everything that is user-dependent. In many situations a unique application login will suffice.

The reason is that managing thousands of users, changing every day, may be hell for a database administrator. This is not so for a service administrator, so delegate all identification, authentication, and authorization issues to the service administrator. This information will lay in a table along with connection information, and a billing application, for example, could exploit it.

Security Issues

Security issues apply to stand-alone applications, JDBC and untrusted applets, and firewalls.

STAND-ALONE APPLICATIONS

Stand-alone Java applications are considered trustworthy. They have full access to the local file system as does any other application. They are allowed to call native libraries and open network connections to any host.

There should be, however, one restriction. As with applets, if an untrusted sun.sql.Driver class is dynamically loaded from a remote networked source, then use that driver only with code loaded from that source.

JDBC AND UNTRUSTED APPLETS

JDBC follows the standard applet security model, which imposes fairly onerous restrictions for untrusted applets. In particular, JDBC uses these rules:

◆ It assumes that normal unsigned applets are untrustworthy.

◆ It does not allow applets to access to local database data such as registry or configuration files.

◆ If a downloaded JDBC Driver registers itself with the JDBC DriverManager, then JDBC will only use that driver to satisfy connection requests from code that has been loaded from the same source as the driver.

◆ It does not allow an untrusted applet to open a database connection to a server that is not the server it was downloaded from.

◆ JDBC does not make any automatic nor implicit use of local credentials when making connections to remote database servers.

JDBC does not encrypt the data it sends over the Internet. Indeed, JDBC is not a network protocol nor a database protocol. If connection encryption is necessary, choose a database that supports encryption in its protocol. In this case, this specific database management system's JDBC driver will encrypt/decrypt the data as necessary.

FIREWALLS

Firewalls protect intranets. They simply filter incoming and outgoing connections with regard to their IP addresses and/or TCP/IP ports. A simple example is the firewall that only allows WWW, Usenet News, and e-mail to be used. It stops all packets running on ports other than 80, 119, and 25, respectively.

Actually, all connection attempts make their requests to these well-known ports. Once the connection is established, it shifts to another free port. JDBC and JDBC drivers use TCP/IP ports to communicate with database servers. The only thing to do when a firewall is present is to allow data to transit on the port used by your database protocol. The database administrator has a good idea of which port(s) are used by the database management system. So, the operation simply consists of opening an adequate door on the firewall machine.

One Hundred Percent Database Independent

In some cases, it is useful to write code that is 100 percent independent of the underlying database. Such a requirement is mandatory for programmers who develop CASE tools, data import/export utilities, or DBMS administration tools in Java.

Fortunately, JDBC is inherently 100 percent database independent. All DBMS-specific features are provided through JDBC drivers that have enough database knowledge to handle these features. The JDBC metadata interfaces are sufficiently complete to build database-independent code in Java.

In the case of applets, the name of the JDBC driver and the database URL string are passed as parameters for maximum flexibility. The only thing to change when switching from one DBMS to another is the HTML file that contains these applet parameter tags. Listing 9-1 is an example:

Listing 9-1: Passing parameters to an applet.

```
. . .
. .  . .
<applet code=myApplet width=500 height=600>
<param name=driver value=connect.sybase.SybaseDriver>
<param name=connection
value='jdbc:sybase://dbms.mydomain.com:8192/demodb;user=guest;
password=guest'>
. . .
. . .
```

The applet must parse its parameters to discover the driver to load and the database URL to use. The driver code (Java classes) does not have to be present on the client; it can reside on the server side and downloads dynamically upon execution of the applet. The code to fetch parameters from an applet, shown in Listing 9-2, is quite simple:

Listing 9-2: Getting parameters from an applet.

```
. . .
. . .
String driver;
String url;
Connection conn;
driver = getParameter("driver");
if (driver != null)
Class.forName(driver).newInstance();
url = getParameter("connection");
if (url != null)
conn = DriverManager.getConnection(url);
. . .
. . .
```

One Hundred Percent Java or Non-100 Percent Java

One hundred percent Java-based applications or applets may run on all-Java network devices such as the Sun Microsystems, Inc.'s JavaStation. Such devices are the first wave of a seismic shift in the computer industry.

JDBC is, fortunately, all-Java. Programs and applets developed with JDBC are portable, but some JDBC drivers are not portable. Indeed, all those using local native libraries are not portable, although they may be available for a variety of platforms. Furthermore, they have to be installed on a client machine before an application can use them. They cannot be downloaded automatically from the network.

The problem is that there are only a few all-Java JDBC drivers available. Others will appear quickly, but what can we do today, for example, to use JDBC within applets to connect to a poorly supported database?

The best solution is to use a middle tier. Many JDBC endorsees now develop and sell three-tier bridges to place in front of common enterprise class database management systems. Many developers offer evaluation copies, making it is easy to experiment and determine which is the right solution for your project. Another solution is to code the middle tier yourself. It is doable using Java RMI. A simple working example is provided later.

Choosing a DBMS

It is important to choose the right DBMS. While many intranet projects are based on existing architectures and databases, projects related to the Internet open the door to change. The following is worth considering when choosing a DBMS:

- Tools to facilitate the importation of external data in various formats, including binary formats, should accompany the DBMS. Such tools are available from both database vendors and third parties.

- The DBMS should be supported on a variety of platforms and operating systems in case the project grows faster than expected and the platform's limits are reached too quickly.

- The DBMS should offer optimum and proven security.

- The DBMS must be able to handle hundreds of simultaneous connections during peaks.

- For greater convenience, the DBMS should be remotely administrable. For Internet service, the service must be provided 24 hours a day.

♦ Other resource-hogging user or network applications running on the same platform should not be affect the DBMS on a stability point-of-view (this is more related to the operating system than to the DBMS software).

♦ The DBMS must support online backup facilities as well as consistency checking and repair.

♦ Replication facility is an extra.

All relational DBMSs (RDBMS) offer nearly equivalent facilities, security, and performance levels. ODBMSs (Object Database Management Systems) are superior to RDBMSs as regards retrieval of multimedia content. A performance improvement factor of 10 or more is sometimes observed, which is important to consider if the database will hold hundreds or thousands of multikilobyte binary objects. ODBMSs are also very attractive to object-oriented developers. Performance sometimes decreases when a large number of relations between entities is present.

Finally, the choice of the DBMS platform seems to be more important than the choice of the DBMS software itself. While personal computer-based DBMSs may be very convenient during the development phase, their cost/performance factor is much higher than open systems-based DBMSs when supporting a relatively high number of simultaneous connections. Do not compare CPU (central processing unit) power because one architecture is not scalable while the other is. Be aware that the I/O (input/output) subsystem is often the bottleneck. Unix is the best platform when thousands of simultaneous TCP/IP network connections are involved because TCP/IP is part of the heart of the operating system.

In addition, you should consider purchasing a DBMS and hardware platform that are fully scalable without involving replication of the data, the DBMS software, and the platform itself. Almost all serious DBMSs may be dynamically reconfigured each time new hardware is added to the platform as, for example, when adding CPU chips on the main board.

Summary

This chapter discussed design issues for the Internet and intranet scenarios, as well as possible implementation choices and platform choices.

This is the end of Part III. The next part is dedicated to complete, working examples using JDBC.

Part III

Working Examples

Chapter 10: Examples

Part III contains numerous working examples, from the simple to the complex, depicting particular aspects of database integration with JDBC. Among other tasks, you will program applications and applets for: handling normal rows of data, handling BLOBs to insert and retrieve multimedia content to and from database tables, respectively, exploring the objects of a DBMS on-the-fly, and for simple database access in a three-tiered environment using distributed Java objects with RMI.

Chapter 10

Examples

IN THIS CHAPTER

This chapter provides many examples of Java applets or stand-alone applications. Each example covers a particular topic discussed in this book. The source code for all the examples is included on the accompanying CD-ROM. In this chapter, we discuss:

- ◆ A simple ISQL clientBullets

- ◆ Handling BLOBS from the command line

- ◆ A Java Automatic Teller Machine

- ◆ Flying with JDBC Airlines

- ◆ A graphical database surfer

- ◆ An advanced example using Remote Method Invocation

Handling Normal Rows

Almost all database applications written in Java will handle normal rows of data. SQL (Structured Query Language) only provides ways of inserting and extracting data in tabular format, while permitting complex queries to be issued.

Simple ISQL Client Application

This example shows how to handle normal rows of data in a simple way. ISQL stands for "Interactive SQL" client, which means that it can be used to send queries to a database and then retrieve the results in a text-based interface. This ISQL client is a stand-alone Java application.

As shown in Figure 10-1, once launched, a number of questions appear on the screen. The questions prompt you for a Java Database Connectivity (JDBC) Uniform Resource Locator (URL), a database log in, and a database password. SQL queries are then entered from the keyboard, and the results immediately appear on the screen. It is really a primitive ISQL client. It supports SQL updates and multiline queries, however.

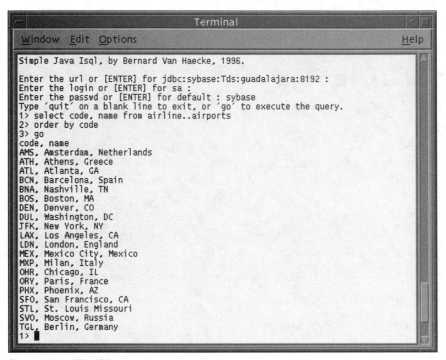

Figure 10-1: The ISQL stand-alone application.

As Figure 10-1 shows, this simple ISQL stand-alone application runs in a terminal window. Its input is taken from the standard input, and its output is directed to the standard output. Default values are provided for connection parameters just for ease of use.

Listing 10-1 gives you an example of an ISQL session. It uses a database with only three tables: clients, accounts, and transaction history. These tables are used in another example later in this chapter.

Listing 10-1: Simple Java ISQL.

```
Enter the url or [ENTER] for jdbc:odbc:netbank :
Enter the login or [ENTER] for dba :
Enter the passwd or [ENTER] for default :
Type 'quit' on a blank line to exit, or 'go' to execute the query.
1> select * from clients
2> go
ownerno, name, address
1, Bernard Van Haecke, Brussels, 1000
2, John Doe, Imola Circuit, KM83
3, Jane Doe, Imola Circuit, KM83
4, Santa Klaus, North Pole, 1
5, Little Duke, Java Islandd, 1
```

```
6, The Bank, Downtown LA
1> select name, acctno, balance
2> from clients, accounts
3> where clients.ownerno = accounts.ownerno
4> order by balance
5> go
name, acctno, balance
Little Duke, 5, -840
Jane Doe, 3, 320600
Bernard Van Haecke, 1, 991900
John Doe, 2, 1256050
Santa Klaus, 4, 8892750
The Bank, 6, 999999995904
1> select distinct typetransaction
2> from history
3> go
typetransaction
Received
Transfert
Withdraw
1> select sum(balance)
2> from accounts
3> go
sum(balance)
1000011464704
1> update accounts
2> set balance = balance + (balance * 0.05)
3> go
6 row(s) affected.
1> quit
```

There is only one class for this example: the class ISQL handles everything. The class constructor initializes the database connection and then calls a method that handles the user's input in a loop to allow entry of multiple queries. Keywords "go" and "quit" are caught to process a query or quit the application. The database connection is closed when a "quit" is issued or a fatal error occurs. Listing 10-2 shows the source code for this ISQL client.

Listing 10-2: An Interactive SQL Client.

```
import java.sql.*;
import java.io.*;
import java.util.*;
public class isql {
  static DataInputStream kbd = new DataInputStream(System.in);
  static String url = "jdbc:odbc:netbank";
  static String driver = "sun.jdbc.odbc.JdbcOdbcDriver";
  static String login = "dba";
  static String passwd = "javabank";
  static Connection curConn = null;
  public static void main(String argv[]) throws IOException
```

```
{
    String temp = "";
    System.out.println("Simple Java Isql, by Bernard Van Haecke,
      1996.\n");
    System.out.print("Enter the url or [ENTER] for " + url + " :
      ");
    System.out.flush();
    temp = kbd.readLine();
    if (!temp.equals("")) url = temp;
    System.out.print("Enter the login or [ENTER] for " + login +
      " : ");
    System.out.flush();
    temp = kbd.readLine();
    if (!temp.equals("")) login = temp;
    System.out.print("Enter the passwd or [ENTER] for default :
      ");
    System.out.flush();
    temp = kbd.readLine();
    if (!temp.equals("")) passwd = temp;
    isql session = new isql();
}
public isql() throws IOException
{
    try {
    Class.forName(driver);
    curConn = DriverManager.getConnection(url, login,  passwd);
    checkForWarnings(curConn.getWarnings ());
    }
    catch(java.lang.Exception ex) {
    System.out.println("url : " + url);
    System.out.println("login : " + login);
    System.out.println("passwd : " + passwd);
    ex.printStackTrace();
    return;
    }
    processQueries();
    finalize();
}
protected void finalize()
{
    try {
            curConn.close();
    }
    catch (SQLException ex) { }
}
private void processQueries() throws IOException
{
    int i = 1;
    String temp = "";
    String query = "";
    String results = "";
```

```
     System.out.println("Type 'quit' on a blank line to exit, or
      'go' to execute the query.");
     do {
             System.out.print(i + "> ");
             System.out.flush();
             temp = kbd.readLine();
             if (temp.equals("quit"))
                     break;
             if (temp.equals("go")) {
                     executeThisQuery(query);
                     i = 1;
                     query = "";
             }
             else {
                     query = query + " " + temp;
                     i++;
             }
     } while (true);
}
private void executeThisQuery(String sqlText)
{
     boolean resultSetIsAvailable;
     boolean moreResultsAvailable;
     int i = 0;
     int res=0;
     try {
             Statement curStmt = curConn.createStatement();
             resultSetIsAvailable = curStmt.execute(sqlText);
             ResultSet rs = null;
             for (moreResultsAvailable = true;
              moreResultsAvailable;)
             {
                     checkForWarnings(curConn.getWarnings());
                     if (resultSetIsAvailable)
                     {
                             if ((rs = curStmt.getResultSet()) !=
                              null)
                             {
                                     // we have a resultset
                                     checkForWarnings(curStmt.getWarni
                                      ngs());
                                     ResultSetMetaData rsmd =
                                      rs.getMetaData();
                                     int numCols =
                                      rsmd.getColumnCount();
                                     // display column headers
                                     for (i = 1; i <= numCols; i++)
                                     {
                                             if (i > 1)
                                               System.out.print(", ");
                                             System.out.print(rsmd.
                                              getColumnLabel(i));
                                     }
```

```
                                    System.out.println("");
                                    // step through the rows
                                    while (rs.next())
                                    {
                                            // process the columns
                                            for (i = 1; i <= numCols;
                                             i++)
                                            {
                                              if (i > 1)
                                                System.out.print(", ");
                                              System.out.print(rs.
                                                getString(i));
                                            }
                                            System.out.println("");
                                    }
                            }
                            else
                            {
                                    if ((res = curStmt.getUpdateCount()) !=
                                     -1)
                                    {
                                            // we have an updatecount
                                            System.out.println(res + "
                                             row(s) affected.");
                                    }
                                    // else no more results
                                    else
                                    {
                                            moreResultsAvailable = false;
                                    }
                            }
                            if (moreResultsAvailable)
                            {
                                    resultSetIsAvailable =
                                     curStmt.getMoreResults();
                            }
                    }
                    if (rs != null) rs.close();
                    curStmt.close();
            }
        catch (SQLException ex) {
                // Unexpected SQL exception.
                ex.printStackTrace ();
        }
        catch (java.lang.Exception ex) {
                // Got some other type of exception. Dump it.
                ex.printStackTrace ();
        }
    }
    private static void checkForWarnings (SQLWarning warn)
            throws SQLException
```

```
{
    while (warn != null) {
        System.out.println(warn);
        warn = warn.getNextWarning();
    }
}
}
```

Simple ISQL Client Applet

Here is another ISQL client. It is different from the previous example because it runs as an applet. Anyone with a Java-enabled World Wide Web (WWW) browser can load the hypertext markup language (HTML) file containing the applet tag that calls this applet. The logic to execute the SQL statements is similar to the logic of the command-line ISQL example.

A 100-percent Java JDBC driver must be supplied with such an applet. The JDBC-ODBC Bridge, for example, would not work because it calls native methods to talk to ODBC. "All-Java" drivers are becoming available as more and more developers implement the JDBC Driver Application Programming Interface (API). Good examples are Sybase's jConnect and Connect Software's FastForward JDBC driver.

It is remarkably simple to provide the 100-percent Java JDBC driver classes to the calling browser: the classes — the JDBC driver package — must be available in the directory where the applet resides. As soon as the Java applet is loaded in the virtual machine running in the WWW browser, the class loader notices that it needs additional classes, and a call to `Class.forName()` dynamically loads the appropriate driver class. The Hypertext Transport Protocol (HTTP) server then sends the requested classes.

Snapshot of the Applet

As shown in Figure 10-2, the applet lets you enter a SQL query in a floating window.

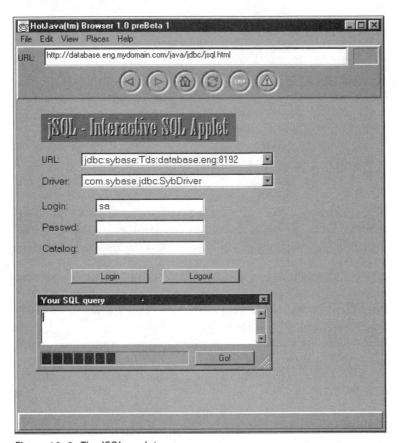

Figure 10-2: The ISQL applet.

Clicking the "Go!" button sends the query to the database and retrieves the results. Figure 10-3 shows the resulting rows of data displayed in another floating window.

The graphical user interface (GUI) part of this applet was done using Marimba Bongo, which generates a 100 percent portable .gui file containing the persistified GUI objects. This file contains a persistent form of the widgets used in this example. The .gui file is editable using Marimba Bongo, a demo version of which is on the CD-ROM accompanying this book. The unzipped Marimba classes must be in the CLASSPATH or available in the applet's home directory on the WWW server to run this example.

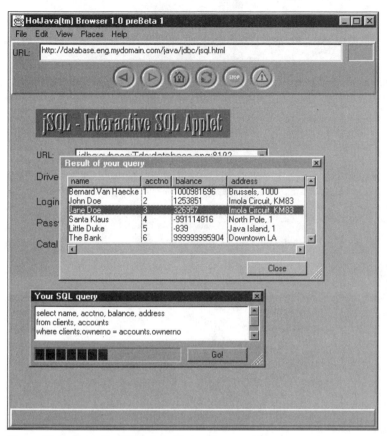

Figure 10-3: Executing SQL statements.

THE HTML FILE

The following is the HTML file that calls the applet. The connection parameters are passed as arguments to the applet for greater convenience. These parameters specify which JDBC driver to load and which database URL to use.

```
<applet
name="jsql"
code="jsql.class"
width="430"
height="390"
align="Top"
alt="If you had a java-enabled browser, you would see an applet
  here."
>
```

```
<param name="driver" value="com.sybase.jdbc.SybDriver">
<param name="url" value="jdbc:sybase:Tds:database.eng:8192">
<param name="login" value="guest">
<param name="password" value="javabank">
<param name="catalog" value="javabank">
<hr>If your browser recognized the applet tag,
you would see an applet here.<hr>
</applet>
```

SOURCE

Listing 10-3 contains the source code for the ISQL applet example. Remember that the Marimba classes must be in the CLASSPATH or in the applet's home directory on the WWW server to run.

Listing 10-3: An Interactive SQL Applet.

```
import java.awt.*;
import java.sql.*;
import java.lang.*;
import java.util.*;
import java.net.*;
import marimba.gui.*;
public class jsql extends java.applet.Applet {
Presentation presentation;
PlayerPanel player;
PlayerUtil util;
Connection conn = null;
DatabaseMetaData mtdt = null;
ResultSet rs = null;
/**
* initialize the applet
*/
public void init() {
try {
     presentation = Presentation.getPresentation(new
       URL(getDocumentBase(), "jsql.gui"));
  }
  catch (MalformedURLException ex) {
      ex.printStackTrace();
  }
  // create a player panel
  setLayout(new BorderLayout());
  add("Center", player = new PlayerPanel());
  // set the presentation
  player.setPresentation(presentation);
  // create a player utility object
  util = new PlayerUtil(player);
  // load applet parameters
((ChoiceWidget)
  util.getWidget("dataURL")).addChoice(getParameter("url"));
```

```
((ChoiceWidget)
 util.getWidget("dataDriver")).addChoice(getParameter("driver"));
 util.setText("dataLogin", getParameter("login"));
 util.setText("dataPasswd", getParameter("password"));
 util.setText("dataCatalog", getParameter("catalog"));
 // add some jdbc connection choices
 // jdbc-odbc bridge
 addDriverInfo("jdbc:odbc:data-source-name",
   "sun.jdbc.odbc.JdbcOdbcDriver");
 // sybase's driver
 addDriverInfo("jdbc:sybase:Tds:host.domain.com:8192",
   "com.sybase.jdbc.SybDriver");
 // connect software's sybase driver
 addDriverInfo("jdbc:sybase://host.domain.com:8192",
   "connect.sybase.SybaseDriver");
 // funny driver
 addDriverInfo("foo:bar:database", "foo.bar.Driver");
}
/**
* add a new entry in the url and driver listboxes
*/
public void addDriverInfo(String url, String driver)
{
// add entry for this driver provider
((ChoiceWidget) util.getWidget("dataURL")).addChoice(url);
((ChoiceWidget) util.getWidget("dataDriver")).addChoice(driver);
}
/**
* we handle all gui events here
*/
public boolean handleEvent(Event evt)
{
try {
 if ((evt.id == Event.ACTION_EVENT) && (evt.target instanceof
  Widget)) {
 Widget w = (Widget)evt.target;
 String nm = w.getName();
 if (nm != null) System.out.println("Event: " + nm);
 // The user has logged in.
 if (nm.equals("dataLoginButton")) {
     String url = util.getText("dataURL").trim();
     String uid = util.getText("dataLogin").trim();
     String pwd = util.getText("dataPasswd").trim();
     String catalog = util.getText("dataCatalog").trim();
     String driver = util.getText("dataDriver").trim();
     try {
            Class.forName(driver);
            conn = DriverManager.getConnection(url, uid, pwd);
            if (conn != null) {
                   mtdt = conn.getMetaData();
                   conn.setCatalog(catalog);
            }
     }
```

```java
        catch (SQLException ex) {
                System.out.println(ex);
        }
        catch (java.lang.Exception ex) {
                System.out.println(ex);
        }
   }
   // The user has clicked logout
   if (nm.equals("dataLogoutButton")) {
       if (conn != null) {
               conn.close();
       }
   }
   // execute the sql query
   if (nm.equals("isqlGoButton")) {
       String query = util.getText("isqlQueryText");
       if (true)
       {
               TableWidget tbl = (TableWidget)
                util.getWidget("isqlResultTable");
               tbl.removeAllRows();
               tbl.removeAllColumns();
               util.show("isqlResultWindow", true);
               ResultSet rs = getSingleRS(query);
               Vector headers = getRSColumnHeadersAsVector(rs);
               int i;
               for (i=0; i<headers.size(); i++)
//                          tbl.addColumn((String)
                                headers.elementAt(i), ((String)
                                headers.elementAt(i)).length());
                    tbl.addColumn((String) headers.elementAt(i));
               Vector rows = getRSRowsAsVector(rs);
               for (i=0; i<rows.size(); i++)
                       tbl.addRow((Vector) rows.elementAt(i));
               rs.close();
       }
   }
   // close the isql result window
   if (nm.equals("resultCloseButton")) {
       util.show("isqlResultWindow", false);
   }
  }
 }
}
catch(java.lang.Exception ex) {
 ex.printStackTrace();
}
return super.handleEvent(evt);
}
/**
* return the resultset of a simple query
*/
public ResultSet getSingleRS(String sqlText)
{
```

```java
    ResultSet rs = null;
    int res;
    try {
        Statement st = conn.createStatement();
        if (st.execute(sqlText)) {
            // okay it's not an update count
            rs = st.getResultSet();
        }
        else if ((res = st.getUpdateCount()) != -1) {
            // it's an update count
            // we could could display it
        }
    } catch (SQLException ex) { ex.printStackTrace(); }
    return rs;
}
/**
* return the column headers of a resultset as vector
*/
public Vector getRSColumnHeadersAsVector(ResultSet rs) {
    int i;
    Vector v = new Vector();
    try {
        ResultSetMetaData rsmd = rs.getMetaData();
        int numCols = rsmd.getColumnCount();
        // fetch column headers
        for (i = 1; i <= numCols; i++)
        {
            v.addElement(rsmd.getColumnLabel(i));
        }
    }
    catch (SQLException ex)
    {
    }
    return v;
}
/**
* return a resultset as vector
*/
public Vector getRSRowsAsVector(ResultSet rs) {
ProgressIndicatorWidget bar = (ProgressIndicatorWidget)
    util.getWidget("sqlProgressBar");
    int barValue = 0;
    Vector v = new Vector();
    Vector r = null;
    int i;
    try {
        ResultSetMetaData rsmd = rs.getMetaData();
        int numCols = rsmd.getColumnCount();
        bar.setValue(0);
        // step through the rows
        while (rs.next())
        {
            // process the columns
```

```
                r = new Vector();
                for (i = 1; i <= numCols; i++)
                {
                        r.addElement(rs.getString(i));
                }
                v.addElement(r);
                if (barValue < 100) {
                        barValue = barValue + 10;
                }
                else {
                        barValue = 0;
                }
                bar.setValue(barValue);
                bar.repaint();
        }
  }
  catch (SQLException ex)
  {
  }
  return v;
}
}
```

Applet: JDBC Airlines

Looking for online airline information? Choose JDBC Airlines! This applet illustrates remote access to a database through a nice user interface. The example runs
as an applet within World Wide Web browsers that support Java. It uses JDBC to
connect and retrieve flight schedules from a database. No middleware is involved.
The JDBC driver used for this example is a 100-percent Java driver that directly
connects to the database server. Figure 10-4 shows the JDBC Airlines applet.

This is an example from Connect Software, Inc. Thanks to its 100-percent Java
drivers, this applet is able to run within any Java-compatible WWW browser.
Again, no specific classes must be preinstalled on the client machine. The JDBC
driver downloads from the Web server along with the applet classes.

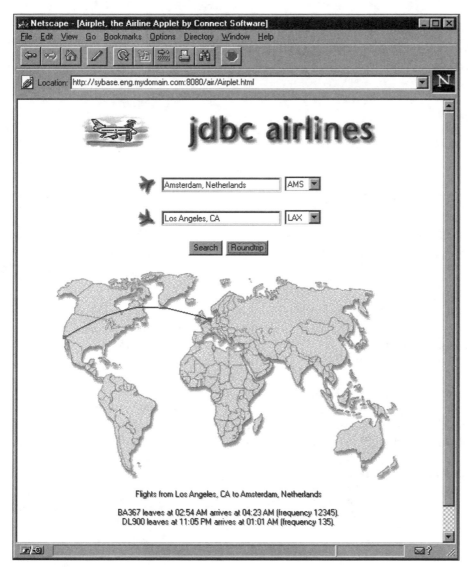

Figure 10-4: Connect Software's JDBC Airlines applet.

THE HTML FILE

The HTML file contains the tag to load the applet as well as parameters that provide connection information to this applet. Such connection information includes
the driver to use to connect to the database and the database's URL.

```
<html>
<head>
<title>
Airplet, the Airline Applet by Connect Software
</title>
</head>
<body bgcolor="#FFFFFF">
<center>
<img src="images/banner.gif">
<p>
<applet code=airplet.Airplet width=500 height=600>
<param name=driver value=connect.sybase.SybaseDriver>
<param name=connection
  value='jdbc:sybase://db.mydomain.com:8192/airline;user=guest;passwo
  rd=guest'>
</center>
</applet>
</html>
```

AIRPLET. JAVA

Airplet.java is the main applet class. Initialization establishes a connection with the database server. As soon as the connection is established, various panels are prepared and displayed. These panels include a panel with name and preset choices for departure and arrival airports, a panel with search and roundtrip buttons, and a panel with maps and routes between airports.

User events are handled when selecting airport choices and clicking search or roundtrip buttons. A search for flights from the origin to the destination is performed. A method is also provided to load map images from the server.

Listing 10-4 shows the source code for the main part of the applet, Airplet.java.

Listing 10-4: Airplet.java.

```
//
// Airplet.java - Connect Software's Airline Applet, a.k.a. jdbc
  airlines
//
// Copyright (C) 1996 by Connect Software. All rights reserved.
//
// Written by Gionata Mettifogo, Peter Ham.
//
// Connect Software, Inc.
// 81 Lansing Street, Suite #411
// San Francisco, CA 94105
// (415) 710-1544 (phone) - (415) 543-6695 (fax)
//
// email: info@connectsw.com - www: http://www.connectsw.com
package airplet; // airplet's package
import java.applet.*; // import a number of java libraries
import java.awt.*;
import java.io.*;
import java.net.*;
```

```java
import java.util.*;
import jdbc.sql.*; // import modified jdbc libraries
public class Airplet extends java.applet.Applet // main applet class
{
 private TextField nameTo = null; // names of departure and arrival
   airports
 private TextField nameFrom = null;
 private AirportChoice choiceTo = null; // preset lists of departure
   and arrival airports
 private AirportChoice choiceFrom = null;
 private FlightsPanel panelFlights = null; // panel containing maps
   and flights listings
 /** Initialize the applet, opens the connection with the database
   and add user interface items in the applet. */
 synchronized public void init()
 {
     airplet = this; // static reference to this airplet
     setBackground(Color.white); // white background for this
      applet
     LayoutManager columnLayout = new ColumnLayout(5,5); // all
      panels go in a single column
     setLayout(columnLayout);
     showStatus("Connecting..."); // let user know we're connecting
      to the database
     try
     {
             String driver = getParameter("driver"); // use sql
              driver specified in 'driver' parameter
             if(driver != null) Class.forName(driver).newInstance();
              // register driver with DriverManager
             String url = getParameter("connection"); // get
              connection's url
             connection = DriverManager.getConnection(url); //
              establish connection with server
     }
     catch(Exception sqlEx)
     {
             System.out.println("Connection failed because " + sqlEx
              + "\n");
     }
     showStatus("Preparing...");
     try
     {
             Panel panelFrom = new Panel(); // create panel with
              name and preset choices for departure's airport
             ImageCanvas imageFrom = new
             ImageCanvas("images/airFrom.gif");
              panelFrom.add(imageFrom);
             nameFrom = new TextField(25); panelFrom.add(nameFrom);
             choiceFrom = new AirportChoice();
              panelFrom.add(choiceFrom);
             Panel panelTo = new Panel(); // create panel with name
              and preset choices for arrival's airport
```

```
                    ImageCanvas imageTo = new
                      ImageCanvas("images/airTo.gif");
                     panelTo.add(imageTo);
                    nameTo = new TextField(25); panelTo.add(nameTo);
                    choiceTo = new AirportChoice(); panelTo.add(choiceTo);
                    Panel panelButtons = new Panel(); // panel with search
                      and roundtrip buttons
                    Button button1 = new Button("Search");
                     panelButtons.add(button1);
                    Button button2 = new Button("Roundtrip");
                     panelButtons.add(button2);
                    panelFlights = new FlightsPanel(); // panel with maps
                      and routes
                    add(panelFrom); // add all panels to the applet
                    add(panelTo);
                    add(panelButtons);
                    add(panelFlights);
                    showStatus("Connect Software, 1996."); // here we are!
            }
        catch(SQLException sqlEx) { showStatus("Sorry, could not
          initialize, e-mail support@connectsw.com"); }
    }
    /** Responds to user selecting an airport in the choice menus or
      clicking search or roundtrip. */
    public boolean action(Event iEvent,Object iArgument)
    {
        if(iEvent.target == choiceFrom) // user picked an origin from
          the choices
        {
                Airport air = choiceFrom.getSelectedAirport();
                nameFrom.setText(air.getName()); // copy origin's name
                  to origin's text field
                return true;
        }
        if(iEvent.target == choiceTo) // user picked a destination
          from the choices
        {
        Airport air = choiceTo.getSelectedAirport();
        nameTo.setText(air.getName()); // copy destination's name to
          destination's text field
        }
        if(iArgument.equals("Search") ||
          iArgument.equals("Roundtrip")) // search for flights from
          origin to destination
        {
                String airFrom = nameFrom.getText();
                if(airFrom.length() < 1) airFrom =
                  choiceFrom.getSelectedItem();
                String airTo = nameTo.getText();
                if(airTo.length() < 1) airTo =
                  choiceTo.getSelectedItem();
        searchFlights(airFrom,airTo,iArgument.equals("Roundtrip"));
        return true;
        }
```

```
            return super.action(iEvent,iArgument); // event was handled
    }
    private void searchFlights(String departingFrom,String
      arrivingTo,boolean roundTrip)
    {
        try
        {
                // System.out.println("Airplet.searchFlights - from " +
                  departingFrom + " to " + arrivingTo);
                Airport airFrom = Airport.getAirport(departingFrom); //
                  find out more about departing airport
                Airport airTo = Airport.getAirport(arrivingTo); // find
                  out more about arriving airport
                if(airFrom != null && airTo != null) // if both
                  airports where found (and they are different)
                {
                        nameFrom.setText(airFrom.getName()); // show
                          complete name and code for departure airport
                        choiceFrom.select(airFrom.getCode());
                        nameTo.setText(airTo.getName()); // show
                          complete name and code for arrival airport
                        choiceTo.select(airTo.getCode());
                        if(roundTrip) // if user requested return trip
                        {
                                panelFlights.setAirports(airTo,airFrom);
                                 // show inverse route
                                }
                        else panelFlights.setAirports(airFrom,
                          airTo); // show normal route
                        layout();
                        }
                }
                catch(SQLException sqlEx) {
                  panelFlights.setText(sqlEx.toString());
        }
    }
    static Statement createStatement() throws SQLException
    {
    return connection.createStatement();
    }
        private static Connection connection = null; // connection to
          the airline database
        /** Loads given image from the network, or file system, and
          returns it. */
        static Image loadImage(String iName)
        {
                if(images == null) // if there's no hash table for
                  images yet
                {
                images = new Hashtable(); // create an empty hash table
                }
        Image image = (Image) images.get(iName); // try to get image
          from the hash table (hash is image's name)
```

```
        if(image == null) // if this image hasn't been loaded yet
        {
                try // catch all loading problems
                {
                        URL url = new URL(airplet.getDocumentBase(),
                         iName); // create url of image on web server
                         or local file system
                        image = airplet.getImage(url); // try to load
                         image
                        airplet.prepareImage(image,airplet);
                }
                catch(Exception e) { }
                if(image != null) // if image was loaded
                {
                        images.put(iName,image); // add it to the hash
                         table so next time we don't have to load it
                }
        }
        return image; // return the image
    }
    static private Hashtable images = null; // an hash table of loaded
     images
    static private Airplet airplet = null; // a static reference to
     this applet (there's only one instance of it running at any time)
}
```

AIRPORT. JAVA

Airport.java holds the information regarding an airport. The constructor executes a query returning airport details such as its code, its name, its description, and its geographical coordinates in terms of x and y positions on different maps.

A hash table of airports is also created in Listing 10-5, which shows the source code of Airport.java.

Listing 10-5: Airport.java.

```
//
// Airport.java - this objects holds information regarding an
 airport
//
// Copyright (C) 1996 by Connect Software. All rights reserved.
//
// Written by Gionata Mettifogo, Peter Ham.
//
package airplet;
import connect.sql.*; // import sql server access classes
import java.awt.*; // java's windowing toolkit and other ui classes
import java.util.*; // utility classes
/** Information regarding an airport. */
class Airport
{
  public Airport(String iAirport) throws SQLException
```

```
{
    iAirport = iAirport.trim(); // remove leading and trailing
    spaces
    ResultSet r = null; Statement s = Airplet.createStatement();
    // use normal statement to query the Airports table
    if(iAirport.length() == 3) // if this is likely to be an
    airport code
    {
        r = s.executeQuery("select * from airports where code =
        '" + iAirport + "'");
        if(r.next() == false) // move over to the first (and
        only) row in the result set
        {
            r = null; // there are no entries with given
            airport code
        }
    }
    if(r == null) // search for airports whose name contain given
    airport string (like %string%)
    {
        r = s.executeQuery("select * from airports where name
        like '%" + iAirport + "%'");
        if(r.next() == false) // move to first (and probably
        only) row in result set
        {
            String nocase = ""; // case insensitive name,
            eg. [mM][iI][lL][aA][nN] instead of Milan
            for(int i = 0 ; i < iAirport.length() ; i++) //
            scan all characters in the string
            {
                String single =
                iAirport.substring(i,i+1); // extract
                character then convert to lowercase and
                uppercase
                String lower = single.toLowerCase(),
                upper = single.toUpperCase();
                if(lower.equals(upper) == false) // if
                lowercase is different from uppercase
                (that is if this character is alpha)
                {
                    nocase += "[" + lower + upper +
                    "]"; // regular expression for
                    both lower or uppercase, e.g.
                    [aA]
                }
                else nocase += single;
            }
            // System.out.println("Airport - searching with
            case insensitive string '" + nocase + "'");
            r = s.executeQuery("select * from airports where
            name like '%" + nocase + "%'");
            if(r.next() == false) r = null; // if this one
            didn't work either there's no such airport
        }
```

```
        }
        if(r != null)
        {
                code = r.getString("code"); // airport code, eg. 'SFO'
                name = r.getString("name"); // airport name, eg. 'San
                 Francisco, CA'
                description = r.getString("description"); //
                 description of this airport
                StringTokenizer sTokenizer = new StringTokenizer
                 (r.getString("maps"),";");
                while(sTokenizer.hasMoreTokens()) // scan each token,
                 maps entry looks something like
                 "california(45,60);usa(123,3);world(56,78)"
                {
                        MapInfo info = new
                         MapInfo(sTokenizer.nextToken()); // create an
                         object containing information regarding this
                         airport on a single map
                        if(maps != null) // if there's other maps
                         already
                        {
                                maps.append(info); // add this map to
                                 the linked list of maps
                        }
                        else maps = info; // this is the first map in
                         the list
                        // System.out.println(code + " map " + info);
                }
        }
        else throw new SQLException("Can't find '" + iAirport + "' in
         the airports database.");
}
private String code, name, description; // airport code, name and
 description, eg. 'SFO', 'San Francisco, CA', 'International
 Airport, ...'
private MapInfo maps; // linked list of maps available for this
 airport (and coordinates on each map) in preferred order (eg.
 'california', 'usa', 'world')
public String getCode()
{
        return code; // return airport code
}
public String getName()
{
        return name;
            }
            public MapInfo getMaps()
            {
                    return maps;
                    }
                    /** Returns airport with the given name or code.
                     */
                    static public Airport getAirport(String iName)
                    {
```

```
        try
            {
            if(airports = null) // if there's no
             hash table for airports
            {
                    airports = new Hashtable(); //
                    create an empty hash table
            }
        Airport airport = (Airport) airports.get(iName);
         // try getting the airport from the hash table
        if(airport = null) // if airport was not found
        {
                airport = new Airport(iName); // create
                a new airport from that name (will
                query the database)
                airports.put(airport.getName(),airport);
                // add airport to the hash table (by
                name)
                airports.put(airport.getCode(),airport);
                // add also by code
        }
        return airport; // return the airport
        }
        catch(SQLException sqlException) { return null; } //
         airport could not be found
    }
    static private Hashtable airports = null; // hash table of
     airports (used to minimize database access)
public String toString()
    {
    return "Airport[" + code + "," + name + "]"; // convert object
     to string
    }
}
```

AIRPORTCHOICE. JAVA

AirportChoice.java class queries the database to build a list of airport codes such as SFO, LAX, or JFK. The list is used within the user interface to let the user choose the departure and arrival airports. Listing 10-6 shows the source code for AirPortChoice.java.

Listing 10-6: AirportChoice.java.

```
//
// AirportChoice.java - user interface widget showing a choice of
 airports
//
// Copyright (C) 1996 by Connect Software. All rights reserved.
//
// Written by Gionata Mettifogo, Peter Ham.
//
package airplet;
```

```
import connect.sql.*; // import jdbc and other sql libraries
import java.awt.*; // java windowing toolkit
/** A choice user interface widget showing a list of available
 airport codes. */
class AirportChoice extends Choice
{
 /**
  * Initialize the choice user interface widget with a list of
   airports
  * available in the database. The method will query the airports
   table
  * of the database, listing all available airports by code.
  */
 public AirportChoice() throws SQLException
 {
     // use sql to select all airport codes from the airports table
       then add them to the widget
     Statement s = Airplet.createStatement(); // scan all the
       airports in the table
     for(ResultSet r = s.executeQuery("select code from airports
       order by code") ; r.next() ; )
     {
         String name = r.getString(1); // name of this airport
         // System.out.println("AirportChoice - " +
          r.getString("code") + " is '" + name + "'");
         addItem(name); // add airport to the choices
     }
     s.close(); // close statement
 }
 /** Returns the Airport corresponding to the entry with the given
   index. */
 public Airport getAirport(int index)
 {
     return Airport.getAirport(getItem(index)); // return Airport
       object
                 }
                 /** Returns the currently selected Airport. */
                 public Airport getSelectedAirport()
                 {
     return getAirport(getSelectedIndex());
 }
}
```

COLUMNLAYOUT. JAVA

ColumnLayout.java class arranges a set of components in a single column. The
source code for this class is in Listing 10-7.

Listing 10-7: ColumnLayout.java.

```
//
// ColumnLayout.java - layout that arranges all components in a
 column
```

```
//
// Copyright (C) 1996 by Connect Software. All rights reserved.
//
// Written by Gionata Mettifogo.
//
package airplet;
import java.awt.*; // import java windowing classes
/** A layout that arranges all components in a single column. */
public class ColumnLayout implements LayoutManager // just another
 layout manager
{
 public ColumnLayout()
 {
     hgap = vgap = 0; // no gap between components
 }
 public ColumnLayout(int hgap,int vgap)
 {
     this.hgap = hgap; this.vgap = vgap; // use this spacing
       between components
 }
 private int hgap, vgap; // horizontal and vertical spacing between
   components
/** Arrange components contained in iParent in a single column
  using their preferred size. */
 public void layoutContainer(Container iParent)
 {
     Insets insets = iParent.insets(); // insets (borders around
       the container)
     Dimension dimension = iParent.size(); // size of parent
       container
     dimension.width -= insets.left + insets.right; // net width of
       container
     for(int i = 0, v = vgap ; i < iParent.countComponents() ; i++)
     {
             Component component = iParent.getComponent(i); // scan
               each component in the container
             Dimension size = component.preferredSize(); // get
               component's preferred size the reshape it
             component.reshape(insets.left,v,dimension.width -
               insets.left - insets.right,size.height);
             component.repaint(); // redraw the component
             v += size.height + vgap; // update vertical origin for
               next component
     }
 }
/** Returns the minimum layout size calculated using each
  component's preferred size. */
 public Dimension minimumLayoutSize(Container iParent)
 {
     Dimension dimension = new Dimension(0,0);
     for(int i = 0 ; i < iParent.countComponents() ; i++) // scan
       components
     {
```

```
            Component component = iParent.getComponent(i);
            Dimension size = component.preferredSize(); // get i-th
              component's size
            dimension.width = Math.max(dimension.width,size.width);
            dimension.height += size.height + vgap; // update height
              including this component
            }
            Insets insets = iParent.insets(); // add insets (border)
            dimension.width += insets.left + insets.right + 2 * hgap;
            dimension.height += insets.top + insets.bottom + vgap;
            return dimension;
    }
    /** Preferred size is just like minimum size but can be as wide as
      the parent component. */
    public Dimension preferredLayoutSize(Container iParent)
    {
            Dimension dimension = minimumLayoutSize(iParent);
            dimension.width = Math.max(iParent.size().width,dimension.
              width);
            return dimension;
    }
    public void addLayoutComponent(String iName,Component iComponent)
    {
    }
    public void removeLayoutComponent(Component iComponent)
    {
    }
}
```

FLIGHT.JAVA

Flight.java contains a constructor that initializes the members of the flight information and passes them as a parameter. It extracts the flight number, departure and arrival, flight frequency, and plane identification. Listing 10-8 shows the source code for this class.

Listing 10-8: Flight.java.

```
//
// Flight.java - holds information regarding a flight
//
// Copyright (C) 1996 by Connect Software. All rights reserved.
//
// Written by Gionata Mettifogo, Peter Ham.
//
package airplet;
import connect.sql.*;                    // import jdbc and other sql
  libraries
class Flight
{
  /**
   * Initialize flight from the information contained in the current
```

```
* row of this result set. The result set is a subset of rows from
* the flights table in the airline database. This method will read
* information on current row (it will not call next).
*
* @param iFlight is a result set whose current row is a flight
*/
public Flight(ResultSet iFlight) throws SQLException
{
    code = iFlight.getString("code"); // get flight number
    from = iFlight.getString("from_city"); to =
      iFlight.getString("to_city");
    departure = iFlight.getTime("departure"); arrival =
      iFlight.getTime("arrival");
    frequency = iFlight.getString("frequency"); // flight
      frequency (eg. which days this flight operates)
    plane = iFlight.getString("plane"); // airplane used
}
String code, from, to; // the flight code/number and city of
  departure/arrival, e.g., 'TWA800'
Time departure, arrival; // departure and arrival time
String frequency; // days when the flight is available, e.g., 123
  for Mon, Tue, Wed
String plane; // airplane used, e.g., "Boeing 767"
public String toString()
{
    return "Flight[" + code + "," + from + " " + departure + "," +
      to + " " + arrival + "," + frequency + "," + plane + "]";
}
}
```

FLIGHTSPANEL.JAVA

FlightsPanel.java class is a panel containing a graphical map. Which map is displayed depends on the departure and destination airport locations. This panel also displays the routes. Listing 10-9 contains the source code for this class.

Listing 10-9: FlightsPanel.java.

```
//
// FlightsPanel.java - a panel showing flights information and
  routes.
//
// Copyright (C) 1996 by Connect Software. All rights reserved.
//
// Written by Gionata Mettifogo, Peter Ham.
//
package airplet; // airplet package
import connect.sql.*; // import connect's jdbc libraries
import java.awt.*; // import java windowing library
class FlightsPanel extends Panel
{
  public FlightsPanel()
  {
```

```
        LayoutManager layout = new ColumnLayout(0,10); // column
          layout with 10 pixels between components
        setLayout(layout); // use this layout for the panel
        map = new MapCanvas(); add(map); // add a map to the panel
        label = new MultilineLabel(Label.CENTER); // label that can
          display multiple lines of text (draw with subtle good
          looking shadow)
        setText("Welcome to jdbc airlines!\n \nPlease pick an origin
          and a destination\nthen click Search or RoundTrip.");
        add(label); // add label to panel
}
/** Converts a time object into a string in the form hh:mm am/pm */
String time2string(Time time)
{
      int hour = time.getHours(); // get hours (0..23) and minutes
        (0..59)
      int minute = time.getMinutes(); // format the string as hh:mm
        then append am or pm
      return (hour % 12 < 10 ? "0" : "") + Integer.toString(hour %
        12) + ":" + (minute < 10 ? "0" : "") +
        Integer.toString(minute) + (hour < 12 ? " AM" : " PM");
}
void setAirports(Airport iFrom,Airport iTo) throws SQLException
{
      String str = null;
      try
      {
            map.setAirports(iFrom,iTo); // show best map for these
              two airports (and a route between them)
            if(iFrom.getCode().equals(iTo.getCode()) = false) // if
              the two airports are not the same
            {
                  FlightsVector flights = new
                    FlightsVector(iFrom,iTo); // create a vector
                    containing all the flights between the two
                    airports
                  int numFlights = flights.size(); // number of
                    flights found
                  if(numFlights > 0) // if there are flights
                  {
                        str = "Flights from " + iFrom.getName()
                          + " to " + iTo.getName() + "\n \n";
                        for(int i = 0 ; i < numFlights ; i++) //
                          scan flights between these two airports
                        {
                              Flight flight = (Flight)
                                flights.elementAt(i); //
                                retrieve i-th flight
                              str += flight.code + " leaves at
                                " +
                                time2string(flight.departure) +
                                " arrives at " +
                                time2string(flight.arrival) + "
                                (frequency " + flight.frequency
                                + ").\n";
```

```
                             }
                      }
                      else str = "There are no flights between " +
                        iFrom.getName() + " and " + iTo.getName() +
                        ".";
               }
               else str = "Please pick two different airports, then
                  retry."; // if there are no flights or airports are
                  the same show an error message
       }
       catch(SQLException sqlEx) // some sql exception was raised,
         notify the user
       {
               str = "Sorry, your request didn't go through,\nthe
                  server is probably down or busy,\nplease try again
                  later.\n \n" + sqlEx;
       }
       setText(str); // show the string with the flights or the
         warning
       layout(); // we may need to redo this panel's layout (the
         label may have changed its size)
  }
  public void setText(String text)
  {
       label.setText(text);
  }
  private MapCanvas map = null; // map and route canvas
  private MultilineLabel label = null; // label with flights or error
    message
}
```

FLIGHTSVECTOR.JAVA

FlightsVector.java is a vector containing all flights between the departure and arrival airports. A query is sent to the database server to get information about flights with the given airport codes for departure and arrival. Listing 10-10 shows the source code for this class.

Listing 10-10: FlightsVector.java.

```
//
// FlightsVector.java - a vector containing a bunch of flights
//
// Copyright (C) 1996 by Connect Software. All rights reserved.
//
// Written by Gionata Mettifogo, Peter Ham.
//
package airplet;
import connect.sql.*; // import jdbc and other sql libraries
import java.util.*; // java utility classes
class FlightsVector extends Vector // this is just a vector of
  Flight objects
{
```

```
/**
    * Initialize this vector with all flights between two given
      airports.
    * The method will select all rows in the flights table having
      the given airport
    * codes in the from_city and to_city fields. An entry in the
      vector will then
    * be created for each flight and each entry will be added to
      the vector.
    *
    * @param iConnection connection to the database
    * @param iFrom the airport we're leaving from
    * @param iTo the airport we're arriving to
    */
public FlightsVector(Airport iFrom,Airport iTo) throws SQLException
{
    // executes something like: select * from flights where
      from_city = 'SFO' and to_city = 'JFK'
    String sql = "select * from flights where from_city = '" +
      iFrom.getCode() + "' and to_city = '" + iTo.getCode() + "'
      order by departure";
    Statement s = Airplet.createStatement(); // create normal sql
      statement
    for(ResultSet r = s.executeQuery(sql) ; r.next() ; ) // scan
      all flights between given airports
    {
            Flight flight = new Flight(r); // create a new flight
              from current row
            // System.out.println("FlightsVector - adding flight "
              + flight + " to vector");
            addElement(flight); // add this flight to the vector
    }
    s.close(); // we don't have to do this (but it could help jdbc
      optimize access)
}
}
```

IMAGECANVAS.JAVA

ImageCanvas.java class is a canvas containing an image. An update method is provided to draw the image using double buffering, if possible. Listing 10-11 shows the source code for this class.

Listing 10-11: ImageCanvas.java.

```
//
// ImageCanvas.java - a canvas that shows an image
//
// Copyright (C) 1996 by Connect Software. All rights reserved.
//
// Written by Gionata Mettifogo, Peter Ham.
//
package airplet;
```

```
import java.applet.*;
import java.awt.*; // java windowing classes
/** A canvas used to display an image. */
public class ImageCanvas extends Canvas // shows a canvas containing
 an image
 {
 /** Initialize canvas showing the image with the given name. */
 public ImageCanvas(String name)
 {
     if(name != null && name.length() > 0) // if a name was
       specified
     {
           setImage(name); // load image
     }
 }
 protected Image image = null; // image shown by this canvas
 /** Display image with given name in the canvas. */
 public void setImage(String iName)
 {
     Image newimage = Airplet.loadImage(iName); // load new image
     if(image != newimage) // if image changed
     {
           image = newimage; repaint(); // refresh the canvas
     }
 }
 /** Update the canvas using double buffering (if enough memory's
  available). */
 synchronized public void update(Graphics iGraphics)
 {
     Dimension d = size();
     if(d.width < 1 || d.height < 1) return; // don't update if
       empty
     Image buf = null;
     try // catch memory full and other problem
     {
           buf = createImage(d.width,d.height); // create
             temporary buffer
     }
     catch(Exception e) { }
     if(buf != null) // if buffer was created
     {
           Graphics bufGr = buf.getGraphics(); // get buffer's
             graPHIC CONTEXT
           bufGr.clearRect(0,0,d.width,d.height); // erase content
             of buffer
           paint(bufGr); // paint into the offscreen buffer
           iGraphics.drawImage(buf,0,0,this); // copy the
             offscreen buffer to the panel
           buf.flush(); // dispose buffer's resources
     }
     else super.update(iGraphics); // if there's not enough memory
       for double buffering let the superclass update as usual
 }
 /** Draw the image centered in the canvas. */
```

```
public void paint(Graphics iGraphics)
{
    if(image != null) // if there is an image
    {
        Dimension d = size(); // calculate image's origin
        d.width -= image.getWidth(this);
        d.height -= image.getHeight(this); // then draw the
            image centered in the canvas
        iGraphics.drawImage(image,d.width,d.height,this);
    }
}
/** Preferred size for this canvas is the size of the image that it
  is showing, if any. */
public Dimension preferredSize()
{
    if(image != null) // if an image was selected return its size
    {
        return new Dimension(image.getWidth(this),image.
            getHeight(this));
    }
    return new Dimension(1,1); // otherwise 1 pixel will do (0
        would be too little, 'cause paint would never be called)
}
}
```

MAPCANVAS.JAVA

MapCanvas.java contains the methods used to display the most appropriate map for the departure and arrival selections. A route is drawn between the two airports. Listing 10-12 shows the source code for this class.

Listing 10-12: MapCanvas.java.

```
//
// MapCanvas.java - a view that shows a map with airports and a
  route
//
// Copyright (C) 1996 by Connect Software. All rights reserved.
//
// Written by Gionata Mettifogo, Peter Ham.
//
package airplet;
import java.awt.*; // import java windowing toolkit
import java.io.*; // I/O streams, exceptions, etc.
import java.applet.*; // applet class
/** A canvas that shows a map and a flight's route. */
class MapCanvas extends ImageCanvas // map class extends canvas
  (drawable view)
{
  public MapCanvas()
  {
      super("images/world.gif"); // display world map until airports
        are selected
```

```
            iconFrom = Airplet.loadImage("images/iconFrom.gif"); // load
              origin and destination icons
            iconTo = Airplet.loadImage("images/iconTo.gif");
}
private Airport airFrom = null; // arrival and departure airports
private Airport airTo = null;
private MapInfo mapFrom = null; // information regarding the
  airports on the map
private MapInfo mapTo = null;
private Image iconFrom = null; // icons for arrival and departure
  points on the map
private Image iconTo = null;
/** Draw a route going from x1,y1 to x2,y2 */
private void drawRoute(Graphics iGraphics,int x1,int y1,int x2,int
  y2)
{
      int xp = x1;
      int yp = y1;
      double arc = Math.min(Math.abs(x1 - x2) * .20 + Math.abs(y1 -
      y2) * .20,30.0);
      for(double p = .1 ; p <= 1.0 ; p += .1) // draw a slanted arc
        as 20 connected lines
      {
              int xc = (int) (x1 + (double) (x2 - x1) * p); //
                calculate parametric position in the line connecting
                origin with arrival
              int yc = (int) (y1 + (double) (y2   y1) * p);
              double pslanted = p; // (p < .75) ? (p * .50 / .75) :
                (.50 + (p - .75) * .50 / .25);
              yc -= (int) (Math.sin(Math.PI * pslanted) * arc); //
                add variable y value to form an arc
              iGraphics.drawLine(xp,yp,xc,yc); // draw current
                segment
              xp = xc; // current position becomes previous position
              yp = yc;
      }
}
/** Draw the map of the region containing both airports and a
  route. */
public void paint(Graphics iGraphics)
{
      super.paint(iGraphics); // draws the map
      if(mapFrom != null && mapTo != null)
      {
              Dimension d = size(); // size of this canvas
              int w = image.getWidth(this), hofs = (d.width - w) / 2;
                // origin of the map in the canvas
              int h = image.getHeight(this), vofs = (d.height - h) /
                2;
              iGraphics.setColor(Color.lightGray);
              drawRoute(iGraphics,hofs + mapFrom.x + 1,vofs +
                mapFrom.y + 1,hofs + mapTo.x + 1,vofs + mapTo.y + 1);
              iGraphics.setColor(Color.black);
```

```
                drawRoute(iGraphics,hofs + mapFrom.x,vofs +
                 mapFrom.y,hofs + mapTo.x,vofs + mapTo.y);
                int xFrom = hofs + mapFrom.x - iconFrom.getWidth(this)
                 / 2;
                int yFrom = vofs + mapFrom.y - iconFrom.getHeight(this)
                 / 2;
                int xTo = hofs + mapTo.x - iconTo.getWidth(this) / 2;
                 // calculate origin and destination icon's position
                int yTo = vofs + mapTo.y - iconTo.getHeight(this) / 2;
                iGraphics.drawImage(iconFrom,xFrom,yFrom,this); // draw
                 origin and destination icons
                iGraphics.drawImage(iconTo,xTo,yTo,this);
        }
    }
    /** Sets departure and arrival airports, selecting and displaying
     the most appropriate map. */
    void setAirports(Airport iFrom,Airport iTo)
    {
        String name = null;
        airFrom = iFrom; airTo = iTo; // set departure and arrival
         airports
        if(airFrom != null && airTo != null) // if departure and
         arrival airports were specified
        {
                for(mapFrom = airFrom.getMaps() ; name == null &&
                 mapFrom != null ; )
                {
                        for(mapTo = airTo.getMaps() ; name == null &&
                         mapTo != null ; )
                        {
                                if(mapFrom.name.equals(mapTo.name))
                                {
                                        name = mapFrom.name;
                                }
                                else mapTo = mapTo.next;
                        }
                        if(name == null) mapFrom = mapFrom.next;
                }
                // System.out.println("MapCanvas.setAirport - " +
                 airFrom + " " + mapFrom + " to " + airTo + " " +
                 mapTo);
        }
        name = "images/" + (name != null ? name : "world") + ".gif";
         // use world's map if there's no better one
        setImage(name); // display new image
    }
    public Dimension preferredSize()
    {
        return new Dimension(500,300); // size of the maps is fixed
    }
}
```

MAPINFO.JAVA
MapInfo.java class extracts the x,y coordinates from the flight's string for a particular graphic map. Listing 10-13 shows its source code.

Listing 10-13: MapInfo.java.

```
//
// MapInfo.java - informations regarding airport's position on a map
//
// Copyright (C) 1996 by Connect Software. All rights reserved.
//
// Written by Gionata Mettifogo, Peter Ham.
//
package airplet; // airplet's package
import java.util.*; // utility classes
/** Information about an airport's position on a map. */
class MapInfo
{
  /** Initialize from a 'map(x,y)' string. */
  MapInfo(String map)
  {
      StringTokenizer sTokenizer = new StringTokenizer(map,"(,)");
       // name is encoded as name(x,y) so use ( and comma as
       separators
      name = sTokenizer.nextToken().toLowerCase(); // name of this
       map (eg. 'usa', 'europe', 'world')
      x = Integer.parseInt(sTokenizer.nextToken()); // coordinate of
       the airport in this map
      y = Integer.parseInt(sTokenizer.nextToken());
  }
  String name; // name of the map
  int x,y; // coordinates of the airport on this map
  MapInfo next = null; // next map (this is a linked list)
  void append(MapInfo item)
  {
      if(next != null) next.append(item); else next = item; //
       appends item at the end of the linked list
  }
  public String toString()
  {
      return "MapInfo[" + name + "," + x + "," + y + "]"; // returns
       MapInfo[name,x,y]
  }
}
```

MULTILINELABEL.JAVA
MultilineLabel.java is simply a label that can display multiple lines of text. It also provides text shadow for the drawn string. Listing 10-14 shows the source code for this class.

Listing 10–14: MultilineLabel.java.

```java
//
// MultilineLabel.java - a label that can draw several lines of text
//
// Copyright (C) 1996 by Connect Software. All rights reserved.
//
// Written by Gionata Mettifogo, Peter Ham.
//
package airplet;
import java.awt.*;
import java.util.*;
public class MultilineLabel extends java.awt.Canvas
{
  public MultilineLabel(int alignment)
  {
      align = alignment;
  }
  private String text; private int align; // text and alignment (see
    constants in Label)
  public void setText(String text)
  {
      this.text = text;
  }
  /** Draw the multiline label aligned as specified during object's
    construction. */
  public void paint(Graphics iGraphics)
  {
      FontMetrics fm = iGraphics.getFontMetrics(); // get
        information on the font's sizes
      StringTokenizer tokens = new StringTokenizer(text,"\n"); //
        separate different lines
      int w = size().width, h = fm.getHeight(); // line height and
        label's width
      for(int y = h ; tokens.hasMoreTokens() ; y += h) // scan all
        lines in the label
      {
              String line = tokens.nextToken(); // retrieve line
              int x = 0;
              if(align == Label.CENTER || align == Label.RIGHT) // if
               line is centered or right aligned
              {
                      x = w - fm.stringWidth(line); if(align ==
                      Label.CENTER) x /= 2; // calculate spacing on
                      left side
              }
              shadowString(iGraphics,line,x,y); // draw the line
      }
  }
  public Dimension preferredSize()
  {
      FontMetrics fm = getGraphics().getFontMetrics(); // get
        information on the font's sizes
      StringTokenizer tokens = new StringTokenizer(text,"\n"); //
        separate different lines
```

```
            Dimension dimension = new Dimension(0,fm.getHeight() *
              tokens.countTokens() + fm.getMaxDescent() + 1);
            while(tokens.hasMoreTokens()) // scan lines
            {
                    String line = tokens.nextToken(); // retrieve line
                    dimension.width =
                      Math.max(fm.stringWidth(line),dimension.width); //
                      width is the length of the longest line
            }
        return dimension;
}
/**
* Draws the given string at the given position using a
* subtle 1 pixel gray shadow. Light comes from the upper
* left corner (where the Apple used to be).
*/
public void shadowString(Graphics iGraphics,String iString,int
  x,int y)
{
        Color color = iGraphics.getColor();
        iGraphics.setColor(Color.lightGray);
        iGraphics.drawString(iString,x+1,y+1);
        iGraphics.setColor(color);
        iGraphics.drawString(iString,x,y);
}
}
```

Handling Multimedia Content

SQL does not provide mechanisms that are powerful enough to handle binary large objects, known as BLOBs. Fortunately, JDBC contains the necessary methods to insert and extract BLOBs.

Sending BLOBS

The next example is a simple command line tool used to insert binary large objects in a table. Any kind of BLOB may be used, including pictures, audio files, binary data, and texts. It is quite simple to use. The tool prompts you for a database URL, a log in, a password, the name of the table to be updated, the BLOB column name, which is the column that holds a BLOB, and the BLOB file name.

A row must exist in the table before trying to insert a BLOB. For example, a table of employees must contain a row for Jones before a picture can be inserted for this employee. To locate this row, the program also prompts for a column name and value, which represent a search criteria. In the case of employee Jones, simply use "name" as column name and "Jones" as column value.

All parameters but the database URL, log in, and password may be passed on the command line. In this case, the program will use the default URL, log in, and password. This method is extremely convenient for inserting multiple BLOBs at once from a shell script.

BATCH COMMAND
Consider this script.

```
java txblob -c employees pict name Jones /tmp/pictures/jones.jpg
java txblob -c employees pict name Dupont /tmp/pictures/dupont.jpg
java txblob -c employees pict name Duke /tmp/pictures/duke.jpg
java txblob -c employees pict name Jack /tmp/pictures/jack.jpg
...
...
```

It inserts the pictures of Jones, Dupont, Duke, and Jack in the table of employees.

SOURCE
Listing 10-15 contains the source code for this example.

Listing 10-15: txblob.java.

```java
import java.sql.*;
import java.io.*;
import java.util.*;
public class txblob {
  static DataInputStream kbd = new DataInputStream(System.in);
  static String url = "jdbc:odbc:netbank";
  static String driver = "sun.jdbc.odbc.JdbcOdbcDriver";
  static String login = "dba";
  static String passwd = "javabank";
  static String filename = "";
  static String tablename = "";
  static String blobcolumnname = "";
  static String selectcolumnname = "";
  static String selectcolumnvalue = "";
  static Connection curConn = null;
  public static void main(String argv[]) throws IOException
  {
      String temp = "";
      if (argv[0].equals("-c")) {
            tablename = argv[1];
            blobcolumnname = argv[2];
            selectcolumnname = argv[3];
            selectcolumnvalue = argv[4];
            filename = argv[5];
      } else {
            System.out.println("Simple tool to insert BLOBS, by
              Bernard Van Haecke, 1996.\n");
            System.out.print("Enter the url or [ENTER] for " + url
              + " : ");
            System.out.flush();
            temp = kbd.readLine();
            if (!temp.equals("")) url = temp;
```

```
                System.out.print("Enter the login or [ENTER] for " +
                  login + " : ");
                System.out.flush();
                temp = kbd.readLine();
                if (!temp.equals("")) login = temp;
                System.out.print("Enter the passwd or [ENTER] for " +
                  passwd + " : ");
                System.out.flush();
                temp = kbd.readLine();
                if (!temp.equals("")) passwd = temp;
                System.out.print("\nEnter the table name : ");
                System.out.flush();
                tablename = kbd.readLine();
                System.out.print("Enter the blob column name : ");
                System.out.flush();
                blobcolumnname = kbd.readLine();
                System.out.print("Enter the row selection criteria
                  column name : ");
                System.out.flush();
                selectcolumnname = kbd.readLine();
                System.out.print("Enter the row selection criteria
                  value : ");
                System.out.flush();
                selectcolumnvalue = kbd.readLine();
                System.out.print("Enter the file name : ");
                System.out.flush();
                filename = kbd.readLine();
        }
        txblob session = new txblob();
}
public txblob() throws IOException
{
        try {
                Class.forName(driver);
                curConn = DriverManager.getConnection(url, login,
                  passwd);
        }
        catch(java.lang.Exception ex) {
                System.out.println("url : " + url);
                System.out.println("login : " + login);
                System.out.println("passwd : " + passwd);
                ex.printStackTrace();
                return;
        }
        processBlob();
        finalize();
}
protected void finalize()
{
        try {
                curConn.close();
        }
        catch (SQLException ex) { }
}
```

```
private void processBlob() throws IOException
{
    try {
            java.io.File blobFile = new java.io.File(filename);
            int blobFileLen = (int) blobFile.length();
            java.io.InputStream fblob = new
             java.io.FileInputStream(blobFile);
            PreparedStatement myStmt = curConn.prepareStatement(
             "UPDATE " + tablename + " SET " + blobcolumnname + " =
             ? WHERE " + selectcolumnname + " = ?");
            myStmt.setBinaryStream(1, fblob, blobFileLen);
            myStmt.setString(2, selectcolumnvalue);
            int res = myStmt.executeUpdate();
            myStmt.close();
    }
    catch (SQLException ex) {
            // Unexpected SQL exception.
            System.out.println(ex);
    }
    catch (java.lang.Exception ex) {
            // Got some other type of exception. Dump it.
            ex.printStackTrace ();
    }
  }
}
```

Retrieving BLOBS

This example is very similar to the previous one. It is a simple command line tool to retrieve binary large objects from a table. It prompts for a database URL, a log in, a password, the name of the table to be updated, the BLOB column name, which is the column that holds a BLOB, and the BLOB file name where this BLOB must be stored.

If a table of employees contains a row for Jones and if a picture is available for this employee, it is possible to retrieve it. To locate this row, the program prompts for a column name and value, which represent a search criteria. In the case of employee Jones, we would simply use "name" as column name and "Jones" as column value.

All parameters but the database URL, log in, and password pass on the command line. In this case, the program uses the default URL, log in, and password. This is extremely convenient for retrieving many BLOBs at once from a shell script.

BATCH COMMAND
Consider the script in Listing 10-16.

Listing 10-16: Batch command.
```
java rxblob -c employees pict name Jones /tmp/pictures/jones.jpg
java rxblob -c employees pict name Dupont /tmp/pictures/dupont.jpg
```

```
java rxblob -c employees pict name Duke /tmp/pictures/duke.jpg
java rxblob -c employees pict name Jack /tmp/pictures/jack.jpg
...
...
```

This batch command retrieves the pictures of Jones, Dupont, Duke, and Jack from the table of employees and stores these pictures in different files. The file name and file type are not stored in the table. We could have stored the file type in the table by simply adding a file type record. In case the client application is not aware of the BLOB format, it is mandatory to store this type information somewhere. It is possible to do so, but, in this case, special fields must be added to the table structure because it is considered extra information regarding BLOBs. Indeed, BLOBs are nothing more than untyped binary data.

It may be a good idea to hold the data type along with BLOBs, particularly when the information is to be extracted and sent to a Web browser. In this case, it is appropriate to store the BLOB's Multimedia Internet Mail Extension (MIME) type in a specific field of the table so the browser knows how to interpret the data [e.g., should it display it as a JPEG (Joint Photographic Experts Group) picture or MPEG (Motion Pictures Experts Group) movie file, or play it as an .au (common audio file on Unix machines) sound file].

SOURCE
Listing 10-17 contains the source code for this example.

Listing 10-17: rxblob.java.

```java
import java.sql.*;
import java.io.*;
import java.util.*;
public class rxblob {
  static DataInputStream kbd = new DataInputStream(System.in);
  static String url = "jdbc:odbc:netbank";
  static String driver = "sun.jdbc.odbc.JdbcOdbcDriver";
  static String login = "dba";
  static String passwd = "javabank";
  static String filename = "";
  static String tablename = "";
  static String blobcolumnname = "";
  static String selectcolumnname = "";
  static String selectcolumnvalue = "";
  static Connection curConn = null;
  public static void main(String argv[]) throws IOException
  {
      String temp = "";
      if ((argv[0] != null) && (argv[0].equals("-c")))
{
            tablename = argv[1];
            blobcolumnname = argv[2];
            selectcolumnname = argv[3];
            selectcolumnvalue = argv[4];
```

```
                        filename = argv[5];
                } else {
                        System.out.println("Simple tool to retrieve BLOBS, by
                         Bernard Van Haecke, 1996.\n");
                        System.out.print("Enter the url or [ENTER] for " + url
                         + " : ");
                        System.out.flush();
                        temp = kbd.readLine();
                        if (!temp.equals("")) url = temp;
                        System.out.print("Enter the login or [ENTER] for " +
                         login + " : ");
                        System.out.flush();
                        temp = kbd.readLine();
                        if (!temp.equals("")) login = temp;
                        System.out.print("Enter the passwd or [ENTER] for " +
                         passwd + " : ");
                        System.out.flush();
                        temp = kbd.readLine();
                        if (!temp.equals("")) passwd = temp;
                        System.out.print("\nEnter the table name : ");
                        System.out.flush();
                        tablename = kbd.readLine();
                        System.out.print("Enter the blob column name : ");
                        System.out.flush();
                        blobcolumnname = kbd.readLine();
                        System.out.print("Enter the row selection criteria
                         column name : ");
                        System.out.flush();
                        selectcolumnname = kbd.readLine();
                        System.out.print("Enter the row selection criteria
                         value : ");
                        System.out.flush();
                        selectcolumnvalue = kbd.readLine();
                        System.out.print("Enter the file name : ");
                        System.out.flush();
                        filename = kbd.readLine();
                }
                rxblob session = new rxblob();
        }
        public rxblob() throws IOException
        {
                try {
                        Class.forName(driver);
                        curConn = DriverManager.getConnection(url, login,
                         passwd);
                }
                catch(java.lang.Exception ex) {
                        System.out.println("url : " + url);
                        System.out.println("login : " + login);
                        System.out.println("passwd : " + passwd);
                        ex.printStackTrace();
                        return;
                }
                processBlob();
```

```java
        finalize();
    }
protected void finalize()
{
    try {
            curConn.close();
    }
    catch (SQLException ex) { }
    }
    private void processBlob() throws IOException
    {
    try {
            java.io.File blobFile = new java.io.File(filename);
            java.io.OutputStream fblob = new
             java.io.FileOutputStream(blobFile);
            java.sql.Statement myStatement =
             curConn.createStatement();
            ResultSet rs = myStatement.executeQuery("SELECT " +
             blobcolumnname + " FROM " + tablename + " WHERE " +
             selectcolumnname + " = " + selectcolumnvalue);
            // we retrieve in 4K chunks
            byte[] buffer = new byte[4096];
            int size;
            if (rs.next()) {
                    // fetch blob
                    java.io.InputStream strin =
                     rs.getBinaryStream(blobcolumnname);
                    for (;;)
                    {
                            size = strin.read(buffer);
                            if (size == 0)
                            {
                            break;
                            }
                            // Send the buffer to some output stream
                            fblob.write(buffer, 0, size);
                    }
            }
            else System.out.println("Row not found.");
            myStatement.close();
            rs.close();
    }
    catch (SQLException ex) {
            // Unexpected SQL exception.
            System.out.println(ex);
    }
    catch (java.lang.Exception ex) {
            // Got some other type of exception. Dump it.
            ex.printStackTrace ();
    }
    }
}
```

Dealing with Database Transactions

As seen in the section dedicated to database transactions, transactions group the execution of a number of SQL statements to maintain consistency in multiuser environments. In the following example, we group multiple SQL INSERT statements to ensure consistent financial transactions by using database transactions.

The Bank of Java

This Java applet is similar to the software provided by banks to their customers to perform operations on their accounts from their home computers with telephones and modems. It was simplified to illustrate database transactions with JDBC.

The main operations are these:

♦ Welcome a client and prompt for the client's ID and PIN code

♦ Look up the client's balance and transaction history in the database

♦ Perform money transfers to other accounts

♦ For fun, withdraw virtual $20 banknotes

The information about clients and their accounts is, of course, stored in a database. The data structure was kept simple to allow a quick understanding of the whole application and the transaction mechanism. Database transactions are performed in the main thread, while a second thread serves as a clock. Each time an update is made to the database, the SQL queries that perform the update are grouped in a single transaction unit. By doing so, no inconsistent update can bring the database to an incoherent state.

If the client-server link is broken in the middle of a transaction, the transaction will be canceled; otherwise, it is committed. Canceling a transaction is called transaction rollback. This mechanism prevents unlogged transfers or unlogged withdrawals. Indeed, transfers and withdrawals are SQL INSERTs in database tables such as accounts and history log.

The GUI part of this applet was written using Marimba Bongo, which generates a 100-percent portable .gui file. This file contains a persistent form of the widgets used in this example. The .gui file can be edited using Marimba Bongo, a demo version of which is on the CD-ROM accompanying this book. The unzipped Marimba classes must be in the CLASSPATH or present on the WWW server to run this example. The GUI part of the application uses the Marimba Bongo classes that are persistified to a portable file, which is the main reason why almost no GUI code is present in the source code. Each GUI control is a Marimba widget, which has a name and various properties that are also persistified in the permanent GUI file.

Figure 10-5 shows the welcome screen. It prompts for an account number and a PIN code. There is a status bar below the validate button. If the PIN code is incorrect, this status bar displays an error message.

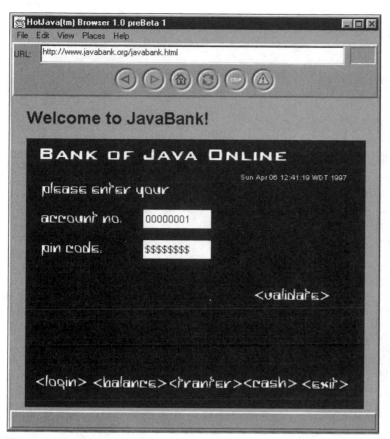

Figure 10-5: JavaBank applet login screen.

The names of the main controls are:

- welcomeAccountNo — a text field to get the account number

- welcomePinCode — a text field to get the personal identification number

- welcomeOkButton — a button to log into the database

- welcomeEndButton — a button to close the database connection and quit the application

- statusBar — a noneditable text field to display various messages

The values associated with these controls are checked and set within the program; the control names refer to them as instances of the Marimba GUI widgets.

Once the client has logged in, a lookup is performed in the database, and the customer's account balance and transaction history are displayed, as shown in Figure 10-6.

Figure 10-6: JavaBank applet account balance.

These are the controls:

- `balanceHistory` — a scrollable text list to display the transaction history for the current account

- `balanceBalance` — a noneditable text field to display the balance of this account

- `balanceRefreshButton` — a button to refresh the history log

- `balanceEndButton` — a button to exit the session

- `statusBar` — a noneditable text field to display various messages

The client's account balance and transaction history display each time the refresh button is pressed.

The next screen panel allows transfers to other accounts. The name and address of the recipient is looked up in the database and displayed in the status bar. Then the amount of money is transferred, as shown in Figure 10-7.

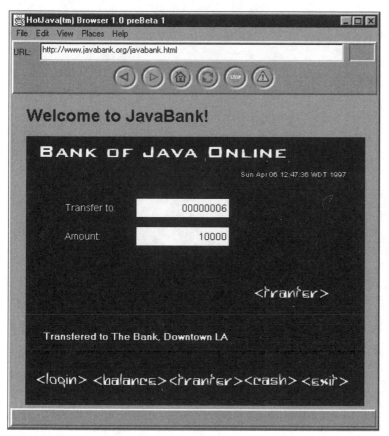

Figure 10-7: JavaBank applet transfer screen.

The control names include:

- ◆ transferAccountNo — a text field for the recipient's account number
- ◆ transferAmount — a text field for the amount of money to transfer
- ◆ transferYesButton — a button to commit the transfer
- ◆ transferEndButton — a button to exit the session
- ◆ statusBar — a noneditable text field to display various messages

This is the automatic teller machine (ATM) panel. After choosing an amount to withdraw and after pressing the withdraw button, a Java banknote appears and scrolls on the screen. Figure 10-8 shows this panel.

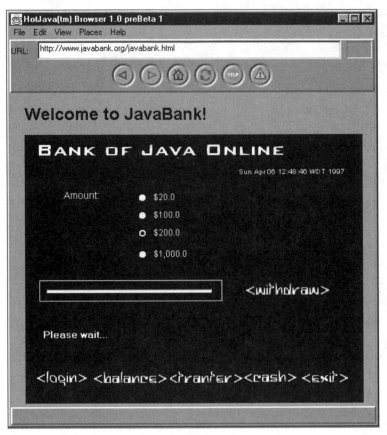

Figure 10-8: JavaBank applet cash withdrawal.

The controls include:

- ◆ withdrawXX, where XX is one of 20, 100, 200, 1,000 — radio buttons used to select the amount of money to withdraw

- ◆ withdrawImage — a picture of a banknote that displays and scrolls when the withdrawal is committed

- ◆ withdrawWithdrawButton — a button to commit the withdrawal

- ◆ withdrawEndButton — a button to exit the session

- ◆ statusBar — a noneditable text field to display various messages

The applet contains two important classes: Account and NetBank. NetBank is the main class, which handles user input, while Account has specific methods to perform usual bank operations on an account. The most essential part of this example, the JDBC and SQL code, is in the Account class.

THE HTML FILE
This is the HTML page that calls the applet.

```html
<html>
<title>JavaBank Applet</title>
<head>
<h1>Welcome to JavaBank!</h1>
</head>
<body>
<applet code=NetBank.class width=480 height=380>
</applet>
</body>
</html>
```

ACCOUNT. JAVA
Listing 10-18 contains the source code for the Account.java class.

Listing 10-18: Account.java.

```java
import java.sql.*;
import java.io.*;
import java.util.*;
import java.net.*;
public class Account {
 long acctNo = 0;
 Connection curConn;
 public Account(String url, String uid, String pwd) {
      try {
              Class.forName("sun.jdbc.odbc.JdbcOdbcDriver");
              curConn = DriverManager.getConnection(url, uid, pwd);
      }
      catch(java.lang.Exception ex) {
              ex.printStackTrace();
      }
 }
 protected void finalize()
 {
      try {
              curConn.close();
      } catch (SQLException ex) { }
 }
 public boolean verifyPinCode(long checkAcctNo, String checkPinCode)
 {
      boolean rc = (0 == 1);
      String acctPinCode = "";
      String curQueryString = "SELECT pincode FROM accounts WHERE
       acctno = " + checkAcctNo;
      try {
              Statement curSt = curConn.createStatement();
              curSt.setQueryTimeout(60);
              ResultSet curRs = curSt.executeQuery(curQueryString);
              while (curRs.next()) {
```

```
                              acctPinCode = curRs.getString("pincode");
            }
            curRs.close();
            curSt.close();
            rc = (checkPinCode.compareTo(acctPinCode) == 0);
      } catch (SQLException ex) { }
      if (rc) {
            acctNo = checkAcctNo;
      }
      return rc;
}
public float checkAcctBalance()
{
      float acctBalance = 0;
      String curQueryString = "SELECT balance FROM accounts WHERE
       acctno = " + acctNo;
      try {
            Statement curSt = curConn.createStatement();
            curSt.setQueryTimeout(60);
            ResultSet curRs = curSt.executeQuery(curQueryString);
            while (curRs.next()) {
                  acctBalance = curRs.getFloat("balance");
            }
            curRs.close();
            curSt.close();
      } catch (SQLException ex) { }
      return (acctBalance);
}
public Vector checkHistory()
{
      Vector acctTransactionHistory = new Vector();
      String curQueryString = "SELECT tdate, typetransaction,
       otheracct, amount, ipaddress FROM history WHERE acctno = " +
       acctNo;
      try {
            Statement curSt = curConn.createStatement();
            curSt.setQueryTimeout(60);
            ResultSet curRs = curSt.executeQuery(curQueryString);
            while (curRs.next()) {
                  acctTransactionHistory.addElement(curRs.getStrin
                  g(1) + " "
                                          + curRs.getString(2) + "
                                          "
                                          + curRs.getString(3) + "
                                          "
                                          + curRs.getString(4) + "
                                          "
                                          + curRs.getString(5));
            }
            curRs.close();
            curSt.close();
      } catch (SQLException ex) { }
      return (acctTransactionHistory);
}
```

```
public Vector checkAcctOwnerName(long checkAcctNo)
{
    Vector acctOwner = new Vector();
    String curQueryString = "SELECT name, address FROM clients
     WHERE ownerno = (SELECT ownerno FROM accounts WHERE acctno =
     " + checkAcctNo + ")";
    try {
            Statement curSt = curConn.createStatement();
            curSt.setQueryTimeout(60);
            ResultSet curRs = curSt.executeQuery(curQueryString);
            while (curRs.next()) {
                    acctOwner.addElement(curRs.getString("name"));
                    acctOwner.addElement(curRs.getString("address"))
                      ;
            }
            curRs.close();
            curSt.close();
    } catch (SQLException ex) { }
    return (acctOwner);
}
public void makeTransfer(long toAcctNo, float amount)
{
    String curUpdateString = "UPDATE accounts SET balance =
     balance + ? WHERE acctno = ?";
    String logInsertString = "INSERT INTO history (tdate, acctno,
     typetransaction, otheracct, amount, ipaddress) VALUES (?, ?,
     ?, ?, ?, ?)";
    try {
            curConn.setTransactionIsolation(Connection.TRANSACTION_
             SERIALIZABLE   );
            curConn.setAutoCommit(false);
            PreparedStatement curSt =
             curConn.prepareStatement(curUpdateString);
            curSt.setQueryTimeout(60);
            curSt.setFloat(1, -amount);
            curSt.setLong(2, acctNo);
            curSt.executeUpdate();
            curSt.setFloat(1, amount);
            curSt.setLong(2, toAcctNo);
            curSt.executeUpdate();
            java.util.Date toDay = new java.util.Date();
            String localHost = "";
            try {
                    localHost =
                      InetAddress.getLocalHost().toString();
            }
            catch (UnknownHostException ex) {
                    localHost = "localhost/127.0.0.1";
            }
            PreparedStatement logSt =
             curConn.prepareStatement(logInsertString);
            logSt.setQueryTimeout(60);
            logSt.setString(1, toDay.toGMTString());
            logSt.setLong(2, acctNo);
```

```
              logSt.setString(3, "Transfert");
              logSt.setLong(4, toAcctNo);
              logSt.setFloat(5, -amount);
              logSt.setString(6, localHost);
              logSt.executeUpdate();
              logSt.setString(1, toDay.toGMTString());
              logSt.setLong(2, toAcctNo);
              logSt.setString(3, "Received");
              logSt.setLong(4, acctNo);
              logSt.setFloat(5, amount);
              logSt.setString(6, localHost);
              logSt.executeUpdate();
              curConn.commit();
              curConn.setTransactionIsolation(Connection.TRANSACTION_
                NONE);
              curSt.close();
              logSt.close();
          } catch (SQLException ex) { }
      }
      public void cashWithdraw(float amount)
      {
          String curUpdateString = "UPDATE accounts SET balance =
            balance + ? WHERE acctno = ?";
          String logInsertString = "INSERT INTO history (tdate, acctno,
            typetransaction, otheracct, amount, ipaddress) VALUES (?, ?,
            ?, ?, ?, ?)";
          try {
              curConn.setTransactionIsolation(Connection.TRANSACTION_
                SERIALIZABLE);
              curConn.setAutoCommit(false);
              PreparedStatement curSt =
                curConn.prepareStatement(curUpdateString);
              curSt.setQueryTimeout(60);
              curSt.setFloat(1, -amount);
              curSt.setLong(2, acctNo);
              curSt.executeUpdate();
              java.util.Date toDay = new java.util.Date();
              String localHost = "";
              try {
                  localHost =
                    InetAddress.getLocalHost().toString();
              }
              catch (UnknownHostException ex) {
                  localHost = "localhost/127.0.0.1";
              }
              PreparedStatement logSt =
                curConn.prepareStatement(logInsertString);
              logSt.setQueryTimeout(60);
              logSt.setString(1, toDay.toGMTString());
              logSt.setLong(2, acctNo);
              logSt.setString(3, "Withdraw");
              logSt.setLong(4, 0);
              logSt.setFloat(5, -amount);
              logSt.setString(6, localHost);
```

```
        logSt.executeUpdate();
        curConn.commit();
        curConn.setTransactionIsolation(Connection.TRANSACTION_
          NONE);
        curSt.close();
        logSt.close();
    } catch (SQLException ex) { }
  }
}
```

NETBANK.JAVA
Listing 10-19 contains the source code for NetBank.java.

Listing 10-19: NetBank.java.

```
import java.awt.*;
import java.sql.*;
import java.lang.*;
import java.util.*;
import java.net.*;
import marimba.gui.*;
public class NetBank extends java.applet.Applet {
Presentation presentation;
PlayerPanel player;
PlayerUtil util;
Account curAcct = null;
float curWithdrawAmount = 0;
public void init()
{
  try {
        presentation = Presentation.getPresentation(new
          URL(getDocumentBase(), "netbank.gui"));
  } catch (MalformedURLException ex) {
   ex.printStackTrace();
  }
  // Create a Player Panel
  setLayout(new BorderLayout());
  add("Center", player = new PlayerPanel());
  // Set the presentation
  player.setPresentation(presentation);
  // Create a Player utillity object
  util = new PlayerUtil(player);
  ((FolderWidget)util.getWidget("netbankFolder")).setTabMode(0);

  // Initialize the clock thread
  TimeT t;
  t = new TimeT((TextBoxWidget)util.getWidget("clockLabel"));
  t.start();
}
public void logoutRequest()
{
  util.setText("welcomeAccountNo", "");
```

```java
        util.setText("welcomePinCode", "");
        util.setText("balanceBalance", "");
        util.setText("balanceHistory", "");
        util.setText("transferAccountNo", "");
        util.setText("transferAmount", "");
        util.setText("statusBar", "");
        curAcct.finalize();
        util.gotoPage("welcomePage");
}
public void displayBalance()
{
  String bal = (new Float(curAcct.checkAcctBalance())).toString();
  util.setText("balanceBalance", bal);
  Vector v = curAcct.checkHistory();
  String s = "";
      for (int i=0; i < v.size(); i++)
      s = s + v.elementAt(i) + "\n";
  util.setText("balanceHistory", s);
  util.setText("statusBar", "");
}
public boolean handleEvent(Event evt)
{
  if ((evt.id == Event.ACTION_EVENT) && (evt.target instanceof
    Widget)) {
   Widget w = (Widget)evt.target;
   String nm = w.getName();
   System.out.println("Event: " + nm);
   // The user has switched pages.
   if (nm.equals("netbankFolder")) {
       util.setText("statusBar", "");
   }
   if (nm.equals("loginPanelButton")) {
       util.gotoPage("welcomePage");
   }
   if (nm.equals("balancePanelButton")) {
       util.gotoPage("balancePage");
   }
   if (nm.equals("transferPanelButton")) {
       util.gotoPage("transferPage");
   }
   if (nm.equals("cashPanelButton")) {
       util.gotoPage("withdrawPage");
   }
   // The user has logged in.
   if (nm.equals("welcomeOkButton")) {
       Long acct = new Long(util.getText("welcomeAccountNo").trim());
       String pin = util.getText("welcomePinCode").trim();
       util.setText("statusBar", "Please wait...");
       if ((acct.longValue() > 0) && (pin.length() > 0))
       {
               curAcct = new Account("jdbc:odbc:netbank", "dba",
                "javabank");
               if (curAcct.verifyPinCode(acct.longValue(), pin))
               {
```

```
                    Vector v =
                     curAcct.checkAcctOwnerName(acct.longValue());
                    util.setText("statusBar", "Welcome " +
                     v.elementAt(0) + ", " + v.elementAt(1));
                    util.gotoPage("balancePage");
                    displayBalance();
            }
            else
            {
                    // wrong info
                    util.setText("statusBar", "Account number or PIN
                     invalid!");
                    logoutRequest();
            }
    }
    else
            util.setText("statusBar", "Please enter your account
             number first!");
}
// The user has clicked refresh
if (nm.equals("balanceRefreshButton")) {
            util.setText("statusBar", "Please wait...");
            displayBalance();
}
// The user has clicked OK to transfer money
if (nm.equals("transferYesButton")) {
    Long acct = new
     Long(util.getText("transferAccountNo").trim());
    Float amnt = new Float(util.getText("transferAmount").trim());
    util.setText("statusBar", "Please wait...");
    if ((acct.longValue() > 0) && (amnt.floatValue() > 0))
    {
            if (0 == 0) // should verify the transferAcctNo
            {
                    curAcct.makeTransfer(acct.longValue(),
                     amnt.floatValue());
                    Vector v =
                     curAcct.checkAcctOwnerName(acct.longValue());
                    util.setText("statusBar", "Transfered to " +
                     v.elementAt(0) + ", " + v.elementAt(1));
                    util.setText("transferAccountNo", "");
                    util.setText("transferAmount", "");
            }
            else
            {
            // acct does not exist in database
                    util.setText("statusBar", "INVALID ACCT NO OR
                     PIN CODE!!!");
            }
    }
    else
            util.setText("statusBar", "Please enter the account
             number first!");
}
```

```
        // Check the selection for cash
        if (nm.equals("withdraw20")) {
            curWithdrawAmount = 20;
        } else if (nm.equals("withdraw100")) {
            curWithdrawAmount = 100;
        } else if (nm.equals("withdraw200")) {
            curWithdrawAmount = 200;
        } else if (nm.equals("withdraw1000")) {
            curWithdrawAmount = 1000;
        }
        // The user has clicked withdraw
        if (nm.equals("withdrawWithdrawButton")) {
            util.setText("statusBar", "Please wait.");
            curAcct.cashWithdraw(curWithdrawAmount);
            util.setText("statusBar", "Please wait...");
            ImageWidget img = (ImageWidget) util.getWidget("bankNote");
            img.show();
            for (int i = 0; i < 3050; i++)
            {
                    img.reshape(60, 120 - (i / 10), 100, 10 + (i / 10));
                    img.repaint();
            }
//img.hide();
        }
        // The user has clicked EndPage to log out
            if (nm.equals("welcomeEndButton")) {
            logoutRequest();
            System.out.println("Ended");
            return true;
        }
    }
    return super.handleEvent(evt);
    }
}
```

TIMET.JAVA

Listing 10-20 contains the source code for TimeT.java.

Listing 10-20: TimeT.java.

```
import java.io.*;
import java.lang.*;
import java.util.*;
import marimba.gui.*;
public class TimeT extends Thread {
  private Thread GetTime;
  private boolean bRun;
  TextBoxWidget tbw;
  public TimeT(TextBoxWidget t) {
      tbw = t;
  }
  public void start() {
```

```
        bRun = true;
        GetTime = new Thread(this);
        GetTime.start();
    }
    public void run() {
        while(bRun)
        {
                try {GetTime.sleep(1000);}
                catch (InterruptedException e) { }
                String today = (new Date()).toString();
                tbw.setText(today);
        }
    }
}
```

THE DATA DEFINITION LANGUAGE FOR THIS EXAMPLE

Some keywords are Transact-SQL. You may want to modify the DDL (Data Definition Language) and DML (Data Manipulation Language) for your DBMS. Listing 10-21 shows how to create tables.

Listing 10-21: DDL to create the tables for the Bank of Java applet.

```
%%%%%%%%%%%%%%%%%%%%%%%%%%%%%%%%%%%%%%%%%%%%%
% Create tables
%%%%%%%%%%%%%%%%%%%%%%%%%%%%%%%%%%%%%%%%%%%%%
CREATE TABLE "accounts"
(
  "acctno"              integer NULL,
  "pincode"             varchar(50) NULL,
  "ownerno"             integer NULL,
  "datecreated"         varchar(50) NULL,
  "balance"             float NULL,
);
CREATE TABLE "clients"
(
  "ownerno"             integer NULL,
  "name"                varchar(50) NULL,
  "address"             varchar(50) NULL,
);
CREATE TABLE "history"
(
  "tdate"               varchar(50) NULL,
  "acctno"              integer NULL,
  "typetransaction"     varchar(20) NULL,
  "otheracct"           integer NULL,
  "amount"              float NULL,
  "ipaddress"           varchar(50) NULL,
);
%%%%%%%%%%%%%%%%%%%%%%%%%%%%%%%%%%%%%%%%%%%%%
% Reload data
%%%%%%%%%%%%%%%%%%%%%%%%%%%%%%%%%%%%%%%%%%%%%
```

```
INSERT INTO "accounts"
 ("acctno","pincode","ownerno","datecreated","balance")
 VALUES ('1','1111','1','','992800');
INSERT INTO "accounts"
 ("acctno","pincode","ownerno","datecreated","balance")
 VALUES ('2','2222','2','','1257450');
INSERT INTO "accounts"
 ("acctno","pincode","ownerno","datecreated","balance")
 VALUES ('3','3333','3','','320700');
INSERT INTO "accounts"
 ("acctno","pincode","ownerno","datecreated","balance")
 VALUES ('4','4444','4','','8900750');
INSERT INTO "accounts"
 ("acctno","pincode","ownerno","datecreated","balance")
 VALUES ('5','5555','5','','-840');
INSERT INTO "accounts"
 ("acctno","pincode","ownerno","datecreated","balance")
 VALUES ('6','6666','6','','999999995904');
INSERT INTO "clients" ("ownerno", "name", "address")
 VALUES ('1','Bernard Van Haecke','Brussels, 1000');
INSERT INTO "clients" ("ownerno", "name", "address")
 VALUES ('2','John Doe','Imola Circuit, KM83');
INSERT INTO "clients" ("ownerno", "name", "address")
 VALUES ('3','Jane Doe','Imola Circuit, KM83');
INSERT INTO "clients" ("ownerno", "name", "address")
 VALUES ('4','Santa Claus','North Pole, 1');
INSERT INTO "clients" ("ownerno", "name", "address")
 VALUES ('5','Little Duke','Java Island, 1');
INSERT INTO "clients" ("ownerno", "name", "address")
 VALUES ('6','The Bank','Downtown LA');
INSERT INTO "history"
 ("tdate","acctno","typetransaction","otheracct","amount","ipaddress
 ")
 VALUES ('23 Oct 1996 20:30:15 GMT','1','Transfert','4','-
 1000','localhost/127.0.0.1');
INSERT INTO "history"
 ("tdate","acctno","typetransaction","otheracct","amount","ipaddress
 ")
 VALUES ('23 Oct 1996 20:30:15
 GMT','4','Received','1','1000','localhost/127.0.0.1');
INSERT INTO "history"
 ("tdate","acctno","typetransaction","otheracct","amount","ipaddress
 ")
 VALUES ('24 Oct 1996 21:18:43 GMT','5','Withdraw','0','-
 20','localhost/127.0.0.1');
```

At the time of this writing, only the JDBC-ODBC bridge and certain ODBC drivers support transaction isolation. Things may change quickly, and by the time you read this chapter, more drivers will support this feature.

Dynamic Database Access

The next example illustrates how to use JDBC's DatabaseMetaData and ResultSetMetaData methods.

A Java Database Explorer

The Java database explorer example runs as a stand-alone application. It can dynamically discover database content thanks to a very intuitive graphical user interface. Numerous JDBC database metadata methods are exploited to enable the exploration of virtually any relational database management system.

The main features of the program are these:

◆ Displays DBMS information such as specifications, supported features, and inherent limitations of the engine

◆ Explores most database objects, including database catalogs, tables, and stored procedures

◆ Gives relational information – that is, primary, imported, and exported keys for all tables

◆ Provides an interactive SQL query and update tool

◆ Displays ResultSets content in raw rows or formatted tabular output

The GUI part of this example was written using Marimba Bongo, which generates a 100-percent portable .gui file. This file contains a persistent form of the widgets used in this example. The .gui file is editable using Marimba Bongo, a demo version of which is on the CD-ROM accompanying this book. The unzipped Marimba classes must be in the CLASSPATH or must be present on the WWW server to run this example. The GUI part of the application uses the Marimba Bongo classes, which are persistified to a portable file. This use is the main reason why almost no GUI code is present in the source. Each GUI control is a Marimba widget that has a name and whose properties are also persistified in the permanent GUI file.

The main database explorer window is divided into three areas:

◆ User login information and controls

◆ Main database navigation widget – the left-sided tree control

◆ The result window

Figure 10-9 depicts the main window of this example.

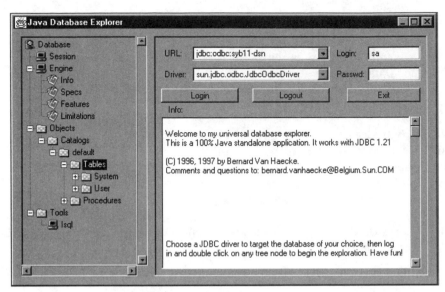

Figure 10-9: Java database explorer main window.

The Screens

The following paragraphs explain how the user interacts with this stand-alone Java application.

LOG IN THE DATABASE

As shown in Figure 10-10, logging into the database engine requires a correct database URL, JDBC driver, user login, and user password. The syntax of the URL is driver-dependant. The login and password are the identification and authorization strings for a particular user in the database management system.

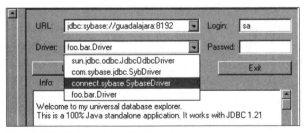

Figure 10-10: Supplying login data.

Press Login to log in to the DBMS. Use Logout to disconnect from the database engine without quitting the application. Another JDBC URL may be entered, and the Login button may be pressed again. Logout may be used as a temporary logout or before logging in as another user. Exit logs the user off the database and closes the application.

THE NAVIGATION GRAPHICAL CONTROL

The tree widget on the left side controls the whole application and navigates within the database. The Session, Engine, and Objects nodes intensively use database metadata methods to get information from the database. Double-clicking on these tree nodes performs all actions. The resulting data displays in the right window.

The main features of this application include:

- ◆ Session information

- ◆ DBMS engine information

- ◆ Database object browsing

- ◆ Interactive SQL query tool

The tree widget shown in Figure 10-11 controls the whole program.

Figure 10-11: The main navigation control widget.

DATABASE ENGINE SPECIFICATIONS AND LIMITATIONS

Four specification sheets are available. The categories are somewhat arbitrary, but it is more convenient to see them split in four screens. Figure 10-12 illustrates one of the four sheets. It shows a small part of the features supported by the database engine. Each topic has its corresponding JDBC database metadata method, which, in general, returns true or false.

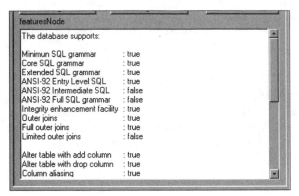

Figure 10–12: Database specs.

BROWSING DATABASE CATALOGS AND THEIR CONTENT

The following items are the most interesting. The main navigation widget allows you to browse through many database objects by expanding and collapsing its nodes. Each activation of a node issues database metadata methods to dynamically discover the database objects. Figure 10-13 shows the database catalog nodes.

Figure 10–13: Database catalog nodes.

Figure 10-14 shows the catalog subnodes.

Figure 10-14: Catalog subnodes.

For example, when double-clicking on the Objects Catalogs node, the program fetches information about database objects such as system tables, user tables, and stored procedures. Catalogs are simply database subspaces. In a DBMS managing multiple databases, a catalog is one database.

As shown in Figure 10-15, all table nodes give useful structure information such as the columns and types it contains, and the primary, imported, and exported keys.

Figure 10-15: Tables.

The procedure node lists all database-stored procedures in the current catalog and displays the results of the `DatabaseMetaData.getProcedureColumns()` method. This is shown in Figure 10-16.

Figure 10-16: Stored procedures.

The procedure node lists all database-stored procedures in the current catalog and displays the results of the `DatabaseMetaData.getProcedureColumns()` method.

EXTRA TOOLS: AN INTERACTIVE SQL GADGET

Figure 10-17 depicts the interactive SQL gadget.

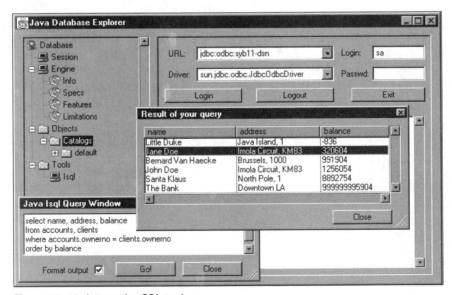

Figure 10-17: Interactive SQL tool.

The tools node contains only one tool, ISQL. This is the interactive ISQL query tool explained earlier. It supports SQL queries and SQL updates that can be entered in the little query window. Figure 10-18 shows the window that accepts SQL statements.

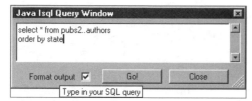

Figure 10-18: SQL query window.

As shown in Figure 10-19, the results finally appear in a nice, formatted spread-sheet-like window. It is possible to sort the data again with a mouse click on any column label.

au_id	au_lname	au_fname	phone	address	city	state	country	p
712-45-1867	del Castillo	Innes	615 996-8275	2286 Cram Pl. #86	Ann Arbor	MI	USA	48
238-95-7766	Carson	Cheryl	415 548-7723	589 Darwin Ln.	Berkeley	CA	USA	94
409-56-7008	Bennet	Abraham	415 658-9932	6223 Bateman St.	Berkeley	CA	USA	94
648-92-1872	Blotchet-Halls	Reginald	503 745-6402	55 Hillsdale Bl.	Corvallis	OR	USA	97
472-27-2349	Gringlesby	Burt	707 938-6445	PO Box 792	Covelo	CA	USA	95
722-51-5454	DeFrance	Michel	219 547-9982	3 Balding Pl.	Gary	IN	USA	46
341-22-1782	Smith	Meander	913 843-0462	10 Mississippi Dr.	Lawrence	KS	USA	66
172-32-1176	White	Johnson	408 496-7223	10932 Bigge Rd.	Menlo Park	CA	USA	94
527-72-3246	Greene	Morningstar	615 297-2723	22 Graybar House Rd.	Nashville	TN	USA	37
213-46-8915	Green	Marjorie	415 986-7020	309 63rd St. #411	Oakland	CA	USA	94
724-08-9931	Stringer	Dirk	415 843-2991	5420 Telegraph Av.	Oakland	CA	USA	94
274-80-9391	Straight	Dick	415 834-2919	5420 College Av.	Oakland	CA	USA	94
724-80-9391	MacFeather	Stearns	415 354-7128	44 Upland Hts.	Oakland	CA	USA	94
756-30-7391	Karsen	Livia	415 534-9219	5720 McAuley St.	Oakland	CA	USA	94

Figure 10-19: SQL results window.

This stand-alone application is easily rewritten to run as an applet within a WWW browser such as Netscape Navigator or Microsoft Internet Explorer. Adding BLOB import/export tools to allow the insertion and retrieval of multimedia content such as pictures is an interesting exercise. See the specific examples on this topic at the beginning of this chapter.

SOURCES

Listing 10-22 contains the source code for the Java database explorer.

Listing 10-22: Jexplorer.java.

```java
import java.io.*;
import java.awt.*;
import java.sql.*;
import java.lang.*;
import java.util.*;
import marimba.gui.*;
/**
```

```
* the main class
*/
public class Jexplorer extends PlayerFrame {
Connection conn = null;
DatabaseMetaData mtdt = null;
ResultSet rs = null;
String text = "";
static final String welcome =
 "\n Welcome to my universal database explorer.\n" +
 " This is a 100% Java stand-alone application. It works with JDBC
   1.21\n\n" +
 " (C) 1996, 1997 by Bernard Van Haecke.\n" +
 " Comments and questions to:
   bernard.vanhaecke@Belgium.Sun.COM\n\n";
static final String extracomment = "\n\n\n\n\n\n" +
 " Choose a JDBC driver to target the database of your choice, then
   log\n" +
 " in and double click on any tree node to begin the exploration.
   Have fun!";
/**
* constructor
*/
public Jexplorer() {
}
/**
* we handle all gui events here
*/
public boolean handleEvent(Event evt)
  {
  try {
  if ((evt.id == Event.ACTION_EVENT) && (evt.target instanceof
   Widget)) {
  Widget w = (Widget)evt.target;
  String nm = w.getName();
  if (nm != null) System.out.println("Event: " + nm);
  // The user has logged in.
  if (nm.equals("dataLoginButton")) {
      String url = util.getText("dataURL").trim();
      String uid = util.getText("dataLogin").trim();
      String pwd = util.getText("dataPasswd").trim();
      String driver = util.getText("dataDriver").trim();
      text = welcome;
      try {
          Class.forName(driver);
          conn = DriverManager.getConnection(url, uid, pwd);
          if (conn != null) {
              text = text + "You are now logged in. Enjoy...";
              mtdt = conn.getMetaData();
          }
      }
      catch (SQLException ex) {
          text = text + "Could not log into the database. Verify
            the parameters:\nURL: " + url + "\nDriver: " + driver
            + "\n\n";
```

```
                    text = text + ex;
                    System.out.println(ex);
        }
        catch (java.lang.Exception ex) {
                    System.out.println(ex);
        }
        util.setText("dataWindowControl", text);
}
// The user has clicked logout
if (nm.equals("dataLogoutButton")) {
    TreeNodeWidget catalogRoot = (TreeNodeWidget)
      util.getWidget("catalogsNode");
    catalogRoot.clear();
    util.show("isqlQueryWindow", false);
    util.show("isqlResultWindow", false);
    if (conn != null) {
                conn.close();
                text = welcome + "You are now logged off. Bye bye...";
    }
    else text = welcome + extracomment;
    util.setText("dataWindowControl", text);
}
// The user has clicked exit
if (nm.equals("dataExitButton")) {
    System.out.println("Normal termination");
    if (conn != null) conn.close();
    System.exit(0);
    return true;
}
// Database Node ////////////////////////////////////////////////
if (nm.equals("databaseNode")) {
    util.setText("dataWindowLabel", nm);
    text = welcome;
    text = text + extracomment;
    util.setText("dataWindowControl", text);
}
// Session Node /////////////////////////////////////////////////
if (nm.equals("sessionNode")) {
    util.setText("dataWindowLabel", nm);
    text ="\nURL in use\t: " + mtdt.getURL() +
            "\nUsername\t: " + mtdt.getUserName();
    util.setText("dataWindowControl", text);
}
// Engine Node //////////////////////////////////////////////////
if (nm.equals("engineNode")) {
    util.setText("dataWindowLabel", nm);
    text = "\nMiscellaneous database engine informations.";
    util.setText("dataWindowControl", text);
}
// give database informations
if (nm.equals("infoNode")) {
    util.setText("dataWindowLabel", nm);
    text = "\nDatabase\t: " + mtdt.getDatabaseProductName() +
            "\nVersion\t: " + mtdt.getDatabaseProductVersion() +
```

```
                  "\n\nDriver\t: " + mtdt.getDriverName() +
                  "\nVersion\t: " + mtdt.getDriverVersion();
         util.setText("dataWindowControl", text);
      }
      // give database specs
      if (nm.equals("specsNode")) {
         util.setText("dataWindowLabel", nm);
         text =  "\nUses local files\t\t\t\t\t: " +
           mtdt.usesLocalFiles() +
                  "\nUses local file per table\t\t\t: " +
                  mtdt.usesLocalFilePerTable() +
                  "\nNulls are sorted high\t\t\t: " +
                  mtdt.nullsAreSortedHigh() +
                  "\nNulls are sorted at end\t\t\t: " +
                  mtdt.nullsAreSortedAtEnd() +
                  "\nSupports mixed case identifiers\t: " +
                  mtdt.supportsMixedCaseIdentifiers() +
                  "\nStores mixed case identifiers\t\t: " +
                  mtdt.storesMixedCaseIdentifiers() +
                  "\nIdentifier quote string\t\t\t: " +
                  mtdt.getIdentifierQuoteString() +
                  "\n\nSupported SQL keywords\t: " +
                  mtdt.getSQLKeywords() +
                  "\n\nNumeric functions\t: " +
                  mtdt.getNumericFunctions() +
                  "\n\nString functions\t: " + mtdt.getStringFunctions()
                  +
                  "\n\nSystem functions\t: " + mtdt.getSystemFunctions()
                  +
                  "\n\nTime and date functions\t: " +
                  mtdt.getTimeDateFunctions();
         util.setText("dataWindowControl", text);
      }
      // give database features
      if (nm.equals("featuresNode")) {
         util.setText("dataWindowLabel", nm);
         text = "\nThe database supports:\n" +
                  "\nMinimun SQL grammar\t\t: " +
                  mtdt.supportsMinimumSQLGrammar() +
                  "\nCore SQL grammar\t\t\t: " +
                  mtdt.supportsCoreSQLGrammar() +
                  "\nExtended SQL grammar\t\t: " +
                  mtdt.supportsExtendedSQLGrammar() +
                  "\nANSI-92 Entry Level SQL\t: " +
                  mtdt.supportsANSI92EntryLevelSQL() +
                  "\nANSI-92 Intermediate SQL\t: " +
                  mtdt.supportsANSI92IntermediateSQL() +
                  "\nANSI-92 Full SQL grammar\t: " +
                  mtdt.supportsANSI92FullSQL() +
                  "\nIntegrity enhancement facility\t: " +
                  mtdt.supportsIntegrityEnhancementFacility() +
                  "\nOuter joins\t\t\t\t: " + mtdt.supportsOuterJoins() +
                  "\nFull outer joins\t\t\t\t: " +
                  mtdt.supportsFullOuterJoins() +
```

```
                        "\nLimited outer joins\t\t\t: " +
                        mtdt.supportsLimitedOuterJoins() +
                        "\n\nAlter table with add column\t: " +
                        mtdt.supportsAlterTableWithAddColumn() +
                        "\nAlter table with drop column\t: " +
                        mtdt.supportsAlterTableWithDropColumn() +
                        "\nColumn aliasing\t\t\t: " +
                        mtdt.supportsColumnAliasing() +
                        "\nTable correlation names\t\t: " +
                        mtdt.supportsTableCorrelationNames() +
                        "\nExpressions in order by\t\t: " +
                        mtdt.supportsExpressionsInOrderBy() +
                        "\nUnrelated order by\t\t: " +
                        mtdt.supportsOrderByUnrelated() +
                        "\nGroup by\t\t\t\t: " + mtdt.supportsGroupBy() +
                        "\nUnrelated group by\t\t: " +
                        mtdt.supportsGroupByUnrelated() +
                        "\nGroup by beyond select\t\t: " +
                        mtdt.supportsGroupByBeyondSelect() +
                        "\nLike escape clause\t\t: " +
                        mtdt.supportsLikeEscapeClause() +
                        "\nMultiple result sets\t\t: " +
                        mtdt.supportsMultipleResultSets() +
                        "\nMultiple transactions\t\t: " +
                        mtdt.supportsMultipleTransactions() +
                        "\nNon nullable columns\t\t: " +
                        mtdt.supportsNonNullableColumns() +
                        "\n\nTerm for schemas\t: " + mtdt.getSchemaTerm() +
                        "\nTerm for procedures\t: " + mtdt.getProcedureTerm() +
                        "\nTerm for catalogs\t: " + mtdt.getCatalogTerm() +
                        "\n\n...";
            util.setText("dataWindowControl", text);
    }
    // give database limitations
    if (nm.equals("limitationsNode")) {
        util.setText("dataWindowLabel", nm);
        text = "\nMaximums:\n" +
                        "\nBinary literal length\t\t: " +
                        mtdt.getMaxBinaryLiteralLength() +
                        "\nCharacter literal length\t: " +
                        mtdt.getMaxCharLiteralLength() +
                        "\nColumn name length\t: " +
                        mtdt.getMaxColumnNameLength() +
                        "\nColumns in group by\t\t: " +
                        mtdt.getMaxColumnsInGroupBy() +
                        "\nColumns in index\t\t: " +
                        mtdt.getMaxColumnsInIndex() +
                        "\nColumns in order by\t\t: " +
                        mtdt.getMaxColumnsInOrderBy() +
                        "\nColumns in select\t\t: " +
                        mtdt.getMaxColumnsInSelect() +
                        "\nColumns in table\t\t: " +
                        mtdt.getMaxColumnsInTable() +
```

```
                      "\nNumber of connections\t: " +
                       mtdt.getMaxConnections() +
                       "\n";
              util.setText("dataWindowControl", text);
      }
      // Object Node /////////////////////////////////////////////////
      if (nm.equals("objectsNode")) {
          util.setText("dataWindowLabel", nm);
          text = "\nDatabase objects.";
          util.setText("dataWindowControl", text);
      }
      // browse database catalogs
      if (nm.equals("catalogsNode")) {
          util.setText("dataWindowLabel", nm);
          text = getRS(mtdt.getCatalogs());
          util.setText("dataWindowControl", text);
          // get a vector of catalogs
          Vector v = getRSColumnAsVector(mtdt.getCatalogs(),
           "TABLE_CAT");
          // Vector v = getRSColumnAsVector(mtdt.getCatalogs(),
           "TABLE_QUALIFIER");
          boolean useCatalog = true;
          // create a default catalog if the database
          // does not support catalogs
          if (v.size() == 0) {
                  useCatalog = false;
                  v.addElement("default");
          }
          // add nodes for each catalog
          TreeNodeWidget catalogRoot = (TreeNodeWidget)
           util.getWidget("catalogsNode");
          if (catalogRoot.hasChildren()) catalogRoot.clear();
          for (int i=0; i < v.size(); i++) {
                  addCatalogNode(catalogRoot, (String) v.elementAt(i));
          }
      }
      // browse tables in this catalog
      if (nm.startsWith("newTableColumnsNode.")) {
          util.setText("dataWindowLabel", nm);
          int p1 = nm.indexOf(".");
          int p2 = nm.indexOf(".", p1 + 1);
          String catalog = nm.substring(p1 + 1, p2);
          if (catalog.equals("null")) catalog = null;
          String table = nm.substring(p2 + 1);
          text = getRS(mtdt.getColumns(catalog, null, table, "%"));
          util.setText("dataWindowControl", text);
      }
      // browse primary keys for this table
      if (nm.startsWith("newTablePrimaryKeysNode.")) {
          util.setText("dataWindowLabel", nm);
          int p1 = nm.indexOf(".");
          int p2 = nm.indexOf(".", p1 + 1);
          String catalog = nm.substring(p1 + 1, p2);
          if (catalog.equals("null")) catalog = null;
```

```
      String table = nm.substring(p2 + 1);
      text = getRS(mtdt.getPrimaryKeys(catalog, null, table));
      util.setText("dataWindowControl", text);
}
// browse imported keys for this table
if (nm.startsWith("newTableImportedKeysNode.")) {
    util.setText("dataWindowLabel", nm);
    int p1 = nm.indexOf(".");
    int p2 = nm.indexOf(".", p1 + 1);
    String catalog = nm.substring(p1 + 1, p2);
    if (catalog.equals("null")) catalog = null;
    String table = nm.substring(p2 + 1);
    text = getRS(mtdt.getImportedKeys(catalog, null, table));
    util.setText("dataWindowControl", text);
}
// browse exported keys for this table
if (nm.startsWith("newTableExportedKeysNode.")) {
    util.setText("dataWindowLabel", nm);
    int p1 = nm.indexOf(".");
    int p2 = nm.indexOf(".", p1 + 1);
    String catalog = nm.substring(p1 + 1, p2);
    if (catalog.equals("null")) catalog = null;
    String table = nm.substring(p2 + 1);
    text = getRS(mtdt.getExportedKeys(catalog, null, table));
    util.setText("dataWindowControl", text);
}
// browse procedures in this catalog
if (nm.startsWith("newProcedureNode.")) {
    util.setText("dataWindowLabel", nm);
    int p1 = nm.indexOf(".");
    int p2 = nm.indexOf(".", p1 + 1);
    String catalog = nm.substring(p1 + 1, p2);
    if (catalog.equals("null")) catalog = null;
    String procedure = nm.substring(p2 + 1);
    text = getRS(mtdt.getProcedureColumns(catalog, null,
      procedure, "%"));
    util.setText("dataWindowControl", text);
}
// Tools Node /////////////////////////////////////////////////
if (nm.equals("toolsNode")) {
    util.setText("dataWindowLabel", nm);
    text = "";
    util.setText("dataWindowControl", text);
}
// display the isql query window
if (nm.equals("isqlNode")) {
    util.setText("dataWindowLabel", nm);
    text = "\nType your queries in the floating query window...";
    util.setText("dataWindowControl", text);
    util.show("isqlQueryWindow", true);
}
// execute the sql query
if (nm.equals("isqlGoButton")) {
    String query = util.getText("isqlQueryText");
```

```
        // test if we want a nicely formatted result
        if (((CheckBoxWidget)
         util.getWidget("isqlFormatCheckBox")).getBooleanValue())
        {
                TableWidget tbl = (TableWidget)
                 util.getWidget("isqlResultTable");
                tbl.removeAllRows();
                tbl.removeAllColumns();
                util.show("isqlResultWindow", true);
                ResultSet rs = getSingleRS(query);
                Vector headers = getRSColumnHeadersAsVector(rs);
                int i;
                for (i=0; i<headers.size(); i++)
//tbl.addColumn((String) headers.elementAt(i), ((String)
 headers.elementAt(i)).length());
                        tbl.addColumn((String) headers.elementAt(i));
                Vector rows = getRSRowsAsVector(rs);
                for (i=0; i<rows.size(); i++)
                        tbl.addRow((Vector) rows.elementAt(i));
        }
        else
        {
                text = getMultipleRS(query);
                util.appendText("dataWindowControl", "\n\n" + text);
        }
    }
    // close the isql query window
    if (nm.equals("isqlCloseButton")) {
        util.show("isqlQueryWindow", false);
        util.show("isqlResultWindow", false);
    }
    // close the isql result window
    if (nm.equals("resultCloseButton")) {
        util.show("isqlResultWindow", false);
    }
    }
    }
    catch(java.lang.Exception ex) {
        // ex.printStackTrace();
    }
    return super.handleEvent(evt);
}
/**
* create a new catalog node
*/
public void addCatalogNode(TreeNodeWidget w, String label)
{
    w.hide();
    String catalogName = label;
    if (label.equals("default")) catalogName = null;
    TreeNodeWidget newCatalogNode = new TreeNodeWidget();
    newCatalogNode.setName("newCatalogNode." + catalogName);
    newCatalogNode.setText(label);
    newCatalogNode.setImage("folder.gif");
```

```
w.addSorted(newCatalogNode);
// add main node for tables
TreeNodeWidget newCatalogTablesNode = addNode(newCatalogNode,
  "newCatalogTablesNode." + catalogName,
     "Tables", "folder.gif");
// add nodes for system tables
TreeNodeWidget newTablesSystemNode = addNode(newCatalogTablesNode,
  "newTablesSystemNode." + catalogName,
     "System", "folder.gif");
String types[] = new String[1];
types[0] = "SYSTEM TABLE";
Vector v = null;
try {
    v = getRSColumnAsVector(mtdt.getTables(catalogName, null, "%",
      types), "TABLE_NAME");
} catch (SQLException ex) { ex.printStackTrace(); }
if (newTablesSystemNode.hasChildren()) newTablesSystemNode.clear();
for (int i=0; i < v.size(); i++) {
    addTableNode(newTablesSystemNode, catalogName, (String)
      v.elementAt(i));
}
// add nodes for system tables
TreeNodeWidget newTablesUserNode = addNode(newCatalogTablesNode,
  "newTablesUserNode." + catalogName,
     "User", "folder.gif");
types[0] = "TABLE";
v = null;
try {
    v = getRSColumnAsVector(mtdt.getTables(catalogName, null, "%",
      types), "TABLE_NAME");
} catch (SQLException ex) { ex.printStackTrace(); }
if (newTablesUserNode.hasChildren()) newTablesUserNode.clear();
for (int i=0; i < v.size(); i++) {
    addTableNode(newTablesUserNode, catalogName, (String)
      v.elementAt(i));
}
// add main node for stored procedures
TreeNodeWidget newCatalogProceduresNode = addNode(newCatalogNode,
  "newCatalogProceduresNode." + catalogName,
     "Procedures", "folder.gif");
// add nodes for procedures
v = null;
try {
    v = getRSColumnAsVector(mtdt.getProcedures(catalogName, null,
     "%"), "PROCEDURE_NAME");
} catch (SQLException ex) { ex.printStackTrace(); }
if (newCatalogProceduresNode.hasChildren())
 newCatalogProceduresNode.clear();
for (int i=0; i < v.size(); i++) {
    addNode(newCatalogProceduresNode, "newProcedureNode." +
     catalogName + "." + (String) v.elementAt(i),
          (String) v.elementAt(i), "archivs.gif");
}
// collapse the catalog leaves
```

```
 w.collapseAll();
 w.show();
}
/**
 * create a new node for a table
 */
public void addTableNode(TreeNodeWidget w, String catalog, String
  label)
{
 TreeNodeWidget newTableNode = new TreeNodeWidget();
 newTableNode.setName("newTableNode." + catalog + "." + label);
 newTableNode.setText(label);
 newTableNode.setImage("table.gif");
 w.addSorted(newTableNode);
 addNode(newTableNode, "newTableColumnsNode." + catalog + "." +
  label,
     "Columns", "archivs.gif");
 addNode(newTableNode, "newTablePrimaryKeysNode." + catalog + "." +
  label,
     "Primary Keys", "archivs.gif");
 addNode(newTableNode, "newTableImportedKeysNode." + catalog + "." +
  label,
     "Imported Keys", "archivs.gif");
 addNode(newTableNode, "newTableExportedKeysNode." + catalog + "." +
  label,
     "Exported Keys", "archivs.gif");
 w.collapseAll();
}
/**
 * add a node
 */
public TreeNodeWidget addNode(TreeNodeWidget w, String name, String
  text, String image) {
 TreeNodeWidget child = new TreeNodeWidget();
 child.setName(name);
 child.setText(text);
 child.setImage(image);
 w.add(child);
 return child;
}
/**
 * transform one column of a resultset into a vector
 */
public Vector getRSColumnAsVector(ResultSet rs, String column)
{
 Vector v = new Vector();
 try {
     while (rs.next()) {
             v.addElement(rs.getString(column));
     }
 } catch (SQLException ex) { ex.printStackTrace(); }
 return v;
}
/**
```

```
* return the resultset of a simple query
*/
public ResultSet getSingleRS(String sqlText)
{
 ResultSet rs = null;
 try {
      Statement st = conn.createStatement();
      if (st.execute(sqlText)) {
              // okay it's not an update count
              rs = st.getResultSet();
      }
 } catch (SQLException ex) { ex.printStackTrace(); }
 return rs;
}
/**
* return the result of a statement as text
* the statement may be an update, a query, or mix
*/
public String getMultipleRS(String sqlText) {
 boolean ResultSetIsAvailable;
 boolean moreResultsAvailable;
 int i = 0;
 int res=0;
 String result = "";
 try {
      Statement curStmt = conn.createStatement();
      ResultSetIsAvailable = curStmt.execute(sqlText);
      ResultSet rs = null;
      for (moreResultsAvailable = true; moreResultsAvailable; )
      {
              if (ResultSetIsAvailable)
              {
                      if ((rs = curStmt.getResultSet()) != null)
                       {
                              // we have a resultset
                              result = getRS(rs);
                       }
              }
              else
              {
                      if ((res = curStmt.getUpdateCount()) != -1)
                              {
                              // we have an updatecount
                              result = res + " row(s) affected.";
                      }
                      // else no more results
                      else
                      {
                              moreResultsAvailable = false;
                      }
              }
              if (moreResultsAvailable)
              {
                      ResultSetIsAvailable = curStmt.getMoreResults();
```

```
            }
        }
        if (rs != null) rs.close();
        curStmt.close();
    }
    catch (SQLException ex) {
        // Unexpected SQL exception.
        // Occurs often with weird jdbc driver implementations.
        // ex.printStackTrace ();
    }
    catch (java.lang.Exception ex) {
        // Got some other type of exception. Dump it.
        // ex.printStackTrace ();
    }
    return result;
}
/**
 * return the result of a query as text
 */
public String getRS(ResultSet rs) {
    String s = "\n";
    int i,j;
    Vector headers = getRSColumnHeadersAsVector(rs);
    Vector rows = getRSRowsAsVector(rs);
    for (i = 0; i < headers.size(); i++)
    {
        if (i > 0) s += ", ";
        s += headers.elementAt(i);
    }
    s += "\n\n";
    for (i = 0; i < rows.size(); i++)
    {
        for (j = 0; j < ((Vector) rows.elementAt(i)).size(); j++)
            {
                if (j > 0) s += ", ";
                s += ((Vector) rows.elementAt(i)).elementAt(j);
            }
        s += "\n";
    }
    return s;
}
/**
 * return the column headers of a resultset as vector
 */
public Vector getRSColumnHeadersAsVector(ResultSet rs) {
    int i;
    Vector v = new Vector();
    try {
        ResultSetMetaData rsmd = rs.getMetaData();
        int numCols = rsmd.getColumnCount();
        // fetch column headers
        for (i = 1; i <= numCols; i++)
        {
                v.addElement(rsmd.getColumnLabel(i));
```

```
        }
    }
    catch (SQLException ex)
    {
    }
    return v;
}
/**
 * return a resultset as vector
 */
public Vector getRSRowsAsVector(ResultSet rs) {
    Vector v = new Vector();
    Vector r = null;
    int i;
    try {
        ResultSetMetaData rsmd = rs.getMetaData();
        int numCols = rsmd.getColumnCount();
        // step through the rows
        while (rs.next())
        {
            // process the columns
            r = new Vector();
            for (i = 1; i <= numCols; i++)
            {
                r.addElement(rs.getString(i));
            }
            v.addElement(r);
        }
        rs.close();
    }
    catch (SQLException ex)
    {
    }
    return v;
}
/**
 * add a new entry in the url and driver listboxes
 */
public void addDriverInfo(String url, String driver)
{
    // add entry for this driver provider
    ((ChoiceWidget) util.getWidget("dataURL")).addChoice(url);
    ((ChoiceWidget) util.getWidget("dataDriver")).addChoice(driver);
}
/**
 * the main program
 */
public static void main(String argv[]) {
    // Create the frame
    Jexplorer frm = new Jexplorer();
    frm.util.setPresentation("Jexplorer.gui");
    frm.util.setText("dataWindowControl", welcome + extracomment);
    // allow miscellaneous drivers and urls to be preset
    // jdbc-odbc bridge
```

```
frm.addDriverInfo("jdbc:odbc:data-source-name",
  "sun.jdbc.odbc.JdbcOdbcDriver");
// sybase's driver
frm.addDriverInfo("jdbc:sybase:Tds:host.domain.com:8192",
  "com.sybase.jdbc.SybDriver");
// connect software's sybase driver
frm.addDriverInfo("jdbc:sybase://host.domain.com:8192",
  "connect.sybase.SybaseDriver");
// funny driver
frm.addDriverInfo("foo:bar:database", "foo.bar.Driver");
frm.show();
}
}
```

Multitier Architectures

In Chapter 8, we discussed different approaches to software partitioning. The next example uses the Remote Method Invocation (RMI) of Java 1.1.

Remote Method Invocation and JDBC

Remote method invocation is now part of Java Development Kit 1.1. As we saw in the chapter discussing three-tiered approaches, RMI allows Java objects to be distributed and shared accross computers and networks. This example uses RMI between the client and the middleware, and JDBC between the middleware and the database server.

RMI combined with JDBC for database access is a simple, but efficient, enabler for software partitioning. Indeed, as in this example, the client performs presentation (GUI) tasks only, the middleware stores the application's logic, and the database provides a persistent and coherent storage for the data.

This example deals with cars. In this example, all the cars are built in hypothetical car factories, and there is one factory for each different car brand. Clients are allowed to invoke various methods on the cars and factories, although these objects are not local client objects to them. They are remote objects. This means that all methods called on these objects are executed where these objects reside – that is, on the RMI server. If parameters must be passed to such methods, they are serialized by RMI and passed to the server object that will deserialize them.

The example has these classes:

◆ Car.java is an interface that extends java.rmi.remote

◆ CarImpl.java implements Car

◆ CarFactory.java is an interface that extends java.rmi.remote

◆ CarFactoryImpl.java implements CarFactory

- ◆ CarSupplierServer.java is a server. It brings car factories to life and makes them reachable through the RMI mechanism

- ◆ CarSales.java is a client that deals with objects such as Car and CarFactories

The client only has access to the Car and CarFactory interfaces. All methods invoked on these objects are actually implemented within the RMI server, which, in turn, performs the calls to the database through JDBC. Figure 10-20 illustrates the whole architecture for this example.

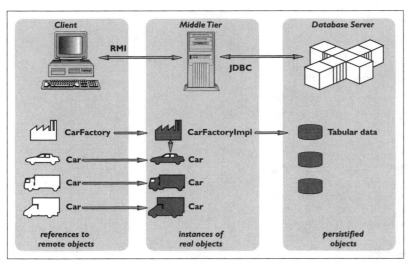

Figure 10-20: Three-tiered architecture of the car factory example.

Instead of providing object persistency at the Car level, a simpler option was choosen: the CarFactory level provides persistent storage. Practically, this means information about the car factories is saved in a database table and loaded by the CarFactoryImpl constructor. The database immediately reflects all updates of the car factories. Another option is to save the different instances of CarFactory in their finalize() method whenever the RMI server program terminates.

DATABASE SIDE

The data structure is quite simple. Here is the SQL to create the table used for this example. The primary key is composed of two fields: serialno and brand.

```
CREATE TABLE cars
(serialno INT
NULL,
brand VARCHAR(12) NULL,
model VARCHAR(12) NULL,
```

```
color VARCHAR(12) NULL,
price INT NULL,
owner VARCHAR(12) NULL)
GO
INSERT INTO cars VALUES
(1000000, 'Volkswagen', 'Golf GL', 'black', NULL, '')
GO
```

The following SQL statement queries the content of the table after a few executions of the RMI client and RMI server:

```
1> SELECT * FROM cars
2> ORDER BY brand, serialno
3> GO
serialno brand model color price owner
———— —————— —————— —————— —————— ——————
1000001 Audi A6 black NULL
1000002 Audi A8 yellow NULL
1000003 Audi A6 black NULL
1000004 Audi A8 yellow NULL
1000005 Audi A6 black NULL
1000006 Audi A8 yellow NULL
1000007 Audi A6 black NULL
1000008 Audi A8 yellow NULL
1000001 BMW 528i fjordgrau NULL
1000002 BMW 750Li articsilber NULL
1000003 BMW 528i fjordgrau NULL
1000004 BMW 750Li articsilber NULL
1000005 BMW 528i fjordgrau NULL
1000006 BMW 750Li articsilber NULL
1000007 BMW 528i fjordgrau NULL
1000008 BMW 750Li articsilber NULL
1000000 Volkswagen Golf GL black NULL
1000001 Volkswagen Golf CL darkred NULL
1000002 Volkswagen Golf CL darkred NULL
1000003 Volkswagen Golf CL darkred NULL
1000004 Volkswagen Golf CL darkred NULL
(21 rows affected)
```

RMI SERVER SIDE

A script file starts the server and an RMI service called the RMI registry. As soon as it launches, the CarSupplierServer object recreates car factories and cars from the data in the database. CarFactory objects are thus created and bound to a name. Client lookups use this name to obtain references to these remote objects. Here is the output of the CarSupplierServer when launched on Unix (Windows users: the RMI registry command must be executed in a separate DOS shell).

```
csh: start
starting registy
[1] 7852
starting CarSupplierServer
press CTRL-C to interrupt server
type: java CarSales to start client
Creating Car Factories
CarFactory: Loaded new Car:Car: model=Audi model=A6 color=black
  serial=1 owner=
CarFactory: Loaded new Car:Car: model=Audi model=A8 color=yellow
  serial=2 owner=
CarFactory: Loaded new Car:Car: model=Audi model=A8 color=yellow
  serial=3 owner=
CarFactory: Loaded new Car:Car: model=Audi model=A8 color=pink
  serial=4 owner=
CarFactory: Loaded new Car:Car: model=BMW model=528i color=fjordgrau
  serial=1 owner=
CarFactory: Loaded new Car:Car: model=BMW model=750Li
  color=articsilber serial=2 owner=
CarFactory: Loaded new Car:Car: model=BMW model=528i
  color=applegreen serial=3 owner=
CarFactory: Loaded new Car:Car: model=BMW model=528i color=sunblue
  serial=5 owner=
CarFactory: Loaded new Car:Car: model=Volkswagen model=Golf TDI
  color=black serial=1000000 owner=
CarFactory: Loaded new Car:Car: model=Volkswagen model=Golf CL
  color=darkred serial=1000001 owner=
CarFactory: Loaded new Car:Car: model=Volkswagen model=Golf TDI
  color=deep space b serial=1000002 owner=
Registring Car Factories
```

CLIENT SIDE

The client programs are started by simply running CarSales as shown in the command line:

```
% java CarSales
```

CarSales calls a lookup method to obtain references to remote objects. Once obtained, these references are used to invoke various methods defined in CarFactory and implemented in CarFactoryImpl.

The window shown in Figure 10-21 appears on the screen, displaying a trace of the different actions the client performs.

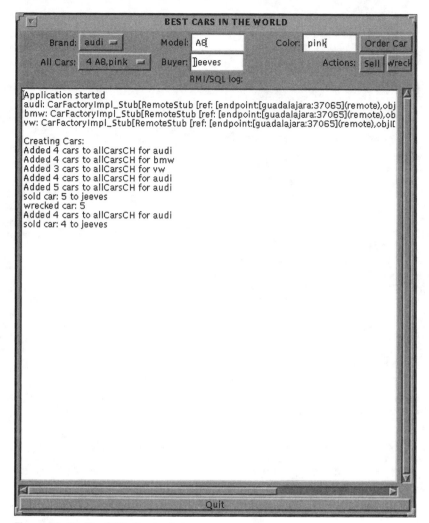

Figure 10–21: The RMI client window.

As soon as the client launches, the RMI server logs all the actions it performs on behalf of the client.

```
CarFactory Audi: request for all cars. 4 returned.
CarFactory BMW: request for all cars. 4 returned.
CarFactory Volkswagen: request for all cars. 3 returned.
CarFactory Audi: request for all cars. 4 returned.
CarFactory: Created new Car:Car: model=Audi model=A8 color=orange
  serial=5 owner=None
CarFactory Audi: request for all cars. 5 returned.
CarFactory: Deleted Car:CarImpl_Stub[RemoteStub [ref:
  [endpoint:[guadalajara:37065](remote),objID:[14]]]]
CarFactory Audi: request for all cars. 4 returned.
```

CAR.JAVA

This is the interface for cars. It extends java.rmi.Remote and is implemented by the CarImpl class. All methods invoked on Car instances trigger respective methods implemented by CarImpl instances. Listing 10-23 shows the source code for Car.java.

Listing 10-23: Car.java.

```
//
// Car.java
//
// (C) 1996 Wim De Munck mailto: wimdm@dm-mediaware.be
//
// Interface describing stub Car functionality
// the actual implementation will be the responibility of
// CarImpl; Car's will be created by a remote factory object:
// CarFactory and CarFactoryImplementation.
//
import java.rmi.Remote;
import java.rmi.RemoteException;
public interface Car extends Remote {
  public int getPrice () throws RemoteException;

  public int getTopSpeed() throws RemoteException;
  public long getSerialNr() throws RemoteException;
  public void sellTo ( String owner ) throws RemoteException;
  public String getOwner ( ) throws RemoteException;

  public String getColor ( ) throws RemoteException;
  public String getModel ( ) throws RemoteException;

  public String getObjectString ( ) throws RemoteException;
}
```

CARIMPL.JAVA

CarImpl.java class implements Car. It contains various methods to perform miscellaneous actions on Cars. Listing 10-24 is the source code for CarImpl.java.

Listing 10-24: CarImpl.java.

```
//
// CarImpl.java
//
// (C) 1996 Wim De Munck mailto: wimdm@dm-mediaware.be
//
import java.rmi.RemoteException;
import java.rmi.server.UnicastRemoteObject;
public class CarImpl extends UnicastRemoteObject implements Car {
  private int price;
  private long serialNr;
  private String brand;
  private String model;
```

```java
    private String color;
    private String owner = null;
    public CarImpl ( String brand, String model, String color, long
      serialNr )
        throws RemoteException {
        this.brand = brand;
        this.model = model;
        this.color = color;
        this.serialNr = serialNr;
    }
    public CarImpl ( String brand, String model, String color, long
      serialNr, String owner )
        throws RemoteException {
        this.brand = brand;
        this.model = model;
        this.color = color;
        this.serialNr = serialNr;
        this.owner = owner;
    }
    public int getPrice () throws RemoteException {
        return 0; // Catalog.getPrice( brand, model );
    }

    public int getTopSpeed() throws RemoteException {
        return 0; // Catalog.getTopSpeed( brand, model );
    }
    public long getSerialNr() throws RemoteException {
        return serialNr;
    }
        public void sellTo ( String owner ) throws RemoteException {
        this.owner = owner;
    }
    public String getOwner ( ) throws RemoteException {
        return owner;
    }
    public String getColor ( ) throws RemoteException {
        return color;
    }
    public String getBrand ( ) throws RemoteException {
        return brand;
    }
    public String getModel ( ) throws RemoteException {
        return model;
    }
    public String toString ( ) {
        return "Car: model=" + brand + " model=" + model + " color=" +
          color +
        " serial=" + serialNr + " owner=" + ((owner == null)? "None" :
          owner);
    }
    public String getObjectString ( ) throws RemoteException {
        return this.toString();
    }
}
```

CARFACTORY.JAVA

The CarFactory class is an interface implemented by CarFactoryImpl. Like the Car interface, CarFactory inherits from java.rmi.Remote. Listing 10-25 is the source code for CarFactory.java.

Listing 10–25: CarFactory.java.

```
//
// CarFactory.java
//
// (C) 1996 Wim De Munck mailto: wimdm@dm-mediaware.be
//
// interface describing stub CarFactory functionality
// the actual implementation will be the responibility of
// CarFactoryImpl.
//
import java.rmi.Remote;
import java.rmi.RemoteException;
import java.sql.*;
public interface CarFactory extends Remote {
  public Car createCar ( String model, String color )
      throws RemoteException, SQLException;
  public Car getCar ( long serialNr )
      throws RemoteException;
  public Car[] getAll () throws RemoteException;
  public boolean deleteCar ( Car car ) throws RemoteException,
    SQLException;
  public String getObjectString () throws RemoteException;
}
```

CARFACTORYIMPL.JAVA

CarFactoryImpl implements CarFactory and provides connectivity to the database through JDBC. It manipulates objects whose lifetime is longer than the application's lifetime. These objects are persistified, stored in a database table, and loaded by the CarFactoryImpl constructor upon initialization.

The methods that perform updates of data call JDBC and execute SQL statements to synchronize the data in the database. Listing 10-26 shows the source code for CarFactoryImpl.java.

Listing 10–26: CarFactoryImpl.java.

```
//
// CarFactoryImpl.java
//
// (C) 1996 Wim De Munck mailto: wimdm@dm-mediaware.be
//
// interface describing stub CarFactory functionality
// the actual implementation will be the responibility of
// CarFactoryImpl.
//
import java.util.Hashtable;
```

```java
import java.util.Enumeration;
import java.rmi.RemoteException;
import java.rmi.server.UnicastRemoteObject;
import java.sql.*;
public class CarFactoryImpl extends UnicastRemoteObject implements
 CarFactory {
 private String brand;
 private long lastSerialNr = 1000000;
 private Hashtable cars = new Hashtable();
 // local variables for connection state
 private Connection conn;
 private String uid = "guest";
 private String pwd = "sybase";
 private String table = "cars";
 // url for sybase's driver
 private String url = "jdbc:sybase:Tds:guadalajara:8192";
 private String driver = "com.sybase.jdbc.SybDriver";
 public CarFactoryImpl ( String brand ) throws RemoteException,
  SQLException, Exception {
     Class.forName(driver);
     conn = DriverManager.getConnection(url, uid, pwd);
     Statement stmt = conn.createStatement();
     ResultSet rs = stmt.executeQuery("SELECT * FROM " + table
     + " WHERE brand = '" + brand + "'");

     while (rs.next()) {
            wakeupCar(rs.getInt("serialno"),
            rs.getString("brand"),
            rs.getString("model"),
            rs.getString("color"),
            rs.getString("owner"));
     }
     rs = stmt.executeQuery("SELECT MAX(serialno) FROM " + table
     + " WHERE brand = '" + brand + "'");
     rs.next();
     lastSerialNr = rs.getLong(1);
     rs.close();
     stmt.close();
     this.brand = brand;
 }
 protected void finalize() throws SQLException {
     conn.close();
 }
 public void wakeupCar ( int sn, String brand, String model, String
   color, String owner )
            throws RemoteException {
            CarImpl car = new CarImpl ( brand, model, color, sn,
             owner );
            cars.put("SN"+car.getSerialNr(), car);
            System.out.println("CarFactory: Loaded new Car:" +
             car);
     }
     public Car createCar ( String model, String color )
     throws RemoteException, SQLException {
```

```java
            CarImpl car = new CarImpl ( brand, model, color,
             ++lastSerialNr );
            Statement stmt = conn.createStatement();
            int res = stmt.executeUpdate("INSERT INTO " + table
            + "(serialno, brand, model, color, owner) VALUES ("
            + car.getSerialNr() + ", '" + brand + "', '" + model
            + "', '" + color + "', '')");
            stmt.close();
            cars.put ( "SN" + car.getSerialNr(), car );
            System.out.println("CarFactory: Created new Car:" +
             car);
            return car;
    }
    public Car getCar ( long serialNr ) throws RemoteException {
    return (Car)cars.get("SN"+serialNr);
}
/**
* get all cars without worrying about synchronization
*/
public Car[] getAll () throws RemoteException {
Car [] allcars = new Car[cars.size()];
int i = 0;
Enumeration e = cars.elements();
while (e.hasMoreElements()) {
            allcars[i++] = (Car)e.nextElement();
            }
    System.out.println("CarFactory " + brand + ": request for all
     cars. " + i + " returned.");
    return allcars;
    }
public boolean deleteCar ( Car car ) throws RemoteException,
  SQLException {
    long sn = car.getSerialNr();
    if ( cars.remove("SN"+ sn) != null ) {
            Statement stmt = conn.createStatement();
            int res = stmt.executeUpdate("DELETE " + table
            + " WHERE brand = '" + brand + "' AND serialno = " + sn
             + "");
            stmt.close();
            System.out.println("CarFactory: Deleted Car:" + car);
            return true;
    }
    else {
            return false;
            }
    }
    public String toString () {
            return "CarFactory: " + brand + " lastNr=" +
             lastSerialNr;
    }
    public String getObjectString () throws RemoteException {
    return this.toString();
}
}
}
```

CARSALES.JAVA

CarSales.java is the client class. CarSales is a stand-alone application that looks up CarFactories in the RMI server to get references to these remote objects.

The application tries to obtain references to three remote CarFactories. Once it obtains the references, actions such as selecting cars, ordering cars, selling cars, and destroying cars may be performed. This RMI client only refers to the CarFactory and Car interfaces, not their actual implementation, which is the main objective of this exercise. The implementation class instances run elsewhere on the network and are seamlessly accessed through RMI. Listing 10-27 shows the source code for CarSales.java.

Listing 10–27: CarSales.java.

```
//
// CarSales.java
//
// (C) 1996 Wim De Munck mailto: wimdm@dm-mediaware.be
//
// This code is not to be distributed without
// explicit confirmation by the auhor.
//
import java.awt.*;
import java.rmi.Naming;
import java.net.MalformedURLException;
import java.rmi.NotBoundException;
import java.net.UnknownHostException;
/**
* CarSales-class connecting to a Remote Object
* registry.
* The Carsales instance allows simple order and selling
* of cars.
*/
public class CarSales extends Frame {
  TextArea ta = new TextArea("Application started");
  Button quitB = new Button ( "Quit" ), orderB = new Button ( "Order
    Car" );
  Button sellB = new Button ( "Sell" );
  Button wreckB = new Button ( "Wreck" );
  Choice brandCH = new Choice (), allCarsCH = new Choice();
  TextField modelTF = new TextField(10), colorTF = new TextField(10);
  TextField buyerTF = new TextField(10);
  CarFactory carFactory[];
  Car cars[] = null;
  /**
  * Construct the CarSales GUI
  */
  public CarSales ( ) {
      super ("BEST CARS IN THE WORLD");
      // Setup the User Interface
      Panel northPan = new Panel ( );
      northPan.setLayout ( new BorderLayout () );
      northPan.add ( "North",
```

```
new Label ("Car Ordering: Select brand and model", Label.LEFT)
 );
northPan.setLayout ( new BorderLayout() );
Panel orderPanel = new Panel ();
//orderPanel.setLayout ( new FlowLayout ( FlowLayout.LEFT ) );
orderPanel.setLayout ( new GridLayout ( 1,7) );
orderPanel.add ( new Label ("Brand:", Label.RIGHT ) );
orderPanel.add ( brandCH );
orderPanel.add ( new Label ("Model:", Label.RIGHT ) );
orderPanel.add ( modelTF );
orderPanel.add ( new Label ("Color:", Label.RIGHT ) );
orderPanel.add ( colorTF );
orderPanel.add ( orderB );
Panel sellPanel = new Panel ();
//sellPanel.setLayout ( new FlowLayout ( FlowLayout.LEFT ) );
sellPanel.setLayout ( new GridLayout ( 1,7) );
sellPanel.add ( new Label ("All Cars:", Label.RIGHT ) );
sellPanel.add ( allCarsCH );
sellPanel.add ( new Label ("Buyer:", Label.RIGHT ) );
sellPanel.add ( buyerTF );
sellPanel.add ( new Label ( "" ) );
sellPanel.add ( new Label( "Actions:", Label.RIGHT ) );
Panel buttonPan = new Panel ( );
buttonPan.setLayout ( new GridLayout ( 1, 2) );
buttonPan.add ( sellB );
buttonPan.add ( wreckB );
sellPanel.add ( buttonPan );
Panel northCenterPanel = new Panel ();
northCenterPanel.setLayout ( new GridLayout ( 2, 1 ) );
northCenterPanel.add ( orderPanel );
northCenterPanel.add ( sellPanel );
northPan.add ( "Center", northCenterPanel );
northPan.add ( "South", new Label ( "RMI/SQL log:",
 Label.CENTER ) );
add("North", northPan );
add("Center", ta);
add("South", quitB );
// In a real application there would be a remote object
// giving us an array or enumeration with all brands.
// In this example we do it hard coded.
String carBrands[] = { "audi", "bmw", "vw" };
carFactory = new CarFactory [ carBrands.length ];
for (int ndx=0; ndx< carBrands.length; ndx ++ ) {
      try {
             brandCH.addItem ( carBrands[ndx] );
             carFactory[ndx] = (CarFactory)
             (java.rmi.Naming.lookup (
              "rmi://serverhost/CarFactory." +
             carBrands[ndx] ) );
             appendTA( carBrands[ndx] + ": " +
              carFactory[ndx]);}
      catch ( java.rmi.RemoteException ex) {
      appendTA( "Constructor() RemoteException: " +
       ex.getMessage() );}
```

```
                        catch ( java.rmi.NotBoundException ex) {
                                appendTA( "Constructor() NotBoundException: " +
                                ex.getMessage() );}
                        catch ( java.net.MalformedURLException ex) {
                                appendTA ( "Constructor() MalformedURLException:
                                "+ ex.getMessage() );
                        }
                } // end for carBrands[ndx]
                try {
                        appendTA("");
                        appendTA("Creating Cars:");
                        updateAllCarsChoice ( ) ;
                        //Car nr1 = audiFact.createCar("A6", "black");}
                catch ( Exception ex) {
                        appendTA( "Constructor() Exception: " + ex.getMessage()
                         );
                        ex.printStackTrace();
                        }
                pack();
                setVisible ( true );  // JDK1.1 replaced deprecated show()
        }
        private void updateAllCarsChoice ( ) {
        int ndx = brandCH.getSelectedIndex();
        int count = 0;
        allCarsCH.removeAll();
        try {
                cars = carFactory[ndx].getAll();
                for ( int i=0 ; i < cars.length; i++ ) {
                allCarsCH.addItem ( "" + cars[i].getSerialNr() + " " +
                cars[i].getModel() + "," + cars[i].getColor() );
                count++;
                }
        }
        catch ( Exception ex ) {
                appendTA ( "updateAllCarChoice() Exception: " +
                 ex.getMessage() );
        }
        if ( count > 0 ) {
                allCarsCH.setEnabled ( true );
                allCarsCH.select( 0 );
                try {
                        buyerTF.setText ( cars[0].getOwner() );
                        colorTF.setText ( cars[0].getColor() );
                        modelTF.setText ( cars[0].getModel() );
                        }
                catch ( Exception ex ) {
                        appendTA ( "updateAllCarChoice() Exception: " +
                         ex.getMessage() );
                }
        }
        else {
                allCarsCH.setEnabled ( false );
                allCarsCH.addItem ( "No Cars Available" );
                }
```

```
    appendTA ( "Added " + count + " cars to allCarsCH for " +
      brandCH.getSelectedItem() );
    }
  private void appendTA ( String text ) {
    ta.setText( ta.getText() + "\n" + text.toString() );
    }
  private void appendTA ( Car car ) {
    try {
          ta.setText( ta.getText() + "\n" + car.getObjectString() ); }
    catch ( java.rmi.RemoteException ex ) {
          ta.setText ( "RemoteException: " + ex.getMessage() );
          ex.printStackTrace();
          }
    }
    // JDK1.02 event-model
    public boolean action ( Event evt, Object arg ) {
          try {
                if ( evt.target == quitB ) {
                      setVisible ( false ); // JDK1.1's setVisible()
                        replaced deprecated hide()
                      dispose();
                      System.exit(0);
                      return true;
                      }
                else if ( evt.target == orderB ) {
                      int factIndex = brandCH.getSelectedIndex();
                      carFactory[factIndex].createCar (
                        modelTF.getText(), colorTF.getText() );
                      updateAllCarsChoice ( ) ;
                      }
                else if ( evt.target == sellB ) {
                      int carIndex = allCarsCH.getSelectedIndex();
                      cars[carIndex].sellTo ( buyerTF.getText() );
                      appendTA ( "sold car: " +
                        cars[carIndex].getSerialNr() + " to " +
                        buyerTF.getText() );
                      }
                else if ( evt.target == wreckB ) {
                      int carIndex = allCarsCH.getSelectedIndex();
                      int factIndex = brandCH.getSelectedIndex();
                      appendTA ( "wrecked car: " +
                        cars[carIndex].getSerialNr() );
                      carFactory[factIndex].deleteCar ( cars[carIndex]
                        );
                      updateAllCarsChoice ( ) ;
                      }
                else if ( evt.target == brandCH ) {
                      colorTF.setText ( "" );
                      modelTF.setText ( "" );
                      updateAllCarsChoice ( ) ;
                      }
                else if ( evt.target == allCarsCH ) {
                      int carIndex = allCarsCH.getSelectedIndex();
                      colorTF.setText ( cars[carIndex].getColor() );
```

```
                              modelTF.setText ( cars[carIndex].getModel() );
                              buyerTF.setText ( cars[carIndex].getOwner() );
                              }
                      }
          catch ( java.rmi.RemoteException ex) {
                      appendTA ( "action() RemoteException: " +
                      ex.getMessage() ); }
          catch ( java.sql.SQLException ex) {
                      appendTA ( "action() SQLException: " + ex.getMessage()
                      );
                      }
          return true;
          }
 public boolean handleEvent ( Event evt ) { // deprecated by
  processEvent( )
 if ( evt.id == Event.WINDOW_DESTROY ) {
 setVisible ( false); // JDK1.1's setVisible() replaced deprecated
  hide( )
 dispose();
 System.exit(0);
 return true;
 }
else {
 return super.handleEvent ( evt );
 }
}

public static void main ( String args[] ) {
// Create GUI-object
CarSales cs = new CarSales();
 }
}
```

CARSUPPLIERSERVER.JAVA

The CarSupplierServer class is the RMI server class. It creates three instances of
CarFactory and binds them to the RMI registry. A simple string names the bindings
to allow clients to perform lookups in the registry. Listing 10-28 shows the source
code for CarSupplierServezr.java.

Listing 10-28: CarSupplierServer.java.

```
//
// CarSupplierServer.java
//
// (C) 1996 Wim De Munck mailto: wimdm@dm-mediaware.be
//
import java.rmi.Naming;
class CarSupplierServer {
  public static void main ( String args[] ) {
```

```
// Install a SecurityManager for this server
    System.setSecurityManager( new java.rmi.RMISecurityManager()
     );
    // create and register all CarFactories
    System.out.println ( "Creating Car Factories" );
    CarFactoryImpl audi, bmw, vw ;
    try {
            audi = new CarFactoryImpl("Audi");
            bmw = new CarFactoryImpl("BMW");
            vw = new CarFactoryImpl("Volkswagen");
    } catch ( Exception ex ) {
            ex.printStackTrace();
            return;
    }
    System.out.println ( "Registring Car Factories" );
    try {
            Naming.bind("CarFactory.audi", audi);
            Naming.bind("CarFactory.bmw", bmw);
            Naming.bind("CarFactory.vw", vw);
    } catch ( java.net.MalformedURLException ex ) {
            ex.printStackTrace();
    } catch ( java.rmi.AlreadyBoundException ex ) {
            ex.printStackTrace();
    } catch ( java.rmi.RemoteException ex) {
            ex.printStackTrace();
    }
  }
}
```

RMI, as defined and implemented by JavaSoft, Inc., is HTTP-proxy aware. The networking layer of RMI provides server- and client-side transparent support for HTTP tunneling that allows applets to communicate with remote methods and remote objects through WWW proxy servers. A final note for those who want to run RMI on a stand-alone machine: A TCP/IP stack must be running on the machine to let RMI clients and servers communicate.

Summary

This chapter provided examples of JDBC in the form of Java applets or stand-alone applications. Each example covered a specific topic discussed in earlier chapters. The source code of all the examples is on the accompanying CD-ROM.

Examples discussed in this chapter include:

- A simple ISQL client

- Handling BLOBS from the command line

- A Java Automatic Teller Machine

◆ Fly with JDBC Airlines

◆ A graphical database surfer

◆ An advanced example using Remote Method Invocation

Part IV

Quick Reference and Appendixes

Quick Reference: JDBC API
Appendix A: JDBC Products and Drivers
Appendix B: Links for Additional Information
Appendix C: Frequently Asked Questions
Appendix D: What's on the CD

Part IV includes the Quick Reference, which covers the JDBC 1.2 API of JavaSoft, and valuable appendixes, which include answers to frequently asked questions and references for additional information about SQL and DBMSs, Objects and DBMSs, and JDBC products and drivers. The CD-ROM contains the source code for all examples, JDBC products, and the common Java utilities such as the JavaSoft, Inc., JDK. See Appendix D, "What's on the CD-ROM," for a detailed list of CD-ROM contents.

Quick Reference

JDBC API: package java.sql

The definitions for interfaces, classes, and methods are based on the Javadoc-generated API specification of JavaSoft. This section covers the JDBC 1.2 API of JavaSoft.

Interface java.sql.CallableStatement

public interface CallableStatement

extends Object

extends PreparedStatement

CallableStatements are used to call SQL stored procedures in a standard way for all DBMSs. Escape syntax is used for procedures that return a result parameter and those that do not return a parameter. If the procedure returns a result, the result parameter must be registered as an OUT parameter.

The set methods inherited from PreparedStatement are used to set IN parameter values. The type of all OUT parameters must be registered prior to executing the stored procedure. Their values are retrieved via the get methods provided here.

A Callable statement may return a ResultSet or multiple ResultSets. Multiple ResultSets are handled using methods inherited from Statement. The OUT parameters must always be retrieved after processing ResultSets and update counts, if any.

```
{?= call <PROCEDURE-NAME>[<ARG1>,<ARG2> , ...]}
{call <PROCEDURE-NAME>[<ARG1>,<ARG2> , ...]}
```

See also: prepareCall, ResultSet

METHODS:

GETBIGDECIMAL
public abstract BigDecimal getBigDecimal(int parameterIndex, int scale) throws SQLException

Get the value of an OUT parameter of type SQL NUMERIC as a java.math.BigDecimal object.

Parameters: parameterIndex — the parameter index begins at 1.

scale — a positive value representing the decimal precision.

Returns: the OUT parameter value; null if its value is SQL NULL

GETBOOLEAN
public abstract boolean getBoolean(int parameterIndex) throws SQLException

Get the value of an OUT parameter of type SQL BIT as a Java boolean.

Parameters: parameterIndex — the parameter index begins at 1.

Returns: the OUT parameter value; false if the value is SQL NULL

GETBYTE
public abstract byte getByte(int parameterIndex) throws SQLException

Get the value of an OUT parameter of type SQL TINYINT as a Java byte.

Parameters: parameterIndex — the parameter index begins at 1.

Returns: the OUT parameter value; 0 if the value is SQL NULL

GETBYTES
public abstract byte[] getBytes(int parameterIndex) throws SQLException

Get the value of an OUT parameter of type SQL BINARY or VARBINARY as a Java byte[].

Parameters: parameterIndex — the parameter index begins at 1.

Returns: the OUT parameter value; null if the value is SQL NULL

GETDATE
public abstract Date getDate(int parameterIndex) throws SQLException

Get the value of an OUT parameter of type SQL DATE as a java.sql.Date object.

Parameters: parameterIndex — the parameter index begins at 1.

Returns: the OUT parameter value; null if the value is SQL NULL

GETDOUBLE
public abstract double getDouble(int parameterIndex) throws SQLException
Get the value of an OUT parameter of type SQL DOUBLE as a Java double.
Parameters: parameterIndex – the parameter index begins at 1.

Returns: the OUT parameter value; 0 if the value is SQL NULL

GETFLOAT
public abstract float getFloat(int parameterIndex) throws SQLException
Get the value of an OUT parameter of type SQL FLOAT as a Java float.
Parameters: parameterIndex – the parameter index begins at 1.

Returns: the OUT parameter value; 0 if the value is SQL NULL

GETINT
public abstract int getInt(int parameterIndex) throws SQLException
Get the value of an OUT parameter of type SQL INTEGER as a Java int.
Parameters: parameterIndex – the parameter index begins at 1.

Returns: the OUT parameter value; 0 if the value is SQL NULL

GETLONG
public abstract long getLong(int parameterIndex) throws SQLException
Get the value of an OUT parameter of type SQL BIGINT as a Java long.
Parameters: parameterIndex – the parameter index begins at 1.

Returns: the OUT parameter value; 0 if the value is SQL NULL

GETOBJECT
public abstract Object getObject(int parameterIndex) throws SQLException
Get the value of an OUT parameter as a Java object.
The object type corresponds to the SQL type that was registered for this parameter using registerOutParameter().
Parameters: parameterIndex – the parameter index begins at 1.

Returns: a java.lang.Object containing the OUT parameter value.

See also: Types

GETSHORT
public abstract short getShort(int parameterIndex) throws SQLException
Get the value of an OUT parameter of type SQL SMALLINT as a Java short.
Parameters: parameterIndex – the parameter index begins at 1.

Returns: the OUT parameter value; 0 if the value is SQL NULL

GETSTRING
public abstract String getString(int parameterIndex) throws SQLException
Get the value of an OUT parameter of type SQL CHAR, VARCHAR, or LONGVAR-
CHAR as a Java String.
Parameters: parameterIndex — the parameter index begins at 1.

Returns: the OUT parameter value; null if the value is SQL NULL

GETTIME
public abstract Time getTime(int parameterIndex) throws SQLException
Get the value of an OUT parameter of type SQL TIME as a java.sql.Time object.
Parameters: parameterIndex — the parameter index begins at 1.

Returns: the OUT parameter value; null if the value is SQL NULL

GETTIMESTAMP
public abstract Timestamp getTimestamp(int parameterIndex) throws SQLException
Get the value of an OUT parameter of type SQL TIMESTAMP as a
java.sql.Timestamp object.
Parameters: parameterIndex — the parameter index begins at 1.

Returns: the OUT parameter value; null if the value is SQL NULL

REGISTEROUTPARAMETER
public abstract void registerOutParameter(int parameterIndex,
int sqlType) throws SQLException
The registerOutParameter() method must be called before executing a stored procedure to register the java.sql.Type of each OUT parameter. This type is used to
retrieve the OUT parameter value with the appropriate getXXX() method.
Parameters: parameterIndex — the parameter index begins at 1.

sqlType — the SQL type code defined by java.sql.Types

See also: Type

REGISTEROUTPARAMETER
public abstract void registerOutParameter(int parameterIndex, int sqlType, int
scale) throws SQLException
This registerOutParameter() method is used for registering Numeric or Decimal
OUT parameters.
Parameters: parameterIndex — the parameter index begins at 1.

sqlType — java.sql.Type.NUMERIC or java.sql.Type.DECIMAL

scale — a positive value representing the desired number of decimal digits

See also: Numeric, Type

WASNULL

   public abstract boolean wasNull() throws SQLException

This method reports whether the last value read was a SQL NULL. A getXXX() must be invoked first.

Returns: true if the last parameter read was SQL NULL

Interface java.sql.Connection

public interface Connection

extends Object

A Connection is a session in a specific database engine. SQL statements and their results are executed within the context of such a Connection.

Information such as database tables, stored procedures, and other database objects may be obtained from a Connection with the getMetaData methods.

All changes are committed after the execution of a statement. This is the default behavior. If autocommit has been disabled, an explicit commit must be done or database changes will not be effective.

See also: getConnection, Statement, ResultSet, DatabaseMetaData

VARIABLES:

TRANSACTION_NONE

   public final static int TRANSACTION_NONE

This constant value is used to specify that transactions are not supported.

TRANSACTION_READ_COMMITTED

   public final static int TRANSACTION_READ_COMMITTED

This constant value is used to specify that only reads on the current row are repeatable. Dirty reads are not allowed, but nonrepeatable and phantom reads can occur.

TRANSACTION_READ_UNCOMMITTED

   public final static int TRANSACTION_READ_UNCOMMITTED

This constant value is used to specify that dirty reads, nonrepeatable reads, and phantom reads can occur.

TRANSACTION_REPEATABLE_READ

   public final static int TRANSACTION_REPEATABLE_READ

This constant value is used to specify that only phantom reads can occur.

TRANSACTION_SERIALIZABLE

   public final static int TRANSACTION_SERIALIZABLE

This constant value is used to specify that dirty reads, nonrepeatable reads, and phantom reads cannot occur.

METHODS:

CLEARWARNINGS
public abstract void clearWarnings() throws SQLException

Clears the chained warnings of a Connection. getWarnings() returns null until a new warning is reported.

CLOSE
public abstract void close() throws SQLException

The close method provides an immediate release for a Connection. All its resources are released upon invocation, including resources maintained by the DBMS and the JDBC driver. Note that a Connection is automatically closed when it is garbage collected.

COMMIT
public abstract void commit() throws SQLException

This method is used to commit transactions. All changes made since the previous commit() or rollback() are made permanent, and any database locks currently held by the Connection are released. Note that all PreparedStatements, CallableStatements, and ResultSets are implicitly closed when a Connection is committed.

See also: setAutoClose, setAutoCommit

CREATESTATEMENT
public abstract Statement createStatement() throws SQLException

This method creates a Statement object used to execute SQL statements without parameters. Unlike PreparedStatement, this method is used for Statements that are executed only once.

Returns: a new Statement object

GETAUTOCLOSE
public abstract boolean getAutoClose() throws SQLException

Checks whether the Connection's state is autoclose.

Returns: Current state of autoclose mode

See also: setAutoClose

GETAUTOCOMMIT
public abstract boolean getAutoCommit() throws SQLException

Checks whether the Connection's state is autocommit.

Returns: Current state of autocommit mode

See also: setAutoCommit

GETCATALOG

public abstract String getCatalog() throws SQLException

If catalogs are supported, this method returns the Connection's current catalog name.

Returns: the current catalog name or null

GETMETADATA

public abstract DatabaseMetaData getMetaData() throws SQLException

The DatabaseMetaData object returned by this method may be used to get information from the database engine. Such information includes a description of tables, stored procedures, keys and indexes, the supported SQL grammar, and so forth. Refer to the DatabaseMetaData interface for more detail.

Returns: a DatabaseMetaData object

GETTRANSACTIONISOLATION

public abstract int getTransactionIsolation() throws SQLException

Return the current transaction isolation mode. The different values are those listed as TRANSACTION_XXX static variables.

Returns: the current transaction mode value

GETWARNINGS

public abstract SQLWarning getWarnings() throws SQLException

Warnings issued by calls on a Connection are chained together. This method returns the first warning that is reported as a SQLWarning.

Returns: the first SQLWarning or null

ISCLOSED

public abstract boolean isClosed() throws SQLException

Checks whether a connection has been closed.

Returns: true if the connection is closed; false if it's still open

ISREADONLY

public abstract boolean isReadOnly() throws SQLException

Checks whether the Connection is in read-only mode.

Returns: true if Connection is read-only

NATIVESQL

public abstract String nativeSQL(String sql) throws SQLException

Under some circumstances specific JDBC drivers may translate the SQL statements into a database's native SQL grammar prior to sending them. This method is useful to obtain the native form of the statement that the driver would have sent.

Parameters: sql — a SQL statement. Note that it may contain '?' parameter placeholders.

Returns: the native form of the statement

PREPARECALL
public abstract CallableStatement prepareCall(String sql) throws SQLException

CallableStatements are used for stored procedure call statements. This method creates such an object that can be used later with appropriate methods to provide IN and OUT parameters to the stored procedure.

Parameters: sql — a SQL statement. Note that it may contain '?' parameter placeholders.

Returns: a new CallableStatement object containing the precompiled SQL statement

PREPARESTATEMENT
public abstract PreparedStatement prepareStatement(String sql) throws SQLException

This method returns a PreparedStatement object. Such objects are useful when a SQL statement must be executed multiple times. The SQL statement is precompiled before it actually receives parameters and is executed. If supported by the driver and by the DBMS, parsing and optimizations are only done once during precompilation.

Parameters: sql — a SQL statement. Note that it is normally used with '?' IN parameter placeholders.

Returns: a new PreparedStatement object containing the precompiled statement

ROLLBACK
public abstract void rollback() throws SQLException

Unlike commit(), rollback() cancels all changes made since the previous commit() or rollback() invocation and releases any database locks currently held by the Connection. This method is used to abort transactions. Note that a Connection's PreparedStatements, CallableStatements, and ResultSets are implicitly closed when it is rollbacked.

See also: setAutoClose, setAutoCommit

SETAUTOCLOSE
public abstract void setAutoClose(boolean autoClose) throws SQLException

When autoclose is disabled, JDBC attempts to keep all Statements and ResultSets open across commits and rollbacks.

Parameters: autoClose — true enables autoclose, false disables autoclose.

See also: supportsOpenCursorsAcrossCommit,
supportsOpenCursorsAcrossRollback, supportsOpenStatementsAcrossCommit,
supportsOpenStatementsAcrossRollback

SETAUTOCOMMIT
public abstract void setAutoCommit(boolean autoCommit) throws
SQLException
SQL statements are executed and committed as individual transactions if a
Connection is in autocommit mode. If not in autocommit mode, the SQL statements
are grouped into transactions that are terminated by either commit() or rollback().
By default, new connections are in autocommit mode. In autocommit mode, a com-
mit always occurs after all results and output parameter values for a specific state-
ment have been retrieved.
Parameters: autoCommit – true enables autocommit; false disables it.

SETCATALOG
public abstract void setCatalog(String catalog) throws SQLException
If the database supports catalogs, this method selects a specific catalog. The
method has no effect if catalogs are not supported.

SETREADONLY
public abstract void setReadOnly(boolean readOnly) throws SQLException
Connections may be set in read-only mode. In this case no database updates are
allowed and performance is often improved. Note that this method cannot be called
while in the middle of a transaction.
Parameters: readOnly – true enables read-only mode; false disables read-only
mode.

SETTRANSACTIONISOLATION
public abstract void setTransactionIsolation(int level) throws SQLException
This method is used to change the transaction isolation level using the TRANS-
ACTION_XXX static variables defined in the beginning of this section. Note that it
cannot be called while in the middle of a transaction.
Parameters: level – a TRANSACTION_XXX isolation value with the exception of
TRANSACTION_NONE

See also: supportsTransactionIsolationLevel

Interface java.sql.DatabaseMetaData

public interface DatabaseMetaData

extends Object

The DatabaseMetaData class provides methods that return information about the database.

A part of its methods return ResultSets. Normal ResultSet methods such as getString() and getInt() must be used to retrieve the data from these ResultSets. A SQLException is thrown if a given form of metadata is not available.

The methods that take String pattern arguments return information using these patterns. Within a pattern String, "%" means match any substring of 0 or more characters, and "_" means match any one character. The various methods that use pattern only return metadata entries matching the search pattern. A search criterion is suppressed if its pattern is set to null.

If a driver does not support a metadata method, an exception is thrown. If such a method normally returns a ResultSet, a ResultSet (which may be empty) is returned or a SQLException is thrown.

VARIABLES:

BESTROWNOTPSEUDO
public final static int bestRowNotPseudo
BEST ROW PSEUDO_COLUMN: It is NOT a pseudocolumn.

BESTROWPSEUDO
public final static int bestRowPseudo
BEST ROW PSEUDO_COLUMN: It is a pseudocolumn.

BESTROWSESSION
public final static int bestRowSession
BEST ROW SCOPE: It is valid for the remainder of the current session.

BESTROWTEMPORARY
public final static int bestRowTemporary
BEST ROW SCOPE: Very temporary, while using row

BESTROWTRANSACTION
public final static int bestRowTransaction
BEST ROW SCOPE: It is valid for the remainder of current transaction.

BESTROWUNKNOWN
public final static int bestRowUnknown
BEST ROW PSEUDO_COLUMN: It may or may not be a pseudocolumn.

COLUMNNONULLS
public final static int columnNoNulls
COLUMN NULLABLE: It might not allow NULL values.

COLUMNNULLABLE
public final static int columnNullable
COLUMN NULLABLE: It definitely allows NULL values.

COLUMNNULLABLEUNKNOWN
public final static int columnNullableUnknown
COLUMN NULLABLE: Its nullability is unknown.

IMPORTEDKEYCASCADE
public final static int importedKeyCascade
IMPORT KEY UPDATE_RULE and DELETE_RULE: For update, change imported key to agree with primary key update. For delete, delete rows that import a deleted key.

IMPORTEDKEYINITIALLYDEFERRED
public final static int importedKeyInitiallyDeferred
IMPORT KEY DEFERRABILITY: See SQL92 for more information.

IMPORTEDKEYINITIALLYIMMEDIATE
public final static int importedKeyInitiallyImmediate
IMPORT KEY DEFERRABILITY: See SQL92 for more information.

IMPORTEDKEYNOACTION
public final static int importedKeyNoAction
IMPORT KEY UPDATE_RULE and DELETE_RULE: Do not allow update or delete of primary key if it has been imported.

IMPORTEDKEYNOTDEFERRABLE
public final static int importedKeyNotDeferrable
IMPORT KEY DEFERRABILITY: See SQL92 for more information.

IMPORTEDKEYRESTRICT
public final static int importedKeyRestrict
IMPORT KEY UPDATE_RULE and DELETE_RULE: Do not allow update or delete of primary key if it has been imported.

IMPORTEDKEYSETDEFAULT
public final static int importedKeySetDefault
IMPORT KEY UPDATE_RULE and DELETE_RULE: Change imported key to default values if its primary key has been updated or deleted.

IMPORTEDKEYSETNULL
public final static int importedKeySetNull
IMPORT KEY UPDATE_RULE and DELETE_RULE: Change imported key to NULL if its primary key has been updated or deleted.

PROCEDURECOLUMNUNKNOWN
public final static int procedureColumnUnknown
COLUMN_TYPE: Unknown type for a procedure's parameter.

PROCEDURECOLUMNIN
public final static int procedureColumnIn
COLUMN_TYPE: It is an IN parameter.

PROCEDURECOLUMNINOUT
public final static int procedureColumnInOut
COLUMN_TYPE: It is an INOUT parameter.

PROCEDURECOLUMNOUT
public final static int procedureColumnOut
COLUMN_TYPE: It is an OUT parameter.

PROCEDURECOLUMNRETURN
public final static int procedureColumnReturn
COLUMN_TYPE: The procedure returns a value.

PROCEDURECOLUMNRESULT
public final static int procedureColumnResult
COLUMN_TYPE: Result column is a ResultSet.

PROCEDURENORESULT
public final static int procedureNoResult
PROCEDURE_TYPE: Procedure does not return a result.

PROCEDURENONULLS
public final static int procedureNoNulls
TYPE NULLABLE: The procedure does not allow NULL values.

PROCEDURENULLABLE
public final static int procedureNullable
TYPE NULLABLE: It allows NULL values.

PROCEDURENULLABLEUNKNOWN
public final static int procedureNullableUnknown
TYPE NULLABLE: Its nullability is unknown.

PROCEDURERESULTUNKNOWN
public final static int procedureResultUnknown
PROCEDURE_TYPE: It may return a result.

PROCEDURERETURNSRESULT
public final static int procedureReturnsResult
PROCEDURE_TYPE: It returns a result.

TABLEINDEXCLUSTERED
public final static short tableIndexClustered
INDEX INFO TYPE: This identifies a clustered index.

TABLEINDEXHASHED
public final static short tableIndexHashed
INDEX INFO TYPE: This identifies a hashed index.

TABLEINDEXOTHER
    public final static short tableIndexOther
INDEX INFO TYPE: This identifies some other form of index

TABLEINDEXSTATISTIC
    public final static short tableIndexStatistic
INDEX INFO TYPE: This identifies table statistics that are returned in conjunction with a table's index descriptions.

TYPENONULLS
    public final static int typeNoNulls
TYPE NULLABLE: It does not allow NULL values.

TYPENULLABLE
    public final static int typeNullable
TYPE NULLABLE: It allows NULL values.

TYPENULLABLEUNKNOWN
    public final static int typeNullableUnknown
TYPE NULLABLE: Its nullability is unknown.

TYPEPREDBASIC
    public final static int typePredBasic
TYPE INFO SEARCHABLE: Supported except for WHERE . . . LIKE

TYPEPREDCHAR
    public final static int typePredChar
TYPE INFO SEARCHABLE: Only supported with WHERE . . . LIKE

TYPEPREDNONE
    public final static int typePredNone
TYPE INFO SEARCHABLE: No support

TYPESEARCHABLE
    public final static int typeSearchable
TYPE INFO SEARCHABLE: Supported for all WHERE

VERSIONCOLUMNNOTPSEUDO
    public final static int versionColumnNotPseudo
VERSION COLUMNS PSEUDO_COLUMN: It is NOT a pseudocolumn

VERSIONCOLUMNPSEUDO
    public final static int versionColumnPseudo
VERSION COLUMNS PSEUDO_COLUMN: It is a pseudocolumn

VERSIONCOLUMNUNKNOWN
    public final static int versionColumnUnknown
VERSION COLUMNS PSEUDO_COLUMN: It may or may not be a pseudocolumn

METHODS:

ALLPROCEDURESARECALLABLE
public abstract boolean allProceduresAreCallable() throws SQLException
Checks whether the current user may call all the procedures returned by getProcedures.
Returns: true if so

ALLTABLESARESELECTABLE
public abstract boolean allTablesAreSelectable() throws SQLException
Checks whether all the tables returned by getTable may be SELECTed by the current user.
Returns: true if so

DATADEFINITIONCAUSESTRANSACTIONCOMMIT
public abstract boolean dataDefinitionCausesTransactionCommit() throws SQLException
Checks whether a data definition statement within a transaction forces the transaction to commit.
Returns: true if so

DATADEFINITIONIGNOREDINTRANSACTIONS
public abstract boolean dataDefinitionIgnoredInTransactions() throws SQLException
Checks whether a data definition statement within a transaction will be ignored.
Returns: true if so

DOESMAXROWSIZEINCLUDEBLOBS
public abstract boolean doesMaxRowSizeIncludeBlobs() throws SQLException
Checks whether getMaxRowSize() includes LONGVARCHAR and LONGVARBINARY blobs.
Returns: true if so

GETBESTROWIDENTIFIER
public abstract ResultSet getBestRowIdentifier(String catalog, String schema, String table, int scope, boolean nullable) throws SQLException
Returns a set of column descriptions that uniquely identifies a row of a table. They are ordered by SCOPE.
The resultset has the following columns:
SCOPE short ⇨ actual scope of result is one of the following:

Σ bestRowTemporary – very temporary, while using row

    Σ bestRowTransaction – valid for remainder of current transaction

    Σ bestRowSession – valid for remainder of current session

COLUMN_NAME String ⇨ column name

DATA_TYPE short ⇨ SQL data type from java.sql.Types

TYPE_NAME String ⇨ Data source dependent type name

COLUMN_SIZE int ⇨ precision

BUFFER_LENGTH int ⇨ not used

DECIMAL_DIGITS short ⇨ scale

PSEUDO_COLUMN short ⇨ a pseudocolumn that can have one of these values:

    Σ bestRowUnknown – may or may not be pseudocolumn

    Σ bestRowNotPseudo – is NOT a pseudocolumn

    Σ bestRowPseudo – is a pseudocolumn

Parameters: catalog – a catalog name; "" retrieves those without a catalog; null means do not use catalogs for the selection criteria.

schema – a schema name; "" retrieves those without a schema

table – a table name

scope – the scope of interest; values are the same as SCOPE.

nullable – include columns that are nullable

Returns: a ResultSet; each row is a column description.

  GETCATALOGS

     public abstract ResultSet getCatalogs() throws SQLException

  Get a table of catalog names available in this database. The results are ordered by catalog name. The catalog column is:

TABLE_CAT String ⇨ catalog name

Returns: a ResultSet containing one row per catalog name

  GETCATALOGSEPARATOR

     public abstract String getCatalogSeparator() throws SQLException

  Get the separator between catalog and table name.

Returns: the catalog separator string

GETCATALOGTERM
    public abstract String getCatalogTerm() throws SQLException
Get the term used for catalogs.
Returns: the vendor term for catalog

GETCOLUMNS
    public abstract ResultSet getColumns(String catalog, String schemaPattern, String tableNamePattern, String columnNamePattern) throws SQLException
Return a ResultSet containing a description of table columns matching the criteria available in a catalog. The ResultSet is ordered TABLE_SCHEM, TABLE_NAME, and ORDINAL_POSITION.
    The ResultSet has the following columns:

TABLE_CAT String ⇨ table catalog (may be null)

TABLE_SCHEM String ⇨ table schema (may be null)

TABLE_NAME String ⇨ table name

COLUMN_NAME String ⇨ column name

DATA_TYPE short ⇨ SQL type from java.sql.Types

TYPE_NAME String ⇨ Data source dependent-type name

COLUMN_SIZE int ⇨ column size; (maximum number of characters for CHAR or DATE type or precision for NUMERIC or DECIMAL types)

BUFFER_LENGTH is not used.

DECIMAL_DIGITS int ⇨ the number of fractional digits

NUM_PREC_RADIX int ⇨ radix (typically either 10 or 2)

NULLABLE int ⇨ has one of these values:

        columnNoNulls – might not allow NULL values

        columnNullable – definitely allows NULL values

        columnNullableUnknown – nullability unknown

REMARKS String ⇨ comment describing column (may be null)

COLUMN_DEF String ⇨ default value (may be null)

SQL_DATA_TYPE int ⇨ unused

SQL_DATETIME_SUB int ⇨ unused

CHAR_OCTET_LENGTH int ⇨ the length of the column in bytes

ORDINAL_POSITION int ⇨ index of column in table (starting at 1)

IS_NULLABLE String ➪ "NO" if NULL values are not allowed; "YES" if the column might allow NULL values; or an empty string if this attribute is unknown

Parameters: catalog — a catalog name; "" retrieves those without a catalog; null means do not use catalogs for the selection criteria.

schemaPattern — a schema name pattern; "" retrieves those without a schema.

tableNamePattern — a table name pattern

columnNamePattern — a column name pattern

Returns: a ResultSet; each row is a column description.

See also: getSearchStringEscape

GETCOLUMNPRIVILEGES

public abstract ResultSet getColumnPrivileges(String catalog, String schema, String table, String columnNamePattern) throws SQLException

Return a description of the access rights for the columns of a table. COLUMN_NAME and PRIVILEGE order the privileges.
The ResultSet contains rows of privileges and has the following columns:

TABLE_CAT String ➪ table catalog (may be null)

TABLE_SCHEM String ➪ table schema (may be null)

TABLE_NAME String ➪ table name

COLUMN_NAME String ➪ column name

GRANTOR ➪ grantor of access (may be null)

GRANTEE String ➪ grantee of access

PRIVILEGE String ➪ name of access (SELECT, INSERT, UPDATE, REFRENCES, . . .)

IS_GRANTABLE String ➪ if grantee is permitted to grant to others, the column contains "YES"; "NO" if it is not permitted, or null if unknown

Parameters: catalog — a catalog name; "" retrieves those without a catalog; null means do not use catalogs for the selection criteria.

schema — a schema name; "" retrieves those without a schema.

table — a table name

columnNamePattern — a column name pattern

Returns: a ResultSet; each row is a description of a column privilege.

See also: getSearchStringEscape

GETCROSSREFERENCE

public abstract ResultSet getCrossReference(String primaryCatalog, String primarySchema, String primaryTable, String foreignCatalog, String foreignSchema, String foreignTable) throws SQLException
Describe the foreign keys of a table and the primary keys of another table they refer to. They are ordered by FKTABLE_CAT, FKTABLE_SCHEM, FKTABLE_NAME, and KEY_SEQ.

The ResultSet contains foreign key column descriptions. It contains the following columns:

PKTABLE_CAT String ⇨ primary key table catalog (may be null)

PKTABLE_SCHEM String ⇨ primary key table schema (may be null)

PKTABLE_NAME String ⇨ primary key table name

PKCOLUMN_NAME String ⇨ primary key column name

FKTABLE_CAT String ⇨ foreign key table catalog (may be null) being exported (may be null)

FKTABLE_SCHEM String ⇨ foreign key table schema (may be null) being exported (may be null)

FKTABLE_NAME String ⇨ foreign key table name being exported

FKCOLUMN_NAME String ⇨ foreign key column name being exported

KEY_SEQ short ⇨ sequence number within foreign key

UPDATE_RULE short ⇨ What happens to foreign key when primary is updated:

> importedKeyNoAction – do not allow update of primary key if it has been imported

> importedKeyCascade – change imported key to agree with primary key update

> importedKeyRestrict – do not allow update of primary key if it has been imported

> importedKeySetDefault – change imported key to default values if its primary key has been updated

> importedKeySetNull – change imported key to NULL if its primary key has been updated

DELETE_RULE short ⇨ What happens to the foreign key when primary is deleted.

> importedKeyNoAction – do not allow delete of primary key if it has been imported

> importedKeyCascade – delete rows that import a deleted key

importedKeyRestrict — do not allow delete of primary key if it has been imported

importedKeySetDefault — change imported key to default if its primary key has been deleted

importedKeySetNull — change imported key to NULL if its primary key has been deleted

FK_NAME String ⇨ foreign key identifier (may be null)

PK_NAME String ⇨ primary key identifier (may be null)

DEFERRABILITY short ⇨ can the evaluation of foreign key constraints be deferred until commit

importedKeyInitiallyDeferred — see SQL92 for definition

importedKeyInitiallyImmediate — see SQL92 for definition

importedKeyNotDeferrable — see SQL92 for definition

Parameters: primaryCatalog — a catalog name; "" retrieves those without a catalog; the catalog name criteria is suppressed if null.

primarySchema — a schema name pattern; "" retrieves those without a schema.

primaryTable — the table name that exports the key

foreignCatalog — a catalog name; "" retrieves those without a catalog; the catalog name criteria is suppressed if null.

foreignSchema — a schema name pattern; "" retrieves those without a schema.

foreignTable — the table name that imports the key

Returns: a ResultSet; each row is a foreign key column description.

See also: getImportedKeys

GETDATABASEPRODUCTNAME
    public abstract String getDatabaseProductName() throws SQLException
Get the name of the database product in use.
Returns: database product name

GETDATABASEPRODUCTVERSION
    public abstract String getDatabaseProductVersion() throws SQLException
Get the version of the database product in use.
Returns: database version

GETDEFAULTTRANSACTIONISOLATION
    public abstract int getDefaultTransactionIsolation() throws SQLException
Get the database's default transaction isolation level. See the possible values in java.sql.Connection.
Returns: the default isolation level

See also: Connection

GETDRIVERNAME
    public abstract String getDriverName() throws SQLException
Get the name of the JDBC driver in use.
Returns: JDBC driver name

GETDRIVERMAJORVERSION
    public abstract int getDriverMajorVersion()
Get the JDBC driver's major version number.
Returns: JDBC driver major version

GETDRIVERMINORVERSION
    public abstract int getDriverMinorVersion()
Get the JDBC driver's minor version number.
Returns: JDBC driver minor version number

GETDRIVERVERSION
    public abstract String getDriverVersion() throws SQLException
Get the version of the JDBC driver in use.
Returns: JDBC driver version

GETEXPORTEDKEYS
    public abstract ResultSet getExportedKeys(String catalog, String schema, String table) throws SQLException
Get a description of foreign key columns that reference a table's primary key columns (the foreign keys exported by a table). They are ordered by FKTABLE_CAT, FKTABLE_SCHEM, FKTABLE_NAME, and KEY_SEQ.
The ResultSet contains foreign key column description. Each row has these columns:

PKTABLE_CAT String ⇨ primary key table catalog (may be null)

PKTABLE_SCHEM String ⇨ primary key table schema (may be null)

PKTABLE_NAME String ⇨ primary key table name

PKCOLUMN_NAME String ⇨ primary key column name

FKTABLE_CAT String ⇨ foreign key table catalog (may be null) being exported (may be null)

FKTABLE_SCHEM String ➪ foreign key table schema (may be null) being exported (may be null)

FKTABLE_NAME String ➪ foreign key table name being exported

FKCOLUMN_NAME String ➪ foreign key column name being exported

KEY_SEQ short ➪ sequence number within foreign key

UPDATE_RULE short ➪ what happens to foreign key when primary is updated:

> importedKeyNoAction — do not allow update of primary key if it has been imported
>
> importedKeyCascade — change imported key to agree with primary key update
>
> importedKeyRestrict — do not allow update of primary key if it has been imported
>
> importedKeySetDefault — change imported key to default values if its primary key has been updated
>
> importedKeySetNull — change imported key to NULL if its primary key has been updated

DELETE_RULE short ➪ what happens to the foreign key when primary is deleted:

> importedKeyNoAction — do not allow delete of primary key if it has been imported
>
> importedKeyCascade — delete rows that import a deleted key
>
> importedKeyRestrict — do not allow delete of primary key if it has been imported
>
> importedKeySetDefault — change imported key to default if its primary key has been deleted
>
> importedKeySetNull — change imported key to NULL if its primary key has been deleted

FK_NAME String ➪ foreign key identifier (may be null)

PK_NAME String ➪ primary key identifier (may be null)

DEFERRABILITY short ➪ can the evaluation of foreign key constraints be deferred until commit

> importedKeyInitiallyDeferred — see SQL92 for definition
>
> importedKeyInitiallyImmediate — see SQL92 for definition
>
> importedKeyNotDeferrable — see SQL92 for definition

Parameters: catalog – a catalog name; "" retrieves those without a catalog; a null means that the catalog name must be suppressed from the selection criteria.

schema – a schema name pattern; "" retrieves those without a schema.

table – a table name

Returns: a ResultSet; each row is a foreign key column description.

See also: getImportedKeys

GETEXTRANAMECHARACTERS
public abstract String getExtraNameCharacters() throws SQLException
The database may allow special characters to be used in unquoted identifiers. This method returns a String containing such characters.
Returns: the string containing the extra characters

GETIDENTIFIERQUOTESTRING
public abstract String getIdentifierQuoteString() throws SQLException
Get the string used to quote SQL identifiers.
Returns: the quoting string or a space character if the database does not support identifier quoting

GETIMPORTEDKEYS
public abstract ResultSet getImportedKeys(String catalog, String schema, String table) throws SQLException
Get a description of the primary key columns referenced by a table's foreign key columns. They are ordered by PKTABLE_CAT, PKTABLE_SCHEM, PKTABLE_NAME, and KEY_SEQ.
The ResultSet contains primary key column descriptions. It has these columns:

PKTABLE_CAT String ⇨ primary key table catalog being imported (may be null)

PKTABLE_SCHEM String ⇨ primary key table schema being imported (may be null)

PKTABLE_NAME String ⇨ primary key table name being imported

PKCOLUMN_NAME String ⇨ primary key column name being imported

FKTABLE_CAT String ⇨ foreign key table catalog (may be null)

FKTABLE_SCHEM String ⇨ foreign key table schema (may be null)

FKTABLE_NAME String ⇨ foreign key table name

FKCOLUMN_NAME String ⇨ foreign key column name

KEY_SEQ short ⇨ sequence number within foreign key

UPDATE_RULE short ⇨ What happens to foreign key when primary is updated:

> importedKeyNoAction — do not allow update of primary key if it has been imported
>
> importedKeyCascade — change imported key to agree with primary key update
>
> importedKeyRestrict — do not allow update of primary key if it has been imported
>
> importedKeySetDefault — change imported key to default values if its primary key has been updated
>
> importedKeySetNull — change imported key to NULL if its primary key has been updated

DELETE_RULE short ⇨ What happens to the foreign key when primary is deleted

> importedKeyNoAction — do not allow delete of primary key if it has been imported
>
> importedKeyCascade — delete rows that import a deleted key
>
> importedKeyRestrict — do not allow delete of primary key if it has been imported
>
> importedKeySetDefault — change imported key to default if its primary key has been deleted
>
> importedKeySetNull — change imported key to NULL if its primary key has been deleted

FK_NAME String ⇨ foreign key name (may be null)

PK_NAME String ⇨ primary key name (may be null)

DEFERRABILITY short ⇨ can the evaluation of foreign key constraints be deferred until commit:

> importedKeyInitiallyDeferred — see SQL92 for definition
>
> importedKeyInitiallyImmediate — see SQL92 for definition
>
> importedKeyNotDeferrable — see SQL92 for definition

Parameters: catalog — a catalog name; "" retrieves those without a catalog; a null means that the catalog name must be suppressed from the selection criteria.

schema — a schema name pattern; "" retrieves those without a schema.

table — a table name

Returns: a ResultSet; each row is a primary key column description.
See also: getExportedKeys

GETINDEXINFO

public abstract ResultSet getIndexInfo(String catalog, String schema, String table, boolean unique, boolean approximate) throws SQLException

Get a description of a table's indices and statistics. They are ordered by NON_UNIQUE, TYPE, INDEX_NAME, and ORDINAL_POSITION.The ResultSet contains index column descriptions. It has the following columns:

TABLE_CAT String ⇨ table catalog (may be null)

TABLE_SCHEM String ⇨ table schema (may be null)

TABLE_NAME String ⇨ table name

NON_UNIQUE boolean ⇨ can index values be nonunique?; false when TYPE is tableIndexStatistic

INDEX_QUALIFIER String ⇨ index catalog (may be null); null when TYPE is tableIndexStatistic

INDEX_NAME String ⇨ index name; null when TYPE is tableIndexStatistic

TYPE short ⇨ index type; the possible values are:

> tableIndexStatistic — this identifies table statistics that are returned in conjunction with a table's index descriptions.

> tableIndexClustered — this is a clustered index.

> tableIndexHashed — this is a hashed index.

> tableIndexOther — this is another type of index.

ORDINAL_POSITION short ⇨ column sequence number within index; zero if TYPE is tableIndexStatistic

COLUMN_NAME String ⇨ column name; null if TYPE is tableIndexStatistic

ASC_OR_DESC String ⇨ column sort sequence — "A" ⇨ ascending, "D" ⇨ descending; may be null if sort sequence is not supported; null if TYPE is tableIndexStatistic

CARDINALITY int ⇨ if TYPE is tableIndexStatisic then this is the number of rows in the table; otherwise, it is the number of unique values in the index.

PAGES int ⇨ if TYPE is tableIndexStatisic then this is the number of pages used for the table; otherwise, it is the number of pages used for the current index.

FILTER_CONDITION String ⇨ filter condition, if any (may be null)

Parameters: catalog — a catalog name; "" retrieves those without a catalog; a null means that the catalog name must be suppressed from the selection criteria.

schema — a schema name pattern; "" retrieves those without a schema.

table — a table name

unique – if true, returns only indices for unique values; if false, returns all indices

approximate – if true, result is allowed to reflect approximate or out of data values; if false, results must be accurate.

Returns: a ResultSet; each row is an index column description.

GETMAXBINARYLITERALLENGTH
public abstract int getMaxBinaryLiteralLength() throws SQLException
Get the maximum number of hex characters allowed in an inline binary literal.
Returns: max literal length

GETMAXCHARLITERALLENGTH
public abstract int getMaxCharLiteralLength() throws SQLException
Get the maximum length for a character literal.
Returns: max literal length

GETMAXCOLUMNNAMELENGTH
public abstract int getMaxColumnNameLength() throws SQLException
Get the maximum length allowed for a column name.
Returns: max literal length

GETMAXCOLUMNSINGROUPBY
public abstract int getMaxColumnsInGroupBy() throws SQLException
Get the maximum number of columns allowed in a "GROUP BY" clause.
Returns: max number of columns

GETMAXCOLUMNSININDEX
public abstract int getMaxColumnsInIndex() throws SQLException
Get the maximum number of columns allowed in an index.
Returns: max columns

GETMAXCOLUMNSINORDERBY
public abstract int getMaxColumnsInOrderBy() throws SQLException
Get the maximum number of columns allowed in an "ORDER BY" clause.
Returns: max columns

GETMAXCOLUMNSINSELECT
public abstract int getMaxColumnsInSelect() throws SQLException
Get the maximum number of columns allowed in a "SELECT" list.
Returns: max columns

GETMAXCOLUMNSINTABLE
public abstract int getMaxColumnsInTable() throws SQLException
Get the maximum number of columns allowed in a table.
Returns: max columns

GETMAXCONNECTIONS
public abstract int getMaxConnections() throws SQLException
Get the maximum number of simultaneous active connections for this database.
Returns: max connections

GETMAXCURSORNAMELENGTH
public abstract int getMaxCursorNameLength() throws SQLException
Get the maximum cursor name length.
Returns: max cursor name length in bytes

GETMAXINDEXLENGTH
public abstract int getMaxIndexLength() throws SQLException
Get the maximum length of an index.
Returns: max index length in bytes

GETMAXPROCEDURENAMELENGTH
public abstract int getMaxProcedureNameLength() throws SQLException
Get the maximum length of a procedure name.
Returns: max name length in bytes

GETMAXCATALOGNAMELENGTH
public abstract int getMaxCatalogNameLength() throws SQLException
Get the maximum length of a catalog name.
Returns: max name length in bytes

GETMAXROWSIZE
public abstract int getMaxRowSize() throws SQLException
Get the maximum length of a single row.
Returns: max row size in bytes

GETMAXSCHEMANAMELENGTH
public abstract int getMaxSchemaNameLength() throws SQLException
Get the maximum length of a schema name.
Returns: max name length in bytes

GETMAXSTATEMENTLENGTH

public abstract int getMaxStatementLength() throws SQLException

Get the maximum length of a SQL statement.

Returns: max length in bytes

GETMAXSTATEMENTS

public abstract int getMaxStatements() throws SQLException

Get the maximum number of simultaneous active statements for this database.

Returns: the maximum

GETMAXTABLENAMELENGTH

public abstract int getMaxTableNameLength() throws SQLException

Get the maximum length of a table name.

Returns: max name length in bytes

GETMAXTABLESINSELECT

public abstract int getMaxTablesInSelect() throws SQLException

Get the maximum number of tables in a SELECT clause.

Returns: the maximum

GETMAXUSERNAMELENGTH

public abstract int getMaxUserNameLength() throws SQLException

Get the maximum length of a user name.

Returns: max name length in bytes

GETNUMERICFUNCTIONS

public abstract String getNumericFunctions() throws SQLException

Get a list of supported math functions.

Returns: the list; separator is a comma.

GETPRIMARYKEYS

public abstract ResultSet getPrimaryKeys(String catalog, String schema, String table) throws SQLException

Get a description of a table's primary key columns. They are ordered by COLUMN_NAME.

The ResultSet contains column descriptions. It has these columns:

TABLE_CAT String ⇨ table catalog (may be null)

TABLE_SCHEM String ⇨ table schema (may be null)

TABLE_NAME String ⇨ table name

COLUMN_NAME String ⇨ column name

KEY_SEQ short ⇨ sequence number within primary key

PK_NAME String ⇨ primary key name (may be null)

Parameters: catalog — a catalog name; "" retrieves those without a catalog; a null means that the catalog name must be suppressed from the selection criteria.

schema — a schema name pattern; "" retrieves those without a schema.

table — a table name

Returns: a ResultSet; each row is a primary key column description.

GETPROCEDURES

public abstract ResultSet getProcedures(String catalog, String schemaPattern, String procedureNamePattern) throws SQLException

Get a description of stored procedures. They are ordered by PROCEDURE_SCHEM, and PROCEDURE_NAME.

The ResultSet contains procedure descriptions. It has these columns:

PROCEDURE_CAT String ⇨ procedure catalog (may be null)

PROCEDURE_SCHEM String ⇨ procedure schema (may be null)

PROCEDURE_NAME String ⇨ procedure name

RESERVED

RESERVED

RESERVED

REMARKS String ⇨ explanatory comment on the procedure

PROCEDURE_TYPE short ⇨ kind of procedure:

procedureResultUnknown — May return a result

procedureNoResult — Does not return a result

procedureReturnsResult — Returns a result

Parameters: catalog — a catalog name; "" retrieves those without a catalog; a null means that the catalog name must be suppressed from the selection criteria.

schemaPattern — a schema name pattern; "" retrieves those without a schema.

procedureNamePattern — a procedure name pattern

Returns: a ResultSet; each row is a procedure description.
See also: getSearchStringEscape

GETPROCEDURECOLUMNS

public abstract ResultSet getProcedureColumns(String catalog, String schemaPattern, String procedureNamePattern, String columnNamePattern) throws SQLException

Get a description of a catalog's stored procedure parameters and result columns. They are ordered by PROCEDURE_SCHEM and PROCEDURE_NAME.

If the procedure has a return value, its description is given first. The remaining descriptions refer to the procedure's parameters.

Each row in the ResultSet is a parameter description or column description with the following fields:

PROCEDURE_CAT String ⇨ procedure catalog (may be null)

PROCEDURE_SCHEM String ⇨ procedure schema (may be null)

PROCEDURE_NAME String ⇨ procedure name

COLUMN_NAME String ⇨ column/parameter name

COLUMN_TYPE Short ⇨ kind of column/parameter:

procedureColumnUnknown – nobody knows

procedureColumnIn – IN parameter

procedureColumnInOut – INOUT parameter

procedureColumnOut – OUT parameter

procedureColumnReturn – procedure return value

procedureColumnResult – result column in ResultSet

DATA_TYPE short ⇨ SQL type from java.sql.Types

TYPE_NAME String ⇨ SQL type name

PRECISION int ⇨ precision

LENGTH int ⇨ length in bytes of data

SCALE short ⇨ scale

RADIX short ⇨ radix

NULLABLE short ⇨ can it contain NULL?

procedureNoNulls – does not allow NULL values

procedureNullable – allows NULL values

procedureNullableUnknown – nullability unknown

REMARKS String ⇨ comment describing parameter/column

Parameters: catalog – a catalog name; "" retrieves those without a catalog; a null means that the catalog name must be suppressed from the selection criteria.

schemaPattern – a schema name pattern; "" retrieves those without a schema.

procedureNamePattern – a procedure name pattern

columnNamePattern – a column name pattern

Returns: a ResultSet; each row is a stored procedure parameter or column description.
See also: getSearchStringEscape

GETPROCEDURETERM
public abstract String getProcedureTerm() throws SQLException
Get the database vendor's preferred term for "procedure."
Returns: the vendor term

GETSCHEMAS
public abstract ResultSet getSchemas() throws SQLException
Get the schema names available in the database in use. The results are ordered by TABLE_SCHEM. The ResultSet contains one column, which is:
TABLE_SCHEM String ⇨ schema name
Returns: a ResultSet; each row has a single String column that is a schema name.

GETSCHEMATERM
public abstract String getSchemaTerm() throws SQLException
Get the database vendor's preferred term for "schema."
Returns: the vendor term

GETSEARCHSTRINGESCAPE
public abstract String getSearchStringEscape() throws SQLException
Get the string that can be used to escape wildcard characters such as "_" or "%" in the string pattern style catalog search parameters.
The "_" character represents any single character.
The "%" character represents any sequence of zero or more characters.
Returns: the string used to escape wildcard characters

GETSTRINGFUNCTIONS
public abstract String getStringFunctions() throws SQLException
Get the list of string functions supported by the database in use.
Returns: the list, which is comma separated

GETSQLKEYWORDS
public abstract String getSQLKeywords() throws SQLException
Get a list of all SQL keywords that are not also SQL92 keywords supported by the database in use.
Returns: the list, comma separated

GETSYSTEMFUNCTIONS
public abstract String getSystemFunctions() throws SQLException
Get the list of system functions supported by the database in use.
Returns: the list, comma separated

GETTABLES
public abstract ResultSet getTables(String catalog, String schemaPattern, String tableNamePattern, String types[]) throws SQLException
Return a list of user or system tables or views available in a catalog. The search criteria are catalog, schema, table name, and table type. The results are ordered by TABLE_TYPE, TABLE_SCHEM, and TABLE_NAME.
The ResultSet has these columns:

TABLE_CAT String ⇨ table catalog (may be null)

TABLE_SCHEM String ⇨ table schema (may be null)

TABLE_NAME String ⇨ table name

TABLE_TYPE String ⇨ table type; possible types are "TABLE," "VIEW," "SYSTEM TABLE," "GLOBAL TEMPORARY," "LOCAL TEMPORARY," "ALIAS," "SYNONYM".

REMARKS String ⇨ explanatory comment on the table

Parameters: catalog — a catalog name; "" retrieves those without a catalog; a null means that the catalog name must be suppressed from the selection criteria.

schemaPattern — a schema name pattern; "" retrieves those without a schema.

tableNamePattern — a table name pattern

types — a list of table types to include or null to return all types

Returns: a ResultSet; each row is a table description
See also: getSearchStringEscape, getTableTypes

GETTABLETYPES
public abstract ResultSet getTableTypes() throws SQLException
Get all the table types available in the current database. The results are ordered by table type. The table type is:

TABLE_TYPE String ⇨ table type; possible types are "TABLE," "VIEW," "SYSTEM TABLE," "GLOBAL TEMPORARY," "LOCAL TEMPORARY," "ALIAS," "SYNONYM"

Returns: a ResultSet; each row contains a table type.

GETTABLEPRIVILEGES
public abstract ResultSet getTablePrivileges(String catalog, String schemaPattern, String tableNamePattern) throws SQLException

Return a description of table privileges. Remark: Privileges may not apply to all columns of the table. They are ordered by TABLE_SCHEM, TABLE_NAME, and PRIVILEGE.

The ResultSet has these columns:

TABLE_CAT String ⇨ table catalog (may be null)

TABLE_SCHEM String ⇨ table schema (may be null)

TABLE_NAME String ⇨ table name

GRANTOR ⇨ grantor of access (may be null)

GRANTEE String ⇨ grantee of access

PRIVILEGE String ⇨ name of access (SELECT, INSERT, UPDATE, REFRENCES, . . .)

IS_GRANTABLE String ⇨ "YES," grantee is permitted to grant to others; "NO," no grant allowed; null, unknown

Parameters: catalog — a catalog name; "" retrieves those without a catalog; a null means that the catalog name must be suppressed from the selection criteria.

schemaPattern — a schema name pattern; "" retrieves those without a schema.

tableNamePattern — a table name pattern

Returns: a ResultSet; each row is a description of a table privilege.

See also: getSearchStringEscape

GETTIMEDATEFUNCTIONS
public abstract String getTimeDateFunctions() throws SQLException
Get a list of time and date functions.
Returns: a comma-separated list of time and date functions

GETTYPEINFO
public abstract ResultSet getTypeInfo() throws SQLException
Get information about all the standard SQL types supported by this database. The results are ordered by DATA_TYPE. Type definitions that are closer to their corresponding java.sql.Types are listed first. The ResultSet contains these columns:

TYPE_NAME String ⇨ type name

DATA_TYPE short ⇨ SQL data type from java.sql.Types

PRECISION int ⇨ maximum precision

LITERAL_PREFIX String ⇨ prefix used to quote a literal (may be null)

LITERAL_SUFFIX String ⇨ suffix used to quote a literal (may be null)

CREATE_PARAMS String ⇨ parameters used to create the type (may be null)

NULLABLE short ⇨ one of these values:

> typeNoNulls – does not allow NULL values
>
> typeNullable – allows NULL values
>
> typeNullableUnknown – nullability unknown

CASE_SENSITIVE boolean ⇨ says if type is case sensitive

SEARCHABLE short ⇨ support in WHERE clause:

> typePredNone – No support
>
> typePredChar – Only supported with WHERE . . LIKE
>
> typePredBasic – Supported except for WHERE . . LIKE
>
> typeSearchable – Supported for all WHERE . .

UNSIGNED_ATTRIBUTE boolean ⇨ true if unsigned

FIXED_PREC_SCALE boolean ⇨ true if the precision is fixed

AUTO_INCREMENT boolean ⇨ true if it can be used for an autoincrement value

LOCAL_TYPE_NAME String ⇨ localized version of type name (may be null)

MINIMUM_SCALE short ⇨ minimum scale supported

MAXIMUM_SCALE short ⇨ maximum scale supported

SQL_DATA_TYPE int ⇨ unused

SQL_DATETIME_SUB int ⇨ unused

NUM_PREC_RADIX int ⇨ radix – usually 2 or 10

Returns: a ResultSet; each row is a description of a SQL type supported by this database.

    GETURL
        public abstract String getURL() throws SQLException
        Get the url for the current database.
Returns: the url or null if it is not possible to find it

GETUSERNAME
   public abstract String getUserName() throws SQLException
Get the database user name for the current session.
Returns: the current session's user name

GETVERSIONCOLUMNS
   public abstract ResultSet getVersionColumns(String catalog, String schema, String table) throws SQLException
Return information about the columns of a table that are automatically updated when any field in a row is updated.
   The ResultSet contains these columns:

SCOPE short ⇨ unused

COLUMN_NAME String ⇨ column name

DATA_TYPE short ⇨ SQL data type from java.sql.Types

TYPE_NAME String ⇨ database type name

COLUMN_SIZE int ⇨ precision

BUFFER_LENGTH int ⇨ length of column value in bytes

DECIMAL_DIGITS short ⇨ scale

PSEUDO_COLUMN short ⇨ the state of a column:

   versionColumnUnknown – may or may not be pseudocolumn

   versionColumnNotPseudo – is not a pseudocolumn

   versionColumnPseudo – is a pseudocolumn

Parameters: catalog – a catalog name; "" retrieves those without a catalog; a null means that the catalog name must be suppressed from the selection criteria.

schema – a schema name; "" retrieves those without a schema.

table – a table name

Returns: a ResultSet; each row is a column description.

ISCATALOGATSTART
   public abstract boolean isCatalogAtStart() throws SQLException
Checks whether a catalog appears at the start of a qualified table name or at the end of a qualified table name.
Returns: true if it appears at the start

ISREADONLY
   public abstract boolean isReadOnly() throws SQLException

Checks whetehr the database is in read-only mode.
Returns: true if so

NULLSARESORTEDATSTART
public abstract boolean nullsAreSortedAtStart() throws SQLException
Checks whether NULL values sorted at the start regardless of sort order.
Returns: true if so

NULLSARESORTEDATEND
public abstract boolean nullsAreSortedAtEnd() throws SQLException
Checks whether NULL values sorted at the end regardless of sort order.
Returns: true if so

NULLSARESORTEDHIGH
public abstract boolean nullsAreSortedHigh() throws SQLException
Checks whether NULL values sorted high.
Returns: true if so

NULLSARESORTEDLOW
public abstract boolean nullsAreSortedLow() throws SQLException
Checks whether NULL values sorted low.
Returns: true if so

NULLPLUSNONNULLISNULL
public abstract boolean nullPlusNonNullIsNull() throws SQLException
Checks whether a concatenation of NULL values is a NULL value.
Returns: true if so

STORESUPPERCASEIDENTIFIERS
public abstract boolean storesUpperCaseIdentifiers() throws SQLException
Checks whether the database automatically converts unquoted SQL identifiers to uppercase.
Returns: true if so

STORESLOWERCASEIDENTIFIERS
public abstract boolean storesLowerCaseIdentifiers() throws SQLException
Checks whether the database automatically converts unquoted SQL identifiers to lowercase.
Returns: true if so

STORESLOWERCASEQUOTEDIDENTIFIERS
public abstract boolean storesLowerCaseQuotedIdentifiers() throws SQLException
Checks whether the database automatically converts quoted SQL identifiers to lower case.
Returns: true if so

STORESMIXEDCASEIDENTIFIERS
public abstract boolean storesMixedCaseIdentifiers() throws SQLException
Checks whether the database stores mixed case unquoted identifers.
Returns: true if so

STORESMIXEDCASEQUOTEDIDENTIFIERS
public abstract boolean storesMixedCaseQuotedIdentifiers() throws SQLException
Checks whether the database stores mixed-case quoted identifiers.
Returns: true if so

STORESUPPERCASEQUOTEDIDENTIFIERS
public abstract boolean storesUpperCaseQuotedIdentifiers() throws SQLException
Checks whether the database automatically converts quoted SQL identifiers to uppercase.
Returns: true if so

SUPPORTSALTERTABLEWITHADDCOLUMN
public abstract boolean supportsAlterTableWithAddColumn() throws SQLException
Checks whether an "ALTER TABLE" clause may be used to add a column.
Returns: true if so

SUPPORTSALTERTABLEWITHDROPCOLUMN
public abstract boolean supportsAlterTableWithDropColumn() throws SQLException
Checks whether "ALTER TABLE" clause may be used to drop a column.
Returns: true if so

SUPPORTSANSI92ENTRYLEVELSQL
public abstract boolean supportsANSI92EntryLevelSQL() throws SQLException
Checks whether the ANSI92 entry level SQL grammar is supported. Must be true for all JDBC-compliant drivers.
Returns: true if so

SUPPORTSANSI92INTERMEDIATESQL
public   abstract   boolean   supportsANSI92IntermediateSQL()   throws
SQLException
Checks whether the ANSI92 intermediate SQL grammar is supported.
Returns: true if so

SUPPORTSANSI92FULLSQL
public abstract boolean supportsANSI92FullSQL() throws SQLException
Checks whether the ANSI92 full SQL grammar is supported.
Returns: true if so

SUPPORTSCATALOGSINDATAMANIPULATION
public   abstract   boolean   supportsCatalogsInDataManipulation()   throws
SQLException
Checks whether a catalog name can be used in a DML statement.
Returns: true if so

SUPPORTSCATALOGSINPROCEDURECALLS
public   abstract   boolean   supportsCatalogsInProcedureCalls()   throws
SQLException
Checks whether a catalog name can be used in a procedure call statement.
Returns: true if so

SUPPORTSCATALOGSINTABLEDEFINITIONS
public   abstract   boolean   supportsCatalogsInTableDefinitions()   throws
SQLException
Checks whether a catalog name can be used in a table definition (DDL) statement.
Returns: true if so

SUPPORTSCATALOGSININDEXDEFINITIONS
public   abstract   boolean   supportsCatalogsInIndexDefinitions()   throws
SQLException
Checks whether a catalog name can be used in an index definition (DDL) statement.
Returns: true if so

SUPPORTSCATALOGSINPRIVILEGEDEFINITIONS
public abstract boolean supportsCatalogsInPrivilegeDefinitions() throws
SQLException

Checks whether a catalog name can be used in a privilege definition statement.
Returns: true if so

SUPPORTSCOLUMNALIASING

public abstract boolean supportsColumnAliasing() throws SQLException
Checks whether column aliasing is supported to provide name to computed columns with the AS SQL keyword.
Returns: true if so

SUPPORTSCONVERT

public abstract boolean supportsConvert() throws SQLException
Checks whether the CONVERT function is supported between SQL types.
Returns: true if so

SUPPORTSCONVERT

public abstract boolean supportsConvert(int fromType, int toType) throws SQLException
Checks whether the CONVERT function is supported between the given SQL types.
Parameters: fromType — the type to convert from

toType — the type to convert to

Returns: true if so

SUPPORTSCORRELATEDSUBQUERIES

public abstract boolean supportsCorrelatedSubqueries() throws SQLException
Checks whether correlated subqueries are supported.
Returns: true if so

SUPPORTSCORESQLGRAMMAR

public abstract boolean supportsCoreSQLGrammar() throws SQLException
Checks whether the ODBC Core SQL grammar is supported.
Returns: true if so

SUPPORTSDATADEFINITIONANDDATAMANIPULATIONTRANSACTIONS

public abstract boolean supportsDataDefinitionAndDataManipulation Transactions() throws SQLException
Checks whether both data definition (DDL) and data manipulation (DML) statements are supported within a transaction.
Returns: true if so

SUPPORTSDATAMANIPULATIONTRANSACTIONSONLY

public abstract boolean supportsDataManipulationTransactionsOnly() throws SQLException

Checks whether only data manipulation statements are supported within a transaction.

Returns: true if so

SUPPORTSDIFFERENTTABLECORRELATIONNAMES

public abstract boolean supportsDifferentTableCorrelationNames() throws SQLException

Checks whether table correlation names are supported and if they must be different from the table names.

Returns: true if so

SUPPORTSEXPRESSIONSINORDERBY

public abstract boolean supportsExpressionsInOrderBy() throws SQLException

Checks whether expressions are supported in ORDER BY lists.

Returns: true if so

SUPPORTSEXTENDEDSQLGRAMMAR

public abstract boolean supportsExtendedSQLGrammar() throws SQLException

Checks whether the ODBC Extended SQL grammar is supported.

Returns: true if so

SUPPORTSFULLOUTERJOINS

public abstract boolean supportsFullOuterJoins() throws SQLException

Checks whether full nested outer joins are supported.

Returns: true if so

SUPPORTSGROUPBY

public abstract boolean supportsGroupBy() throws SQLException

Checks whether the SQL GROUP BY clause is supported.

Returns: true if so

SUPPORTSGROUPBYUNRELATED

public abstract boolean supportsGroupByUnrelated() throws SQLException

Checks whether a GROUP BY clause can use columns that are not in the SELECT statement.

Returns: true if so

SUPPORTSGROUPBYBEYONDSELECT

public abstract boolean supportsGroupByBeyondSelect() throws SQLException

Checks whether a GROUP BY clause can add columns that are not in the SELECT statement, provided it specifies all the columns in the SELECT clause.

Returns: true if so

SUPPORTSINTEGRITYENHANCEMENTFACILITY

public abstract boolean supportsIntegrityEnhancementFacility() throws SQLException

Checks whether the SQL Integrity Enhancement Facility is supported.

Returns: true if so

SUPPORTSLIKEESCAPECLAUSE

public abstract boolean supportsLikeEscapeClause() throws SQLException

Checks whether the escape character is supported in "LIKE" clauses.

Returns: true if so

SUPPORTSLIMITEDOUTERJOINS

public abstract boolean supportsLimitedOuterJoins() throws SQLException

Checks whether there is limited support for outer joins.

Returns: true if so

SUPPORTSMINIMUMSQLGRAMMAR

public abstract boolean supportsMinimumSQLGrammar() throws SQLException

Checks whether the ODBC Minimum SQL grammar is supported. Must be true for all JDBC-compliant drivers.

Returns: true if so

SUPPORTSMIXEDCASEIDENTIFIERS

public abstract boolean supportsMixedCaseIdentifiers() throws SQLException

Checks whether the database supports unquoted mixed-case identifiers.

Returns: true if so

SUPPORTSMIXEDCASEQUOTEDIDENTIFIERS

public abstract boolean supportsMixedCaseQuotedIdentifiers() throws SQLException

Checks whether the database supports mixed-case quoted identifiers.

Returns: true if so

SUPPORTSMULTIPLERESULTSETS
public abstract boolean supportsMultipleResultSets() throws SQLException
Checks whether multiple ResultSets returned after a single execute are supported.
Returns: true if so

SUPPORTSMULTIPLETRANSACTIONS
public abstract boolean supportsMultipleTransactions() throws SQLException
Checks whether multiple transactions are supported simultaneously on different connections.
Returns: true if so

SUPPORTSNONNULLABLECOLUMNS
public abstract boolean supportsNonNullableColumns() throws SQLException
Checks whether columns can be defined as non-nullable.
Returns: true if so

SUPPORTSOPENCURSORSACROSSCOMMIT
public   abstract   boolean   supportsOpenCursorsAcrossCommit()   throws SQLException
Checks whether cursors can remain open across commits.
Returns: true if so

See also: disableAutoClose

SUPPORTSOPENCURSORSACROSSROLLBACK
public   abstract   boolean   supportsOpenCursorsAcrossRollback()   throws SQLException
Checks whether cursors can remain open across rollbacks.
Returns: true if so

See also: disableAutoClose

SUPPORTSOPENSTATEMENTSACROSSCOMMIT
public   abstract   boolean   supportsOpenStatementsAcrossCommit()   throws SQLException
Checks whether statements can remain open across commits.
Returns: true if so

See also: disableAutoClose

SUPPORTSOPENSTATEMENTSACROSSROLLBACK
public abstract boolean supportsOpenStatementsAcrossRollback() throws SQLException
Checks whether statements can remain open across rollbacks.
Returns: true if so

See also: disableAutoClose

SUPPORTSORDERBYUNRELATED
public abstract boolean supportsOrderByUnrelated() throws SQLException
Checks whether an ORDER BY clause can use columns that are not in the SELECT statement.
Returns: true if so

SUPPORTSOUTERJOINS
public abstract boolean supportsOuterJoins() throws SQLException
Checks whether the database supports outer joins.
Returns: true if so

SUPPORTSPOSITIONEDDELETE
public abstract boolean supportsPositionedDelete() throws SQLException
Checks whether the database supports positioned DELETE.
Returns: true if so

SUPPORTSPOSITIONEDUPDATE
public abstract boolean supportsPositionedUpdate() throws SQLException
Checks whether the database supports positioned UPDATE.
Returns: true if so

SUPPORTSSCHEMASINDATAMANIPULATION
public abstract boolean supportsSchemasInDataManipulation() throws SQLException
Checks whether a schema name can be used in a data manipulation (DML) statement.
Returns: true if so

SUPPORTSSCHEMASINPROCEDURECALLS
public abstract boolean supportsSchemasInProcedureCalls() throws SQLException
Checks whether a schema name can be used in a procedure call statement.
Returns: true if so

SUPPORTSSCHEMASINTABLEDEFINITIONS

public abstract boolean supportsSchemasInTableDefinitions() throws SQLException

Checks whether a schema name can be used in a table definition (DDL) statement.

Returns: true if so

SUPPORTSSCHEMASININDEXDEFINITIONS

public abstract boolean supportsSchemasInIndexDefinitions() throws SQLException

Checks whether a schema name can be used in an index definition (DDL) statement.

Returns: true if so

SUPPORTSSCHEMASINPRIVILEGEDEFINITIONS

public abstract boolean supportsSchemasInPrivilegeDefinitions() throws SQLException

Checks whether a schema name can be used in a privilege definition statement.

Returns: true if so

SUPPORTSSELECTFORUPDATE

public abstract boolean supportsSelectForUpdate() throws SQLException

Checks whether the database supports SELECT for UPDATE clauses.

Returns: true if so

SUPPORTSSTOREDPROCEDURES

public abstract boolean supportsStoredProcedures() throws SQLException

Checks whether the stored procedure escape syntax can be used to call stored procedures.

Returns: true if so

SUPPORTSSUBQUERIESINCOMPARISONS

public abstract boolean supportsSubqueriesInComparisons() throws SQLException

Checks whether subqueries are supported in comparison expressions.

Returns: true if so

SUPPORTSSUBQUERIESINEXISTS

public abstract boolean supportsSubqueriesInExists() throws SQLException

Checks whether subqueries are supported in exists expressions.

Returns: true if so

SUPPORTSSUBQUERIESININS
public abstract boolean supportsSubqueriesInIns() throws SQLException
Checks whether subqueries are supported in IN statements.
Returns: true if so

SUPPORTSSUBQUERIESINQUANTIFIEDS
public abstract boolean supportsSubqueriesInQuantifieds() throws SQLException
Checks whether subqueries are supported in quantified expressions.
Returns: true if so

SUPPORTSTABLECORRELATIONNAMES
public abstract boolean supportsTableCorrelationNames() throws SQLException
Checks whether table correlation names are supported.
Returns: true if so

SUPPORTSTRANSACTIONS
public abstract boolean supportsTransactions() throws SQLException
Checks whether the database supports transactions.
Returns: true if transactions are supported

SUPPORTSTRANSACTIONISOLATIONLEVEL
public abstract boolean supportsTransactionIsolationLevel(int level) throws SQLException
Checks whether the database supports the given transaction isolation level.
Parameters: level — the values are defined in java.sql.Connection.

Returns: true if so

See also: Connection

SUPPORTSUNION
public abstract boolean supportsUnion() throws SQLException
Checks whether the database supports SQL UNION.
Returns: true if so

SUPPORTSUNIONALL
public abstract boolean supportsUnionAll() throws SQLException
Checks whether the database supports SQL UNION ALL.
Returns: true if so

USESLOCALFILES
public abstract boolean usesLocalFiles() throws SQLException
Checks whether the database stores tables in a local file.
Returns: true if so

USESLOCALFILEPERTABLE
public abstract boolean usesLocalFilePerTable() throws SQLException
Checks whether the database uses a file for each table.
Returns: true if the database uses a local file for each table

Interface java.sql.Driver

public interface Driver

extends Object

Drivers are loaded by the DriverManager to provide connections to specific databases. A user can load and register a JDBC driver by calling Class.forName("a.specific.driver"). The DriverManager will use this driver if it can successfully connect to a given database URL.
See also: DriverManager, Connection

METHODS:

ACCEPTSURL
public abstract boolean acceptsURL(String url) throws SQLException
This method is used to check whether this URL syntax is recognized by the driver and if it is capable of opening a connection to it. A driver will usually return true if it is able to understand the subprotocol field of the given URL.
Parameters: url — the URL of the database

Returns: true if this driver can connect to the given URL

CONNECT
public abstract Connection connect(String url, Properties info) throws SQLException
This method is used to get a Connection object for a particular database URL. The DriverManager invokes this method for all Drivers that are loaded, and receives either a null if the Driver is not appropriate for this connection or a Connection object in the opposite case. Note that a SQLException is thrown by the Driver if it has trouble connecting to the database.

Connection arguments may be passed as tag/value pairs via java.util.Properties. At minimum, "user" and "password" properties are included in the Properties.
Parameters: url — the URL of the database to connect to

info — a list of tag/value pairs as connection arguments

Returns: a Connection to the URL

GETMAJORVERSION
public abstract int getMajorVersion()
Get the driver's major version number.

GETMINORVERSION
public abstract int getMinorVersion()
Get the driver's minor version number.

GETPROPERTYINFO
public abstract DriverPropertyInfo[] getPropertyInfo(String url, Properties info) throws SQLException
Get the necessary properties that must be provided to use this Driver. The property list may vary according to the values supplied so far, so it may be necessary to iterate though several calls to this method to discover all the mandatory properties.
Parameters: url — the URL of the database to connect to

info — a list of tag/value pair properties

Returns: an array of DriverPropertyInfo objects; this array may be empty if no properties are required.

JDBCCOMPLIANT
public abstract boolean jdbcCompliant()
Report whether the Driver is a genuine JDBC COMPLIANT[TM] driver.
The Driver reports true only if it passes the JDBC compliance tests, meaning that it provides full support for both the JDBC API and for SQL 92 Entry Level.
Returns: true if so

Interface java.sql.PreparedStatement

public interface PreparedStatement

extends Object

extends Statement

It is possible to precompile SQL statements and execute them with different parameters as many times as wanted. setXXX methods are used to set IN parameter values. They must specify types compatible with the defined SQL type of the input parameter.

Arbitrary parameter type conversions are allowed, but then the setObject method should be used with a SQL type to specify the target type.

See also: prepareStatement, ResultSet

METHODS:

CLEARPARAMETERS

public abstract void clearParameters() throws SQLException

clearParameters() immediately releases the resources used by the current parameter values. Parameter values are not automatically cleared after execution of a preparedStatement, so they can be used for repeated use.

Returns: nothing

EXECUTE

public abstract boolean execute() throws SQLException

This method executes the statement with the IN parameter values just set, if any. Note that execute is normally used for prepared statements that return multiple results.

Returns: true if the next result is a ResultSet; false if it is an update count or there is no more result

See also: execute

EXECUTEQUERY

public abstract ResultSet executeQuery() throws SQLException

executeQuery() is used to execute prepared SQL queries (SELECT only). It returns a ResultSet.

Returns: a ResultSet that contains the data produced by the query; never null

EXECUTEUPDATE

public abstract int executeUpdate() throws SQLException

executeUpdate is used to execute a SQL INSERT, UPDATE, or DELETE statement. It also supports SQL statements that return nothing, such as SQL DDL.

Returns: the number of rows affected for INSERT, UPDATE, or DELETE; or 0 for SQL statements that return nothing

SETASCIISTREAM

public abstract void setAsciiStream(int parameterIndex, InputStream x, int length) throws SQLException

setAsciiStream() is used to set very large LONGVARCHAR parameters. The ASCII data may be sent using a java.io.inputStream. JDBC stops sending data when it reaches EOF (end of file). ASCII characters are converted to the database CHAR format.

Parameters: parameterIndex — the parameter index begins at 1.

x — the ascii data stream

length — the data length in bytes

SETBIGDECIMAL

public abstract void setBigDecimal(int parameterIndex, BigDecimal x) throws SQLException

Supplies a java.math.BigDecimal value that will be converted to a SQL NUMERIC value when sent to the database.

Parameters: parameterIndex — the parameter index begins at 1.

x — the parameter value

SETBINARYSTREAM

public abstract void setBinaryStream(int parameterIndex, InputStream x, int length) throws SQLException

setBinaryStream() is used to set very large LONGVARBINARY parameters. The binary data may be sent using a java.io.inputStream. JDBC stops sending data when it reaches EOF (end of file).

Parameters: parameterIndex — the parameter index begins at 1.

x — the binary data stream

length — the data length in bytes

SETBOOLEAN

public abstract void setBoolean(int parameterIndex, boolean x) throws SQLException

Supplies a Java boolean value that is converted to a SQL BIT value when sent to the database.

Parameters: parameterIndex — the parameter index begins at 1.

x — the parameter value

SETBYTE
   public abstract void setByte(int parameterIndex, byte x) throws SQLException
Supplies a Java byte value that is converted to a SQL TINYINT value when sent to the database.
Parameters: parameterIndex − the parameter index begins at 1.

x − the parameter value

SETBYTES
   public abstract void setBytes(int parameterIndex, byte x[]) throws SQLException
Supplies a Java array of bytes that is converted to a SQL VARBINARY or LONG-VARBINARY when sent to the database.
Parameters: parameterIndex − the parameter index begins at 1.

x − the parameter value

SETDATE
   public abstract void setDate(int parameterIndex, Date x) throws SQLException
Supplies a java.sql.Date value that is converted to a SQL DATE value when sent to the database.
Parameters: parameterIndex − the parameter index begins at 1.

x − the parameter value

SETDOUBLE
   public abstract void setDouble(int parameterIndex, double x) throws SQLException
Supplies a Java double value that is converted to a SQL DOUBLE value when sent to the database.
Parameters: parameterIndex − the parameter index begins at 1.

x − the parameter value

SETFLOAT
   public abstract void setFloat(int parameterIndex, float x) throws SQLException
Supplies a Java float value that is converted to a SQL FLOAT value when sent to the database.
Parameters: parameterIndex − the parameter index begins at 1.

x − the parameter value

SETINT
public abstract void setInt(int parameterIndex, int x) throws SQLException
Supplies a Java int value that is converted to a SQL INTEGER value when sent to the database.
Parameters: parameterIndex – the parameter index begins at 1.

x – the parameter value

SETLONG
public abstract void setLong(int parameterIndex, long x) throws SQLException
Supplies a Java long value that is converted to a SQL BIGINT value when sent to the database.
Parameters: parameterIndex – the parameter index begins at 1.

x – the parameter value

SETNULL
public abstract void setNull(int parameterIndex, int sqlType) throws SQLException
Supplies a SQL NULL value. The parameter's SQL type must be supplied.
Parameters: parameterIndex – the parameter index begins at 1.

sqlType – a SQL type code (see java.sql.Types)

SETOBJECT
public abstract void setObject(int parameterIndex, Object x,int targetSqlType, int scale) throws SQLException
Supplies a parameter value using an object that is converted to the targetSqlType when sent to the database. Abstract data types may be passed using a Driver specific Java type and using java.sql.types.OTHER as targetSqlType.
Parameters: parameterIndex – the parameter index begins at 1.

x – the object containing the input parameter value

targetSqlType – a SQL-type code (see java.sql.Types)

scale – Number of digits after the decimal for java.sql.Types.DECIMAL or java.sql.Types.NUMERIC types. Ignored for other types.

See also: Types

SETOBJECT
public abstract void setObject(int parameterIndex, Object x, int targetSqlType) throws SQLException
Same as setObject() but assumes scale of zero.

SETOBJECT

public abstract void setObject(int parameterIndex, Object x) throws SQLException

Same as setObject() but uses the standard mapping from Java Object types to SQL types.

Parameters: parameterIndex — the parameter index begins at 1.

x — the object containing the input parameter value

SETSHORT

public abstract void setShort(int parameterIndex, short x) throws SQLException

Supplies a Java short value that is converted to a SQL SMALLINT value when sent to the database.

Parameters: parameterIndex — the parameter index begins at 1.

x — the parameter value

SETSTRING

public abstract void setString(int parameterIndex, String x) throws SQLException

Supplies a Java String value that is converted to a SQL VARCHAR or LONGVAR-CHAR value when sent to the database.

Parameters: parameterIndex — the parameter index begins at 1.

x — the parameter value

SETTIME

public abstract void setTime(int parameterIndex, Time x) throws SQLException

Supplies a java.sql.Time value that is converted to a SQL TIME value when sent to the database.

Parameters: parameterIndex — the parameter index begins at 1.

x — the parameter value

SETTIMESTAMP

public abstract void setTimestamp(int parameterIndex, Timestamp x) throws SQLException

Supplies a java.sql.Timestamp value that is converted to a SQL TIMESTAMP value when sent to the database.

Parameters: parameterIndex — the parameter index begins at 1.

x — the parameter value

SETUNICODESTREAM
public abstract void setUnicodeStream(int parameterIndex, InputStream x,int length) throws SQLException

setUnicodeStream() is used to set very large LONGVARCHAR parameters. The UNICODE data may be sent using a java.io.inputStream. JDBC stops sending data when it reaches EOF (end of file). UNICODE characters are converted to the database CHAR format.

Parameters: parameterIndex – the parameter index begins at 1.

x – the unicode data stream

length – the data length in bytes

Interface java.sql.ResultSet

public interface ResultSet

extends Object

SQL queries and many DatabaseMetaData methods return rows of data in ResultSet objects. Such rows must be retrieved in sequence using the ResultSet methods. The next() method is used to scroll through the rows. A ResultSet maintains a cursor pointing to its current row of data. The cursor is initially positioned before the first row. The "next" method moves the cursor to the next row.

Column values must also be retrieved one by one. The getXXX methods make it possible to access these columns either using the index number of the column or the name of the column (which is case insensitive). Using the column index is the most efficient. Note that the first column is numbered 1. The column values must be retrieved from left to right and only once per column.

See also: executeQuery, getResultSet, ResultSetMetaData

METHODS:

CLEARWARNINGS
public abstract void clearWarnings() throws SQLException

Clears all SQLWarnings. getWarning() will return null after a clearWarning().

Returns: nothing

CLOSE
public abstract void close() throws SQLException

Releases all resources associated to the ResultSet. Normally, a ResultSet is automatically closed by the Statement that generated it when that Statement is closed,

reexecuted, or is used to retrieve the next result from a sequence of multiple results. The garbage collector also closes ResultSets when they are no longer used.
Returns: nothing

FINDCOLUMN
   public abstract int findColumn(String columnName) throws SQLException
Return the column index from its column name.
Parameters: columnName – the name of the column

Returns: the column index

GETASCIISTREAM
   public abstract InputStream getAsciiStream(int columnIndex) throws SQLException
This method can be used to retrieve large LONGVARCHAR values. If necessary, the JDBC driver converts the data from database format to ASCII.
Parameters: columnIndex – the column index begins at 1.

Returns: a Java input stream; if the value is SQL NULL, then the result is null.

GETASCIISTREAM
   public abstract InputStream getAsciiStream(String columnName) throws SQLException
This method can be used to retrieve large LONGVARCHAR values. If necessary, the JDBC driver converts the data from database format to ASCII.
Parameters: columnName – the name of the column

Returns: a Java input stream; if the value is SQL NULL, then the result is null.,

GETBIGDECIMAL
   public abstract BigDecimal getBigDecimal(int columnIndex, int scale) throws SQLException
Get the value of a column as a java.math.BigDecimal object.
Parameters: columnIndex – the column index begins at 1.

scale – the number of digits to the right of the decimal

Returns: the column value; if the value is SQL NULL, then the result is null.

GETBIGDECIMAL
   public abstract BigDecimal getBigDecimal(String columnName, int scale) throws SQLException
Get the value of a column as a java.math.BigDecimal object.

Parameters: columnName — the name of the column

scale — the number of digits to the right of the decimal

Returns: the column value; if the value is SQL NULL, then the result is null.

GETBINARYSTREAM
public abstract InputStream getBinaryStream(int columnIndex) throws SQLException
This method can be used to retrieve large LONGVARBINARY values.
Parameters: columnIndex — the column index begins at 1.

Returns: a Java input stream that delivers the database column value as a stream of uninterpreted bytes; if the value is SQL NULL, then the result is null.

GETBINARYSTREAM
public abstract InputStream getBinaryStream(String columnName) throws SQLException
This method can be used to retrieve large LONGVARBINARY values.
Parameters: columnName — the name of the column

Returns: a Java input stream that delivers the database column value as a stream of uninterpreted bytes. If the value is SQL NULL, then the result is null.

GETBOOLEAN
public abstract boolean getBoolean(int columnIndex) throws SQLException
Get the value of a column as a Java boolean.
Parameters: columnIndex — the column index begins at 1.

Returns: the column value; if the value is SQL NULL, then the result is false.

GETBOOLEAN
public abstract boolean getBoolean(String columnName) throws SQLException
Get the value of a column as a Java boolean.
Parameters: columnName — the name of the column

Returns: the column value; if the value is SQL NULL, then the result is false.

GETBYTE
public abstract byte getByte(int columnIndex) throws SQLException
Get the value of a column as a Java byte.
Parameters: columnIndex — the column index begins at 1.

Returns: the column value; if the value is SQL NULL, then the result is 0.

GETBYTE
    public abstract byte getByte(String columnName) throws SQLException
    Get the value of a column as a Java byte.
Parameters: columnName – the name of the column

Returns: the column value; if the value is SQL NULL, then the result is 0.

GETBYTES
    public abstract byte[] getBytes(int columnIndex) throws SQLException
    Get the value of a column as an array of Java bytes representing the raw values returned by the driver.
Parameters: columnIndex – the column index begins at 1.

Returns: the column value; if the value is SQL NULL, then the result is null.

GETBYTES
    public abstract byte[] getBytes(String columnName) throws SQLException
    Get the value of a column as an array of Java bytes representing the raw values returned by the driver.
Parameters: columnName – the name of the column

Returns: the column value; if the value is SQL NULL, then the result is null.

GETCURSORNAME
    public abstract String getCursorName() throws SQLException
    JDBC supports positioned updates and positioned deletes. This method returns the name of the current SQL cursor used for this ResultSet.
Returns: the ResultSet's SQL cursor name

GETDATE
    public abstract Date getDate(int columnIndex) throws SQLException
    Get the value of a column as a java.sql.Date object.
Parameters: columnIndex – the column index begins at 1.

Returns: the column value; if the value is SQL NULL, then the result is null.

GETDATE
    public abstract Date getDate(String columnName) throws SQLException
    Get the value of a column as a java.sql.Date object.
Parameters: columnName – the name of the column

Returns: the column value; if the value is SQL NULL, then the result is null.

GETDOUBLE

public abstract double getDouble(int columnIndex) throws SQLException
Get the value of a column as a Java double.

Parameters: columnIndex – the column index begins at 1.

Returns: the column value; if the value is SQL NULL, then the result is 0.

GETDOUBLE

public abstract double getDouble(String columnName) throws SQLException
Get the value of a column as a Java double.

Parameters: columnName – the name of the column

Returns: the column value; if the value is SQL NULL, then the result is 0.

GETFLOAT

public abstract float getFloat(int columnIndex) throws SQLException
Get the value of a column as a Java float.

Parameters: columnIndex – the column index begins at 1.

Returns: the column value; if the value is SQL NULL, then the result is 0.

GETFLOAT

public abstract float getFloat(String columnName) throws SQLException
Get the value of a column as a Java float.

Parameters: columnName – the name of the column

Returns: the column value; if the value is SQL NULL, then the result is 0.

GETINT

public abstract int getInt(int columnIndex) throws SQLException
Get the value of a column as a Java int.

Parameters: columnIndex – the column index begins at 1.

Returns: the column value; if the value is SQL NULL, then the result is 0.

GETINT

public abstract int getInt(String columnName) throws SQLException
Get the value of a column as a Java int.

Parameters: columnName – the name of the column

Returns: the column value; if the value is SQL NULL, then the result is 0.

GETLONG
   public abstract long getLong(int columnIndex) throws SQLException
   Get the value of a column as a Java long.
Parameters: columnIndex – the column index begins at 1.

Returns: the column value; if the value is SQL NULL, then the result is 0.

GETLONG
   public abstract long getLong(String columnName) throws SQLException
   Get the value of a column as a Java long.
Parameters: columnName – the name of the column

Returns: the column value; if the value is SQL NULL, then the result is 0.

GETSHORT
   public abstract short getShort(int columnIndex) throws SQLException
   Get the value of a column as a Java short.
Parameters: columnIndex – the column index begins at 1.

Returns: the column value; if the value is SQL NULL, then the result is 0.

GETSHORT
   public abstract short getShort(String columnName) throws SQLException
   Get the value of a column as a Java short.
Parameters: columnName – the name of the column

Returns: the column value; if the value is SQL NULL, then the result is 0.

GETSTRING
   public abstract String getString(int columnIndex) throws SQLException
   Get the value of a column as a Java String.
Parameters: columnIndex – the column index begins at 1.

Returns: the column value; if the value is SQL NULL, then the result is 0.

GETSTRING
   public abstract String getString(String columnName) throws SQLException
   Get the value of a column as a Java String.
Parameters: columnName – the name of the column

Returns: the column value; if the value is SQL NULL, then the result is null.

GETTIME
public abstract Time getTime(int columnIndex) throws SQLException
Get the value of a column as a java.sql.Time object.
Parameters: columnIndex – the column index begins at 1.

Returns: the column value; if the value is SQL NULL, then the result is null.

GETTIME
public abstract Time getTime(String columnName) throws SQLException
Get the value of a column as a java.sql.Time object.
Parameters: columnName – the name of the column

Returns: the column value; if the value is SQL NULL, then the result is null.

GETTIMESTAMP
public abstract Timestamp getTimestamp(int columnIndex) throws SQLException
Get the value of a column as a java.sql.Timestamp object.
Parameters: columnIndex – the column index begins at 1.

Returns: the column value; if the value is SQL NULL, then the result is null.

GETTIMESTAMP
public abstract Timestamp getTimestamp(String columnName) throws SQLException
Get the value of a column as a java.sql.Timestamp object.
Parameters: columnName – the name of the column

Returns: the column value; if the value is SQL NULL, then the result is null.

GETUNICODESTREAM
public abstract InputStream getUnicodeStream(int columnIndex) throws SQLException
This method can be used to retrieve large LONGVARCHAR values. If necessary, the JDBC driver converts the data from database format to Unicode.
Parameters: columnIndex – the column index begins at 1.

Returns: a Java input stream; if the value is SQL NULL, then the result is null.

GETUNICODESTREAM
public abstract InputStream getUnicodeStream(String columnName) throws SQLException
This method can be used to retrieve large LONGVARCHAR values. If necessary, the JDBC driver converts the data from database format to Unicode.

Parameters: columnName — the name of the column

Returns: a Java input stream the column value; if the value is SQL NULL, then the result is null.

GETMETADATA
public abstract ResultSetMetaData getMetaData() throws SQLException
A ResultSetMetaData object dynamically provides information regarding a ResultSet. This method returns such an object. It is useful, for example, for getting the number of columns and their types from a ResultSet.
Returns: a ResultSetMetaData object

GETOBJECT
public abstract Object getObject(int columnIndex) throws SQLException
Get the value of a column as a Java object. The type of the Java object is the Java object type corresponding to the column's SQL type according to standard JDBC-type mapping. It can also be used to read database-specific abstract data types.
Parameters: columnIndex — the column index begins at 1.

Returns: a java.lang.Object holding the column value

GETOBJECT
public abstract Object getObject(String columnName) throws SQLException
Get the value of a column as a Java object. The type of the Java object is the Java object type corresponding to the column's SQL type according to the standard JDBC-type mapping. It can also be used to read database-specific abstract data types.
Parameters: columnName — the name of the column

Returns: a java.lang.Object holding the column value

GETWARNINGS
public abstract SQLWarning getWarnings() throws SQLException
Get the first warning reported by calls on the current ResultSet. The next warnings are chained to this SQLWarning and are automatically cleared each time a new row is read.
Returns: the first SQLWarning or null

NEXT
public abstract boolean next() throws SQLException
This method is used to scan a ResultSet's rows. The first call to this method makes the first row the current row; the second call makes the second row the cur-

rent row, and so forth. Note that the next() method automatically closes input streams used in conjunction with the getXXXStream() methods and clears the warning chain of the ResultSet.

Returns: true if the new current row is valid; false when there are no more rows

WASNULL
public abstract boolean wasNull() throws SQLException
If a column contains a SQL NULL value, this method returns true. wasNull() cannot be invoked before getting the column's value with one of the getXXX() methods.

Returns: true if last column read was SQL NULL

Interface java.sql.ResultSetMetaData

public interface ResultSetMetaData

extends Object

All ResultSetMetaData methods return information related to ResultSets. They may be used to dynamically discover the characteristics of a ResultSet.

VARIABLES:

COLUMNNONULLS
public final static int columnNoNulls
NULL values are not allowed.

COLUMNNULLABLE
public final static int columnNullable
 NULL values are allowed.

COLUMNNULLABLEUNKNOWN
public final static int columnNullableUnknown
The nullability is unknown.

METHODS:

GETCATALOGNAME
public abstract String getCatalogName(int column) throws SQLException
Get the column's table's catalog name.

Parameters: columnIndex – the column index begins at 1.

Returns: column name; "" if no catalog name available

GETCOLUMNCOUNT

public abstract int getColumnCount() throws SQLException
Get the number of columns in the ResultSet.

Returns: the number

GETCOLUMNDISPLAYSIZE

public abstract int getColumnDisplaySize(int column) throws SQLException
Get the column's normal maximum width in chararcters.

Parameters: columnIndex – the column index begins at 1.

Returns: the maximum width

GETCOLUMNLABEL

public abstract String getColumnLabel(int column) throws SQLException
Get the suggested column label.

Parameters: columnIndex – the column index begins at 1.

Returns: the suggested column label

GETCOLUMNNAME

public abstract String getColumnName(int column) throws SQLException
Get a column's name.

Parameters: columnIndex – the column index begins at 1.

Returns: the column name

GETCOLUMNTYPE

public abstract int getColumnType(int column) throws SQLException
Get a column's SQL type.

Parameters: columnIndex – the column index begins at 1.

Returns: the SQL type

See also: Types

GETCOLUMNTYPENAME

public abstract String getColumnTypeName(int column) throws SQLException
Get a column's data source specific type name.

Parameters: columnIndex – the column index begins at 1.

Returns: the type name

GETPRECISION
public abstract int getPrecision(int column) throws SQLException
Get a column's number of decimal digits.
Parameters: columnIndex – the column index begins at 1.

Returns: the precision

GETSCALE
public abstract int getScale(int column) throws SQLException
Get a column's number of digits to right of decimal.
Parameters: columnIndex – the column index begins at 1.

Returns: the scale

GETSCHEMANAME
public abstract String getSchemaName(int column) throws SQLException
Get a column's table's schema.
Parameters: columnIndex – the column index begins at 1.

Returns: the schema name; "" if no schema name available

GETTABLENAME
public abstract String getTableName(int column) throws SQLException
Get a column's table name.
Returns: the table name; "" if not available

ISAUTOINCREMENT
public abstract boolean isAutoIncrement(int column) throws SQLException
Checks whether the column's value is auto-incremented.
Parameters: columnIndex – the column index begins at 1.

Returns: true if so

ISCASESENSITIVE
public abstract boolean isCaseSensitive(int column) throws SQLException
Checks whether a column is case sensitive.
Parameters: columnIndex – the column index begins at 1.

Returns: true if so

ISCURRENCY
public abstract boolean isCurrency(int column) throws SQLException
Checks whether the column is a currency value.

Parameters: columnIndex — the column index begins at 1.

Returns: true if so

ISDEFINITELYWRITABLE
public abstract boolean isDefinitelyWritable(int column) throws SQLException
Checks whether an update of the column will definitely succeed.
Parameters: columnIndex — the column index begins at 1.

Returns: true if so

ISNULLABLE
public abstract int isNullable(int column) throws SQLException
Checks whether this column may be set to SQL NULL.
Parameters: columnIndex — the column index begins at 1.

Returns: columnNoNulls, columnNullable, or columnNullableUnknown

ISREADONLY
public abstract boolean isReadOnly(int column) throws SQLException
Checks whether a column is definitely not writeable.
Parameters: columnIndex — the column index begins at 1.

Returns: true if so

ISSEARCHABLE
public abstract boolean isSearchable(int column) throws SQLException
Checks whether the column may be used in a SQL WHERE clause.
Parameters: columnIndex — the column index begins at 1.

Returns: true if so

ISSIGNED
public abstract boolean isSigned(int column) throws SQLException
Checks whether the column is signed.
Parameters: columnIndex — the column index begins at 1.

Returns: true if so

ISWRITABLE
public abstract boolean isWritable(int column) throws SQLException
Checks whether a column's value is possibly updatable.

Parameters: columnIndex — the column index begins at 1.

Returns: true if so

Interface java.sql.Statement

public interface Statement

extends Object

Statement objects are used to create database and driver resources before and during the execution of static SQL statements. They are also used to obtain the SQL statements' results after being executed within the database. The results, if they are of the form of rows of data, must be retrieved using ResultSets. Note that a SQL statement may return multiple results, but not at the same time. If necessary, instantiate different Statement objects to fetch different ResultSets simultaneously. **See also:** createStatement, ResultSet

METHODS:

CANCEL
    public abstract void cancel() throws SQLException
cancel() is used to terminate the execution of a statement. It can only be used within a thread separate from that executing the statement.

CLEARWARNINGS
    public abstract void clearWarnings() throws SQLException
Clears the chain of SQLWarnings for the current Statement.

CLOSE
    public abstract void close() throws SQLException
close() releases a Statements' database and JDBC driver resources, as well as its Statement, if one exists.

EXECUTE
    public abstract boolean execute(String sql) throws SQLException
This method executes a SQL statement. The statement may return multiple results, that is, results sets and update counts. In this case, the execute(), getMoreResults(), getResultSet(), and getUpdateCount() methods let you fetch those results. execute() indicates whether the first result is a ResultSet or an update count. getResultSet() and getUpdateCount() are used to retrieve the result, and getMoreResults() is used to discover subsequent results, if any.
Parameters: sql — SQL statement

Returns: true if the first result is a ResultSet; false if it is an integer

See also: getResultSet, getUpdateCount, getMoreResults

EXECUTEQUERY

public abstract ResultSet executeQuery(String sql) throws SQLException
Unlike execute(), executeQuery() is used to execute a SQL statement that returns a single ResultSet.
Parameters: sql — a SQL SELECT statement

Returns: a ResultSet containing the result rows, if any

EXECUTEUPDATE

public abstract int executeUpdate(String sql) throws SQLException
Execute a statement that returns an update count or just nothing (for example: SQL INSERT, UPDATE, or DELETE statements, or a SQL DDL statement such as CREATE TABLE).
Parameters: sql — a SQL statement that returns an integer or nothing

Returns: the update count for SQL INSERT, UPDATE, or DELETE; 0 for others

GETRESULTSET

public abstract ResultSet getResultSet() throws SQLException
getResultSet() is used to get the current result as a ResultSet. It can only be called once per result.
Returns: the current result as a ResultSet, or null if the result is an integer or there are no more results
See also: execute

GETUPDATECOUNT

public abstract int getUpdateCount() throws SQLException
getUpdateCount() returns the current result as an update count that represents the number of rows affected by the statement. getUpdateCount may also return -1 if the result is a ResultSet or there are no more results. It can only be called once per result.
Returns: the current result as an update count or -1 if it is a ResultSet or there are no more results
See also: execute

GETMAXFIELDSIZE

public abstract int getMaxFieldSize() throws SQLException
This method returns the maximum length of data returned for any column value. It only applies to BINARY, VARBINARY, LONGVARBINARY, CHAR, VARCHAR, and LONGVARCHAR columns.
Returns: the current maximum column size limit or zero if unlimited

GETMAXROWS
public abstract int getMaxRows() throws SQLException

This method returns the maximum number of rows allowed for a ResultSet. Excessive rows are discarded.

Returns: the current maximum row limit or zero if unlimited

GETMORERESULTS
public abstract boolean getMoreResults() throws SQLException

getMoreResults() is used to navigate results. If true is returned, the current result is a ResultSet. If false, the result is an update count or there are no more results (there are no more results when (!getMoreResults() && (getUpdateCount() == -1)). Note that getMoreResults() implicitly closes any current ResultSet obtained with getResultSet.

Returns: true if the next result is a ResultSet, or false if it is an integer or there are no more results

See also: execute

GETQUERYTIMEOUT
public abstract int getQueryTimeout() throws SQLException

A driver can wait a number of seconds for a Statement to execute. If the limit is exceeded, a SQLException is thrown.

Returns: the current query timeout limit in seconds or zero if unlimited

GETWARNINGS
public abstract SQLWarning getWarnings() throws SQLException

Statement and ResultSet warnings are chained together. This method is used to get the first SQLWarning of the chain. The chain is cleared each time a statement is executed.

Returns: the first SQLWarning or null

SETCURSORNAME
public abstract void setCursorName(String name) throws SQLException

This method sets the SQL cursor name for the current Statement. The cursor name can then be used in SQL positioned update or delete statements to identify the current row in the ResultSet. Note that cursor names must be unique within a Connection.

Parameters: name — the cursor name

SETESCAPEPROCESSING
public abstract void setEscapeProcessing(boolean enable) throws SQLException

A driver does escape substitution by default unless this method has been invoked with a parameter of Boolean value false.
Parameters: enable – true enables escape substitution: false disables it.

SETMAXFIELDSIZE
public abstract void setMaxFieldSize(int max) throws SQLException
Limit the size of data that can be returned for any column value. This only applies to BINARY, VARBINARY, LONGVARBINARY, CHAR, VARCHAR, and LONG-VARCHAR columns.
Parameters: max – the maximum column size limit or zero for unlimited

SETMAXROWS
public abstract void setMaxRows(int max) throws SQLException
setMaxRows() can be used to limit the rows returned by a query. Excessive rows are silently discarded.
Parameters: max – the maximum rows limit or zero for unlimited

SETQUERYTIMEOUT
public abstract void setQueryTimeout(int seconds) throws SQLException
A driver can wait a number of seconds for a Statement to execute. If the limit is exceeded, a SQLException is thrown.
Parameters: seconds – the query timeout limit in seconds or zero for unlimited

Class java.sql.Date

java.lang.Object
 └ java.util.Date
 └ java.sql.Date
public class Date

extends Date

This class extends the standard java.util.date class to represent SQL DATE types. It supports the JDBC escape syntax for date values.

CONSTRUCTORS:

DATE
public Date(int year, int month, int day)
Create a Date object
Parameters: year – year-1900

month – 0 to 11

day – 1 to 31

DATE
   public Date(long date)
Create a Date object using a milliseconds time value.
Parameters: date — milliseconds since January 1, 1970, 00:00:00 GMT

METHODS:

TOSTRING
   public String toString()
Convert a date to "YYYY-MM-DD" format.
Returns: a formatted date String

Overrides: toString in class Date

VALUEOF
   public static Date valueOf(String s)
Convert a "YYYY-MM-DD" formatted string to a Date value.
Parameters: s — date in format "YYYY-MM-DD"

Returns: a Date

Class java.sql.DriverManager

java.lang.Object
  └ java.sql.DriverManager
public class DriverManager

extends Object

The DriverManager manages JDBC drivers and database connection requests. Although the drivers may be registered and loaded with the class.forName() method, the DriverManager uses the "jdbc.drivers" property during its initialization phase to find a suitable one for the connection which is requested.
See also: Driver, Connection

METHODS:

DEREGISTERDRIVER
   public static void deregisterDriver(Driver driver) throws SQLException
Remove a Driver from the DriverManager's list. In the case of applets, only Drivers from the applet's own classloader may be deregistered.
Parameters: driver — a JDBC Driver

GETCONNECTION

public static synchronized Connection getConnection(String url, Properties info) throws SQLException

getConnection() returns a Connection object if the DriverManager is able to find an appropriate driver for the requested connection.

Parameters: url – a database URL

info – a list of string tag/value pairs as connection arguments

Returns: a Connection to the database URL

GETCONNECTION

public static synchronized Connection getConnection(String url, String user, String password) throws SQLException

getConnection() returns a Connection object if the DriverManager is able to find an appropriate driver for the requested connection.

Parameters: url – a database URL

user – a database user's login

password – the user's password

Returns: a Connection to the database URL

GETCONNECTION

public static synchronized Connection getConnection(String url) throws SQLException

getConnection() returns a Connection object if the DriverManager is able to find an appropriate driver for the requested connection.

Parameters: url – a database URL usually containing user and password strings

Returns: a Connection to the database URL

GETDRIVER

public static Driver getDriver(String url) throws SQLException

This method is used to locate a Driver that is able to connect to the database URL. The Driver is selected from the set of registered Drivers.

Parameters: url – a database URL

Returns: a Driver able to connect to the URL

GETDRIVERS

public static Enumeration getDrivers()

Get an Enumeration of the JDBC drivers that are currently loaded.

Returns: the list of JDBC Driver's loaded

GETLOGINTIMEOUT
public static int getLoginTimeout()
Get the maximum time in seconds that all drivers can wait when attempting to log in to a database.
Returns: the login time limit

GETLOGSTREAM
public static PrintStream getLogStream()
The DriverManager and JDBC drivers can give detailed information on what they do during a connection. This method returns the PrintStream used by the DriverManager and the drivers.
Returns: the logging/tracing PrintStream or null if logging/tracing is disabled

PRINTLN
public static void println(Stringmessage)
Print a string to the current JDBC log stream.
Parameters: message – a log message

REGISTERDRIVER
public static synchronized void registerDriver(Driverdriver) throws SQLException
JDBC drivers must register themselves with the DriverManager in order to be candidates for subsequent connections.
Parameters: driver – a JDBC Driver

SETLOGINTIMEOUT
public static void setLoginTimeout(int seconds)
Set the maximum time in seconds that all drivers can wait when attempting to log in to a database.
Parameters: seconds – the login time limit

SETLOGSTREAM
public static void setLogStream(PrintStreamout)
The DriverManager and JDBC drivers can give detailed information on what they do during a connection. This method sets the PrintStream used by the DriverManager and the drivers.
Parameters: out – the logging/tracing PrintStream or null to disable the logging/tracing facility

Class java.sql.DriverPropertyInfo

java.lang.Object
  └ java.sql.DriverPropertyInfo
public class DriverPropertyInfo

extends Object

The DriverPropertyInfo class is used to specify one tag name/value pair plus its description, possible choices for values, and so forth. Use java.sql.Driver.getPropertyInfo() to obtain an array of DriverPropertyInfo objects. Note the public variables of DriverPropertyInfo.

VARIABLES:

CHOICES
    public String choices[]
This is an array of the possible values for this property. If no choice is possible, then choices[] is null.

DESCRIPTION
    public String description
A description of this property

NAME
    public String name
The name of this property

REQUIRED
    public boolean required
This variable is set to true if a value must be supplied for this property during Driver.connect. The property is optional in the opposite case.

VALUE
    public String value
This string contains the current value of the property. It may be null if no value is known.

CONSTRUCTORS:

DRIVERPROPERTYINFO
    public DriverPropertyInfo(String name, String value)
Construct a DriverPropertyInfo object, giving it a name and a value.
Parameters: name − the name of the property

value − the value of the property

Class java.sql.Time

java.lang.Object
 └ java.util.Date
  └ java.sql.Time
public class Time

extends Date

This class extends the standard java.util.date class to represent SQL TIME types. Only hours, minutes, and seconds are handled. It supports the JDBC escape syntax for time values.

CONSTRUCTORS:

TIME
public Time(int hour, int minute, int second)
Construct a Time object.
Parameters: hour − 0 to 23

minute − 0 to 59

second − 0 to 59

TIME
public Time(long time)
Construct a Time object using a milliseconds time value since January 1, 1970, 00:00:00 GMT.
Parameters: time − milliseconds since January 1, 1970, 00:00:00 GMT

METHODS:

TOSTRING
public String toString()
Convert the time to "HH:MM:SS" format.
Returns: a "HH:MM:SS" formatted time String

Overrides: toString in class Date

VALUEOF
public static Time valueOf(String s)
Convert an "HH:MM:SS" formatted string to a Time value.
Parameters: s − time in "HH:MM:SS" format

Returns: a Time object

Class java.sql.Timestamp

java.lang.Object
└ java.util.Date
 └ java.sql.Timestamp
public class Timestamp

extends Date

This class extends the standard java.util.date to represent SQL TIMESTAMP types. It supports subsecond precision and the JDBC escape syntax for time values.

CONSTRUCTORS:

TIMESTAMP
   public Timestamp(int year, int month, int date, int hour, int minute, int second, int nano)
Construct a Timestamp object.
Parameters:
year − year-1900

month − 0 to 11

day − 1 to 31

hour − 0 to 23

minute − 0 to 59

second − 0 to 59

nano − 0 to 999,999,999

TIMESTAMP
   public Timestamp(long time)
Construct a Timestamp object using a milliseconds time value.
Parameters: time − milliseconds since January 1, 1970, 00:00:00 GMT

METHODS:

EQUALS
   public boolean equals(Timestamp ts)
Compare the current Timestamp object with another.
Parameters: ts − the Timestamp value to compare with

Returns: true if they are equal

GETNANOS
   public int getNanos()
Get the Timestamp's nanosecond value.
Returns: the Timestamp's nanosecond value

SETNANOS
   public void setNanos(int n)
Set the Timestamp's nanosecond value.
Parameters: n – the Timestamp's nanosecond value

TOSTRING
   public String toString()
Convert a Timestamp to "YYYY-MM-DD HH:MM:SS.F" format.
Returns: a "YYYY-MM-DD HH:MM:SS.F" formatted timestamp String

Overrides: toString in class Date

VALUEOF
   public static Timestamp valueOf(String s)
Convert a "YYYY-MM-DD HH:MM:SS.F" formatted string to a Timestamp value.
Parameters: s – timestamp formatted as "YYYY-MM-DD HH:MM:SS.F"

Returns: a Timestamp

Class java.sql.Types

java.lang.Object
  └ java.sql.Types
public class Types

extends Object

The SQL types constants and their values are defined in this class. The constant values are equivalent to those defined by XOPEN.

VARIABLES:

BIGINT
   public final static int BIGINT = -5

BINARY
   public final static int BINARY = -2

BIT
   public final static int BIT = -7

CHAR
    public final static int CHAR = 1

DATE
    public final static int DATE = 91

DECIMAL
    public final static int DECIMAL = 3

DOUBLE
    public final static int DOUBLE = 8

FLOAT
    public final static int FLOAT = 6

INTEGER
    public final static int INTEGER = 4

LONGVARCHAR
    public final static int LONGVARCHAR = -4

LONGVARBINARY
    public final static int LONGVARBINARY = -1

NULL
    public final static int NULL = 0

NUMERIC
    public final static int NUMERIC = 2

OTHER
    public final static int OTHER
Use getObject() and setObject() to access columns of SQL type OTHER.

REAL
    public final static int REAL = 7

SMALLINT
    public final static int SMALLINT = 5

TIME
    public final static int TIME = 92

TIMESTAMP
    public final static int TIMESTAMP = 93

TINYINT
    public final static int TINYINT = -6

VARBINARY
    public final static int VARBINARY = -3

VARCHAR
    public final static int VARCHAR = 12

Class java.sql.DataTruncation

java.lang.Object
 └ java.lang.Throwable
  └ java.lang.Exception
   └ java.sql.SQLException
    └ java.sql.SQLWarning
     └ java.sql.DataTruncation
public class DataTruncation

extends SQLWarning

If JDBC unexpectedly truncates a data value during a write, a DataTruncation exception is thrown. If this occurs during a read, a DataTruncation warning is created. The SQLstate value is set to "01004" for a DataTruncation.

CONSTRUCTORS:

DATATRUNCATION
    public DataTruncation(int index, boolean parameter, boolean read, int dataSize, int transferSize)
    Construct a DataTruncation object with "01004" as SQLState and "Data truncation" as reason.
Parameters:
index – the index of the parameter or column value for which a truncation occurred

parameter – true if the truncation occurred when accessing a parameter

read – true if the truncation occurred during a database read

dataSize – the size of the data before being truncated

transferSize – the size after truncation

METHODS:

GETDATASIZE
    public int getDataSize()
    Get the original data length in bytes.
Returns: the DataTruncation's dataSize value or -1 if unknown

GETINDEX
    public int getIndex()
Get the index of the column or parameter that was truncated.

Returns: the DataTruncation's index value or -1 if unknown

GETPARAMETER
    public boolean getParameter()
Checks whether the truncation occurred when reading or writing a parameter's value.
Returns: true if the truncated value was a parameter or false if it was a column

GETREAD
    public boolean getRead()
Checks whether the truncation occurred when reading a parameter or a column.
Returns: true if the value was truncated during a database read or false if the truncation occurred during a database write

GETTRANSFERSIZE
    public int getTransferSize()
Get the number of bytes of data transferred.
Returns: the number of bytes of data transferred or -1 if unknown

Class java.sql.SQLException

java.lang.Object
 └ java.lang.Throwable
 └ java.lang.Exception
 └ java.sql.SQLException
public class SQLException

extends Exception

This type of exception is thrown when database access errors happen. The SQLException supplies details in order to discover the reason why it was thrown. Several methods exist to obtain such information. Note that SQLExceptions are chained together.

CONSTRUCTORS:

SQLEXCEPTION
    public SQLException(String reason, String SQLState, int vendorCode)
Create a SQLException object providing a reason, an XOPEN SQLState, and a vendor code.
Parameters: reason — a short message for this exception

SQLState — an XOPEN code to identify this exception

vendorCode — a database vendor exception code

SQLEXCEPTION
>   public SQLException(String reason, String SQLState)
Create a SQLException object providing a reason and an XOPEN SQLState. The vendorCode is set to 0.
Parameters: reason – a short message for this exception

SQLState – an XOPEN code to identify this exception

SQLEXCEPTION
>   public SQLException(String reason)
Create a SQLException object providing a reason. The SQLState is set to null and the vendorCode is set to 0.
Parameters: reason – a short message for this exception

SQLEXCEPTION
>   public SQLException()
Create a SQLException object without providing additional information. The message and the SQLState are set to null and the vendorCode is set to 0.

METHODS:

GETERRORCODE
>   public int getErrorCode()
Get the vendor code for this exception.
Returns: the vendorCode value for this exception

GETNEXTEXCEPTION
>   public SQLException getNextException()
Get the exception chained to this one.
Returns: the next SQLException

GETSQLSTATE
>   public String getSQLState()
Get the SQLState for this exception.
Returns: the SQLState value for this exception

SETNEXTEXCEPTION
>   public synchronized void setNextException(SQLException ex)
Add an SQLException to the end of the chain of SQLExceptions.
Parameters: ex – a new SQLException

Class java.sql.SQLWarning

java.lang.Object
 └ java.lang.Throwable
  └ java.lang.Exception
   └ java.sql.SQLException
    └ java.sql.SQLWarning
public class SQLWarning

extends SQLException

SQLWarnings happen when database access warnings occur. The SQLWarnings are chained together and do not cause an exception to be thrown. It supplies details in order to discover the reason why it was created. Several methods exist to obtain such information.
See also: getWarnings

CONSTRUCTORS:

SQLWARNING
  public SQLWarning(String reason, String SQLstate, int vendorCode)
Create a SQLWarning object providing a reason, an XOPEN SQLState, and a vendor code.
Parameters: reason — a short message for this warning

SQLState — an XOPEN code to identify this warning

vendorCode — a database vendor warning code

SQLWARNING
  public SQLWarning(String reason, String SQLstate)
Create a SQLWarning object providing a reason and an XOPEN SQLState. The vendor code is set to 0.
Parameters: reason — a short message for this warning

SQLState — an XOPEN code to identify this warning

SQLWARNING
  public SQLWarning(String reason)
Create a SQLWarning object providing a reason. The XOPEN SQLState is set to null and the vendor code is set to 0.
Parameters: reason — a short message for this warning

SQLState — an XOPEN code to identify this warning

SQLWARNING
   public SQLWarning()
Create a SQLWarning object without providing additional information. The reason and XOPEN SQLState are set to null and the vendor code is set to 0.

METHODS:

GETNEXTWARNING
   public SQLWarning getNextWarning()
Get the warning chained to this one.
Returns: the next SQLWarning

SETNEXTWARNING
   public void setNextWarning(SQLWarning w)
Add a SQLWarning to the end of the chain of SQLWarnings.
Parameters: w — a new SQLWarning

Appendix A

JDBC Products and Drivers

The best place to go to when looking for specific Java Database Connectivity (JDBC) driver implementations is Javasoft, where the JDBC team frequently updates a list of JDBC driver vendors.

> **Javasoft, Inc.,** `http://splash.javasoft.com/jdbc/`
> Product name: JDBC API
> Web site: `http://www.javasoft.com/jdbc`
> E-mail: `java@java.sun.com`
> Address: 2550 Garcia Avenue
>   Mountain View, CA 94043-1100
> Phone: 415-960-1300
> Fax: 415-969-9131

The latest version of JDBC is available from Javasoft as well.

Table A-1 is a list of JDBC driver vendors listed according to the database management system (DBMS) they support and the type of JDBC driver implementation they develop:

- Type 1 is a **JDBC-ODBC Bridge**. It uses native, non-Java libraries and is platform-dependent.

- Type 2 is **native- API, partly-Java.** It uses native code too.

- Type 3 is a **net-protocol all-Java driver** but needs a middleware net server between the client and the DBMS.

- Type 4 is a **native-protocol all-Java driver**. It directly connects to the DBMS and is the most portable JDBC solution. It is the best solution for projects which have to be compliant with the 100 percent Pure Java initiative.

TABLE A-1 JDBC DRIVER VENDORS

DBMS	Type 1	Type 2	Type 3	Type 4
Adabas				SAS/ACCESS
DB2		IBM	IBM, Intersolv	

(continued)

339

TABLE **A-1** *(Continued)*

DBMS	Type 1	Type 2	Type 3	Type 4
DMSII			Asgard	
Essentia			Intersoft	
Informix			Agave, IDS, I-Kinetics, Intersolv, OpenLink, SCO	SAS/ACCESS
Ingres			Caribou, Intersolv, OpenLink, SCO	SAS/ACCESS
InterBase			SCO	Borland
miniSQL				Imaginary
Oracle		Intersolv, WebLogic	Agave, IDS, I-Kinetics, Intersolv, OpenLink, SCO, Symantec	SAS/ACCESS
Postgress			OpenLink	
SAS				SAS
Sybase		Intersolv, WebLogic	Agave, IDS, I-Kinetics, Intersolv, OpenLink, SCO, Sybase, Symantec	Connect SW, Sybase
SQL Server		WebLogic	IDS, Intersolv, OpenLink, Symantec	Connect SW
Unify			OpenLink	
Watcom			Sybase, Symantec	Sybase
Yard SQL				Yard Software

DBMS	Type 1	Type 2	Type 3	Type 4
via ODBC	JavaSoft		Agave, DataRamp,IDS, I-Kinetics, StormCloud, Symantec, Visigenic, WebLogic	

As of the writing of this book, these companies endorsed the JDBC API and are building JDBC compliant products, including JDBC drivers:

Agave Software Design

Product type:	Middleware
Product name:	JDBC Netserver
Web site:	http://www.agave.com
E-mail:	info@agave.com
Address:	720 Avenue F, Suite 104
	Plano, TX 75074
Phone:	972-424-6662
Fax:	972-424-6662

Borland International, Inc.

Product type:	Driver, middleware
Product name:	InterClient
Web site:	http://www.borland.com
E-mail:	customer-service@borland.com
Address:	100 Borland Way
	Scotts Valley, CA 95066-3249
Phone:	408-431-1000
Fax:	408-431-1000

Bulletproof Corporation

Product type:	Driver, ODBC middleware
Product name:	JAGG
Web site:	http://bulletproof.com/jagg
E-mail:	support@bulletproof.com
Address:	15732 Los Gatos Blvd., Suite 525
	Los Gatos, CA 95032
Phone:	408-395-5524
Fax:	408-395-6026

Caribou Lake Software
Product type: Various
Product name: SQL Runner, JSQL/Ingres
Web site: http://www.cariboulake.com
E-mail: info@cariboulake.com, sales@cariboulake.com

Centura Software Corporation
Product type: DBMS
Product Name: Centura
Web site: http://www.centurasoft.com
E-mail: info_usa@centurasoft.com
Address: 1060 Marsh Road
                   Menlo Park, CA 94025
Phone: 800-444-8782

Connect Software, Inc.
Product type: Premier 100 percent pure Java Type 4 JDBC drivers, con-
                   necting directly to major Relational DBMSs, including
                   Sybase and Microsoft SQL Server
Product name: Connect JDBC Driver
Web site: http://www.connectsw.com
E-mail: info@connectsw.com
Address: 81 Lansing Street, Suite 411
                   San Francisco, CA 94105
Phone: 415-710-1544
Fax: 415-543-6695

Cyber SQL Corporation
Product type: Database-oriented Java class library
Product name: ActiveWeb
Web site: http://www.cybersql.com
E-mail: feedback@www.cybersql.com

DataRamp, Inc.
Product type: ODBC pipeline
Product name: DataRamp
Web site: http://dataramp.com
E-mail: sales@dataramp.com
Address: 25 Burlington Mall Road
                   Burlington, MA 01803
Phone: 616-273-3772
Fax: 617-270-9169

Dharma Systems, Inc.
Product type: Various
Product name: ODBC SQL

Web site:	http://www.dharmas.com
E-mail:	info@dharmas.com
Address:	15 Trafalgar Square
	Nashua, NH 03063
Phone:	603-886-1400
Fax:	603-883-6904

Esker, Inc.

Product type:	Various
Web site:	http://www.esker.com, http://www.esker.fr
E-mail:	info@esker.com, info@esker.fr
Address:	350 Sansome Street, Suite 210
	San Francisco, CA 94104
Phone:	415-675-7771
Fax:	415-675-7775

GWE Technologies

Product type:	DBMS, 100 percent Java JDBC driver
Web site:	http://www.gwe.co.uk/java/jdbc
E-mail:	gwe@wales.com
Address:	Llys Y Fedwen, Park Menai, Bangor,
	North Wales, LL57 4BF, UK
Phone:	+44-(0)-1248-671001
Fax:	+44-(0)-1248-671102

I-Kinetics

Product type:	100 percent pure Java JDBC Common Object Request Broker Archetecture (CORBA)-based driver
Product name:	OPENjdbc
Web site:	http://www.i-kinetics.com
E-mail:	info@i-kinetics.com
Address:	17 New England Executive Park
	Burlington, MA 01803
Phone:	617-270-1300
Fax:	617-270-4979

IBM Corporation

Product type:	Various, DBMS, connectivity tools
Product name:	DB2, Net.Data
	Web site: http://www.software.ibm.com/data/db2/index.html
E-mail:	askibm@info.ibm.com
Address:	Old Orchard Road
	Armonk, NY 10504
Phone:	520-574-4600

IDS Software
Product type: Server, Middleware, Web/database integration
Product name: IDS Server, IDS JDBC Driver
Web site: http://www.idssoftware.com
E-mail: info@idssoftware.com
Address: 11309 Elmcrest Street
                    El Monte, CA 91732
Phone: 818-401-2648
Fax: Unknown

Imaginary
Product type: 100 percent Java JDBC driver for mSQL
Product name: mSQL-JDBC
Web site: http://www.imaginary.com/~borg/Java
E-mail: borg@imaginary.com

Information Builders
Product type: Various, connectivity tools
Product name: WebFOCUS
Web site: http://www.ibi.com
E-mail: info@ibi.com
Address: 1250 Broadway
                    New York, NY 10001-3782
Phone: 212-279-2382
Fax: 212-967-6406

Informix Software, Inc.
Product type: DBMS, connectivity tools
Product name: Informix Webkits
Web site: http://www.informix.com
E-mail: info@informix.com
Address: 4100 Bohannon Drive
                    Menlo Park, CA 94025
Phone: 415-926-6300

Intersoft Argentina
Product type: Various, DBMS for Linux, JDBC driver
Product name: Essentia-JDBC
Web site: http://www.inter-soft.com/eng/products/system/
                    essentia/
E-mail: info@inter-soft.com
Address: Calle Brisas del Prado, Residencias Bucare, Piso 8D
                    Terrazas del club Hipico, Caracas, Venezuela
Phone: +58-2-978-4921
Fax: +58-16-38-3114

Intersolv

Product type:	Connectivity tools, JDBC-ODBC bridge
Product name:	JDBC-ODBC bridge
Web site:	http://www.intersolv.com
E-mail:	jdbc_answerline@intersolv.com
Address:	9420 Key West Avenue
	Rockville, MD 20850
Phone:	800-547-4000
Fax:	301-838-5064

Ken North Seminars

Product type:	Miscellaneous
Product name:	SQL API Benchmark Kit
Web site:	http://ourworld.compuserve.com/homepages/
	Ken_North

Net Dynamics

Product type:	Web/Database development tools, N-Tier solutions
Product name:	NetDynamics
Web site:	http://www.netdynamics.com/press/reviews/
	jdbcfinal.html
E-mail:	info@netdynamics.com
Address:	185 Constitution Drive
	Menlo Park, CA 94025
Phone:	415-462-7600
Fax:	415-617-5920

O2 Technology

Product type:	ODBMS, connectivity tools, Java-relational bindings
Product name:	Java Relational Binding API
Web site:	http://www.o2tech.com
E-mail:	o2info@o2tech.com
Address:	3600 West Bayshore Road, Suite 106
	Palo Alto, CA 94303
Phone:	415-842-7000
Fax:	415-842-7001

Object Design, Inc.

Product type:	ODBMS, connectivity tools, Java object persistence
Product name:	ObjectStore PSE and ObjectStore PSE for Java
Web site:	http://www.odi.com
E-mail:	info@odi.com
Address:	25 Mall Road
	Burlington, MA 01803
Phone:	617-674-5000
Fax:	617-674-5010

Open Horizon, Inc.

Product type:	Middleware, secure connectivity
Product name:	Ambrosia, Connection
Web site:	http://www.openhorizon.com
E-mail:	info@openhorizon.com
Address:	601 Gateway Boulevard, Suite 800
	South San Francisco, CA 94080
Phone:	415-869-2200
Fax:	415-869-2201

OpenLink Software, Inc.

Product type:	Middleware
Product name:	OpenLink ODBC, OpenLink UDBC
Web site:	http://www.openlinksw.com
E-mail:	oiyoha@openlink.co.uk
Address:	10 Burlington Mall Rd., Suite 265
	Burlington, MA 01803
Phone:	617-273-0900
Fax:	617-229-8030

Oracle Corporation

Product type:	DBMS, connectivity tools
Product name:	Universal Server, WebServer, PowerBrowser
Web site:	http://www.oracle.com
E-mail:	info@oracle.com
Address:	500 Oracle Parkway
	Redwood Shores, CA 94065
Phone:	415-506-7000
Fax:	415-506-7200

Persistence Software, Inc.

Product type:	Object-Relational mapping
Product name:	Persistence, LiveObjectCache for CORBA
Web site:	http://www.persistence.com
E-mail:	info@persistence.com
Address:	1720 S. Amphlett Blvd., Suite 300
	San Mateo, CA 94402
Phone:	415-372-3600
Fax:	415-341-8432

Presence Information Design

Product type:	JDBC driver for Oracle
Product name:	PB&J
Web site:	http://cloud9.presence.com/pbj
E-mail:	pbj@presence.com
Phone:	818-405-9971
Fax:	818-405-1817

PRO-C, Inc.

Product type:	Java code generator
Product name:	WinGEN and WinGEN Lite for Java
Web site:	http://www.pro-c.com
E-mail:	sales@pro-c.com
Address:	1st National Plaza,
	100 W. Kennedy Blvd.
	Tampa, FL 33602-5832
Phone:	813-227-7762
Fax:	813-223-1562

Recital Corporation

Product type:	Various
Product name:	Kaleidoscope and JDBC drivers
Web site:	http://www.recital.com
E-mail:	info@recital.com
Address:	85 Constitution Lane
	Danvers, MA 01923
Phone:	508-750-1066
Fax:	508-762-0119

RogueWave Software Inc.

Product type:	Various class libraries
Product name:	JDBTools
Web site:	http://www.roguewave.com
E-mail:	sales@roguewave.com,
	international_sales@roguewave.com
Address:	850 S.W. 35th Street
	Corvallis, OR 97333
Phone:	541-754-5010
Fax:	541-757-6650

Sanga Corporation

Product type:	Web/Database connectivity components
Product name:	Sanga Pages
Web site:	http://www.sangacorp.com/products.html
E-mail:	info@sangacorp.com
Address:	24 New England Executive Park
	2nd Floor
	Burlington, MA 01803
Phone:	617-272-8500
Fax:	617-272-9800

SAS Institute, Inc.

Product type:	Connectivity
Product name:	SHARE*NET Driver for JDBC
Web site:	http://www.sas.com
E-mail:	webwrk-l@vm.sas.com
Address:	SAS Campus Drive
	Cary, NC 27513
Phone:	919-677-8000
Fax:	919-677-8123

The Santa Cruz Operation, Inc.

Product type:	Various, middleware
Product name:	SQL-Retriever
Web site:	http://www.vision.sco.com/brochure/sqlretriever.html
Address:	400 Encinal Street, PO Box 1900
	Santa Cruz, CA 95061-1900
Phone:	408-425-7222
Fax:	408-458-4227

StormCloud Development Corporation

Product type:	Web/Database development environment
Product name:	WebDBC
Web site:	http://www.stormcloud.com
E-mail:	info@stormcloud.com
Address:	316 Occidental Avenue South, Suite 406
	Seattle, WA 98104
Phone:	206-812-0177
Fax:	206-812-0170

Sybase, Inc.

Product type:	DBMS and connectivity tools
Product name:	SQL Server 10, System XI, Web.SQL
Web site:	http://www.sybase.com
E-mail:	sales@sybase.com
Address:	6475 Christie Avenue
	Emeryville, CA 94608
Phone:	510-922-3500
Fax:	510-658-9441

Symantec

Product type:	Java development tool
Product name:	Symantec Cafe
Web site:	http://cafe.symantec.com/cafe/
Address:	10201 Torre Avenue
	Cupertino, CA 95014-2132

Phone:	408-253-9600
Fax:	408-253-3968

Thought, Inc.

Product type:	Middleware, secure connectivity
Product name:	CocoBase
Web site:	http://www.thoughtinc.com
E-mail:	info@thoughtinc.com
Address:	2222 Leavenworth Street, Suite 304
	San Francisco, CA 94133
Phone:	415-928-4224
Fax:	415-567-9945

Thunderstone

Product type:	Information retrieval
Product name:	Metamorph, Texis
Web site:	http://www.thunderstone.com
E-mail:	info@thunderstone.com
Address:	11115 Edgewater Drive
	Cleveland, OH 44102
Phone:	216-631-8544
Fax:	216-281-0828

Visigenic Software, Inc.

Product type:	Middleware
Product name:	VisiBroker for Java, VisiChannel
Web site:	http://www.visigenic.com
E-mail:	info@visigenic.com
Address:	951 Mariner's Island Blvd., Suite 120
	San Mateo, CA 94404
Phone:	415-286-1900
Fax:	415-286-2464

Weblogic, Inc.

Product type:	Pure Java JDBC drivers, middleware
Product name:	jdbcKona, jdbcKona/T3, dbKona, htmlKona
Web site:	http://www.weblogic.com
E-mail:	info@weblogic.com
Address:	180 Montgomery Street, Suite 180
	San Francisco, CA 94104
Phone:	415-394-8616
Fax:	415-394-8619

XDB Systems, Inc.

Product type:	Web/Database connectivity tools
Product name:	JetConnect, JetAssist, HeatShield

Web site: http://www.xdb.com
E-mail: moreinfo@xdb.com
Address: 9861 Broken Land Parkway
                    Columbia, MD 21046
Phone: 410-312-9300
Fax: 410-312-9505

YARD Software GmbH
Product type: JDBC driver for YARD DBMS
Product name: YARD-JDBC
Web site: http://www.yard.de
E-mail: info@yard.de
Address: Wikingerstr. 18
                    51107 Köln, Germany
Phone: +49-221-98664-0
Fax: +49-221-98664-99

Other organizations and companies make specifications or build Java versions of database-oriented tools, distributed object request brokers, or client-server tools and components. In this book we mentioned:

Object Database Management Group
Web site: http://www.odmg.org
E-mail: info@odmg.org
Address: 14041 Burnhaven Drive, Suite 105
                    Burnsville, MN 55337
Phone: 612-953-7250
Fax: 612-397-7146

Marimba, Inc.
Product type: Java development and connectivity tools
Product name: Bongo, Castanet
Web site: http://www.marimba.com
E-mail: info@marimba.com
Address: 445 Sherman Avenue
                    Palo Alto, CA 94306
Phone: 415-328-JAVA
Fax: 415-328-5295

Platinum Technology, Inc.
Product type: Java OO CASE tool
Product name: Paradigm Plus
Web site: http://www.platinum.com
E-mail: info@platinum.com
Phone: 630-620-5000
Fax: 800-442-4230

Trifox, Inc.

Product type:	Middleware, TP Monitor
Product name:	Vortex for Java
Web site:	http://www.trifox.com/vtxjava.html
E-mail:	info@trifox.com
Address:	851 E. Hamilton Avenue #230
	Campbell, CA 95008
Phone:	408-369-2300
Fax:	408-369-2333

Appendix B

Links for Additional Information

For More Information About SQL and DBMSs

Standards:

Database Language—SQL with Integrity Enhancement, ANSI, 1989 ANSI X3.135-1989

X/Open and SQL Access Group SQL CAE specification, 1992

Database Language—SQL: ANSI X3H2 and ISO/IEC JTC1/SC21/WG3 9075:1992 (SQL-92)

For More Information About Objects and DBMSs

Standards:

Object Database Management Group: ODMG's specifications, http://www.odmg.org

Object Database Management Group: ODMG Java Binding, http://www.odmg.org/java.html

Object Management Group: CORBA 2.0 Architecture and Specification, http://www.omg.org

Appendix C

Frequently Asked Questions

The following are frequently asked questions about JDBC.

Q: Is it possible to access databases with JDBC from an applet?

A: Yes, it is possible provided that the driver in use is a 100-percent Java driver. The driver is called a native-protocol all-Java driver. The problem with a native-API partly-Java driver or a protocol bridge is that it uses native libraries to connect to the DBMS and interact with it. It is not allowed to call native libraries from an applet for security reasons.

Q: I use Solaris 2.4. Can I use the JDBC-ODBC bridge to connect to a Sybase database?

A: Yes, provided that you have an appropriate ODBC driver manager and driver for your platform. These components have nothing to do with Java and are available on the market. This answer is true for a variety of Unix platforms and DBMSs.

Q: May I run my WWW server and DBMS server on different machines?

A: If the goal is to let an applet communicate with a database, the database should be located on the same server the applet came from. For security reasons an applet cannot open sockets to arbitrary hosts. However, it is possible to place the DBMS elsewhere provided that a middle tier is placed on the WWW server machine. This tier would forward calls to the DBMS.

Q: What is involved with installation on the database server side?

A: Nothing special. You just need the appropriate DBMS connectivity software that allows clients to connect to it. The client's JDBC driver should be compatible with this software.

Q: My CLASSPATH environment variable points to the .java files, but the code does not compile. What's wrong?

A: The CLASSPATH environment variable should point to all the .class files that the Java application, applet, or servlet will use.

Q: When I try to use a JDBC–ODBC bridge, I always get this SQLException:
SQLState: IM002
Message: [Microsoft][ODBC Driver Manager] Data Source Name not found
Vendor: 0
A: The sub-subprotocol field of the URL is the Data Source Name as defined within the ODBC Driver Manager. This only works with the 32-bit version of the driver manager.

Q: I use a native driver but I get errors related to a missing shared library. What can I do?
A: Files such as libXXX.so should be reachable by following the LD_LIBRARY_PATH environment variable. Correct its value to make the path point to where the files are located and try again.

Q: I use a native driver but I get errors saying that it is unable to load a DLL. What's wrong?
A: Files such as DLLs should be located in your windows\system directory or where they are reachable by following the PATH. Correct this and try again.

Q: My browser won't launch my applet when reading from a local file.
A: Browsers are usually able to launch applets that come from the local file system but some of them won't open socket connections to connect to a remote server for security reasons. JDBC Drivers use sockets to establish connections on TCP/IP networks.

Q: I am not able to call database metadata methods. I get an error message that says "Driver not capable." What's wrong?
A: When the driver is not capable, it may be because it does not support this function or because the DBMS does not support the function. You should not use database metadata in this case.

Appendix D

What's on the CD-ROM

The CD-ROM contains the source code for all examples, JDBC products, and the common Java utilities such as the JavaSoft, Inc. JDK. Refer to the specific product documentation for information about installing on your platform. The CD_ROM contains the following:

◆ ReadMe.txt   Description of the products contained on the CD-ROM.

◆ legal.txt   Java™ Binary Code License.

Source Code Files

◆ src/fragments/   This directory contains the source code for the code fragments in this book.

◆ src/examples/   This directory contains the complete examples explained in this book.

◆ ./isql   Isql is a tool for issuing SQL statements interactively. The applet and application are included.

◆ ./airlines   JDBC Airlines illustrates a real-world applet. Copyright © 1996–1997 by Connect Software, Inc. For 100% Java drivers, see http://www.connectsw.com.

◆ ./blobs   These are command-line tools to insert and extract batches of multimedia files (.GIF, .WAV, .MPEG, .AU, .WRL, ...) in/from database tables.

◆ ./bank   The "Welcome to the Bank of Java" applet illustrates database transaction isolation.

◆ /jexplore   JExplorer features lots of graphical tools to navigate a database using JDBC metadata interfaces.

◆ ./rmi   The "Best Cars In The World" example illustrates how to develop with JDBC and the Remote Method Invocation of Java. (Portions Copyright © 1997 De Munck Mediaware)

JDBC Products

- ◆ jdbc/jdbc   This directory contains the JDBC classes of JavaSoft, Inc. in ZIP and tar.Z formats.

- ◆ jdbc/jdbcodbc/   This directory contains the JDBC-ODBC bridge of JavaSoft, Inc. and Intersolv, Inc. in ZIP and tar.Z formats.

- ◆ jdbc/drivers/   This directory contains George Reese's mSQL-JDBC driver for miniSQL based on Darryl Collins's mSQL-Java.

- ◆ dbms/minisql/   This directory contains the miniSQL database management system from Hughes Technologies Ltd. in tar.gz formats.

Java Utilities

- ◆ java/jdk/   This directory contains the Java Development Kit 1.1.1 of JavaSoft, Inc. The files are self-extracting archives.

- ◆ java/bongo/   This directory contains a demo version of Bongo 1.0 of Marimba, Inc.

Other Tools

- ◆ misc/winzip/   This directory contains a shareware evaluation version of WinZip for Windows 95, Windows NT and Windows 3.1. WinZipTM is a registred trademark of Nico Mak Computing, Inc. (Copyright © 1997 Nico Mak Computing, Inc.)

Index

Numbers

A

B

(continued)

my2cents.idgbooks.com

Register This Book — And Win!

Visit **http://my2cents.idgbooks.com** to register this book and we'll automatically enter you in our monthly prize giveaway. It's also your opportunity to give us feedback: let us know what you thought of this book and how you would like to see other topics covered.

Discover IDG Books Online!

The IDG Books Online Web site is your online resource for tackling technology — at home and at the office.

Ten Productive and Career-Enhancing Things You Can Do at www.idgbooks.com

1. Nab source code for your own programming projects.

2. Download software.

3. Read Web exclusives: special articles and book excerpts by IDG Books Worldwide authors.

4. Take advantage of resources to help you advance your career as a Novell or Microsoft professional.

5. Buy IDG Books Worldwide titles or find a convenient bookstore that carries them.

6. Register your book and win a prize.

7. Chat live online with authors.

8. Sign up for regular e-mail updates about our latest books.

9. Suggest a book you'd like to read or write.

10. Give us your 2¢ about our books and about our Web site.

Not on the Web yet? It's easy to get started with *Discover the Internet*, at local retailers everywhere.

Java™ Development Kit Version 1.1.1 Binary Code License

This binary code license ("License") contains rights and restrictions associated with use of the accompanying software and documentation ("Software"). Read the License carefully before installing the Software. By installing the Software, you agree to the terms and conditions of the License.

1. <u>Limited License Grant</u>. Sun grants to you ("Licensee") a nonexclusive, nontransferable limited license to use the Software without fee for evaluation of the Software and for development of Java™ compatible applets and applications. Licensee may make one archival copy of the Software. Licensee may not redistribute the Software in whole or in part, either separately or included with a product. Refer to the Java Runtime Environment Version 1.1.1 binary code license (http://www.javasoft.com/products/ JDK/1.1.1/index.html) for the availability of runtime code that may be distributed with Java compatible applets and applications.

2. <u>Java Platform Interface</u>. Licensee may not modify the Java Platform Interface ("JPI", identified as classes contained within the "java" package or any subpackages of the "java" package) by creating additional classes within the JPI or otherwise causing the addition to or modification of the classes in the JPI. In the event that Licensee creates any Java-related API and distributes such API to others for applet or application development, Licensee must promptly publish an accurate specification for such API for free use by all developers of Java-based software.

3. <u>Restrictions</u>. Software is confidential, copyrighted information of Sun and title to all copies is retained by Sun and/or its licensors. Licensee shall not modify, decompile, disassemble, decrypt, extract, or otherwise reverse engineer Software. Software may not be leased, assigned, or sublicensed, in whole or in part. Software is not designed or intended for use in online control of aircraft, air traffic, aircraft navigation, or aircraft communications; or in the design, construction, operation, or maintenance of any nuclear facility. Licensee warrants that it will not use or redistribute the Software for such purposes.

4. <u>Trademarks and Logos</u>. This License does not authorize Licensee to use any Sun name, trademark, or logo. Licensee acknowledges that Sun owns the Java trademark and all Java-related trademarks, logos, and icons including the Coffee Cup and Duke ("Java Marks") and agrees to: (i) to comply with the Java Trademark Guidelines at http://java.com/trademarks.html; (ii) not do anything harmful to or inconsistent with Sun's rights in the Java Marks; and (iii) assist Sun in protecting those rights, including assigning to Sun any rights acquired by Licensee in any Java Mark.

5. **Disclaimer of Warranty**. Software is provided "AS IS," without a warranty of any kind.

ALL EXPRESS OR IMPLIED REPRESENTATIONS AND WARRANTIES, INCLUDING ANY IMPLIED WARRANTY OF MERCHANTABILITY, FITNESS FOR A PARTICULAR PURPOSE OR NONINFRINGEMENT, ARE HEREBY EXCLUDED.

6. **Limitation of Liability.** SUN AND ALL ITS LICNESORS SHALL NOT BE LIABLE FOR ANY DAMAGES SUFFERED BY LICENSEE OR ANY THIRD PARTY AS A RESULT OF USING OR DISTRIBUTING SOFTWARE. IN NO EVENT WILL SUN OR ITS LICENSORS BE LIABLE FOR ANY LOST REVENUE, PROFIT, OR DATA; OR FOR DIRECT, INDIRECT, SPE-CIAL, CONSEQUENTIAL, INCIDENTAL OR PUNITIVE DAMAGES, HOWEVER CAUSED AND REGARDLESS OF THE THEORY OF LIABILITY, ARISING OUT OF THE USE OF OR INABILITY TO USE SOFTWARE, EVEN IF SUN HAS BEEN ADVISED OF THE POSSIB-LITY OF SUCH DAMAGES.

7. **Termination.** Licensee may terminate this License at any time by destroying all copies of Software. This License will terminate immediately without notice from Sun if Licensee fails to comply with any provision of this License. Upon such termination, Licensee must destroy all copies of Software.

8. **Export Regulations.** Software, including technical data, is subject to U.S. export control laws, including the U.S. Export Administration Act and its associated regulations, and may be subject to export or import regulations in other countries. Licensee agrees to comply strictly with all such regulations and acknowledges that it has the responsibility to obtain licenses to export, reexport, or import Software. Software may not be down-loaded, or otherwise exported or reexported (i) into, or to a national or resident of, Cuba, Iraq, Iran, North Korea, Libya, Sudan, Syria, or any country to which the U.S. has embargoed goods; or (ii) to anyone on the U.S. Treasury Department's list of Specially Designated Nations or the U.S. Commerce Department's Table of Denial Orders.

9. **Restricted Rights.** Use, duplication or disclosure by the U.S. government is subject to the restrictions as set forth in the Rights in Technical Data and Computer Software Clauses in DFARS 252.227-7013(c)(1)(ii) and FAR 52.227-19(c) (2) as applicable.

10. **Governing Law.** Any action related to this License will be governed by California law and controlling U.S. federal law. No choice of law rules of any jurisdiction will apply.

11. **Severability.** If any of the above provisions are held to be in violation of applicable law, void, or unenforceable in any jurisdiction, then such provisions are herewith waived to the extent necessary for the License to be otherwise enforceable in such juris-diction. However, if in Sun's opinion deletion of any provisions of the License by oper-ation of this paragraph unreasonably compromises the rights or increase the liabilities of Sun or its licensors, Sun reserves the right to terminate the License and refund the fee paid by Licensee, if any, as Licensee's sole and exclusive remedy.

IDG BOOKS WORLDWIDE, INC.
END-USER LICENSE AGREEMENT

READ THIS. You should carefully read these terms and conditions before opening the software packet(s) included with this book ("Book"). This is a license agreement ("Agreement") between you and IDG Books Worldwide, Inc. ("IDGB"). By opening the accompanying software packet(s), you acknowledge that you have read and accept the following terms and conditions. If you do not agree and do not want to be bound by such terms and conditions, promptly return the Book and the unopened software packet(s) to the place you obtained them for a full refund.

1. <u>License Grant</u>. IDGB grants to you (either an individual or entity) a nonexclusive license to use one copy of the enclosed software program(s) (collectively, the "Software") solely for your own personal or business purposes on a single computer (whether a standard computer or a workstation component of a multiuser network). The Software is in use on a computer when it is loaded into temporary memory (RAM) or installed into permanent memory (hard disk, CD-ROM, or other storage device). IDGB reserves all rights not expressly granted herein.

2. <u>Ownership</u>. IDGB is the owner of all right, title, and interest, including copyright, in and to the compilation of the Software recorded on the disk(s) or CD-ROM ("Software Media"). Copyright to the individual programs recorded on the Software Media is owned by the author or other authorized copyright owner of each program. Ownership of the Software and all proprietary rights relating thereto remain with IDGB and its licensers.

3. <u>Restrictions on Use and Transfer</u>.

   (a) You may only (i) make one copy of the Software for backup or archival purposes, or (ii) transfer the Software to a single hard disk, provided that you keep the original for backup or archival purposes. You may not (i) rent or lease the Software, (ii) copy or reproduce the Software through a LAN or other network system or through any computer subscriber system or bulletin-board system, or (iii) modify, adapt, or create derivative works based on the Software.

   (b) You may not reverse engineer, decompile, or disassemble the Software. You may transfer the Software and user documentation on a permanent basis, provided that the transferee agrees to accept the terms and conditions of this Agreement and you retain no copies. If the Software is an update or has been updated, any transfer must include the most recent update and all prior versions.

4. <u>Restrictions on Use of Individual Programs</u>. You must follow the individual requirements and restrictions detailed for each individual program in Appendix D, "What's on the CD-ROM," of this Book. These limitations are also contained in the individual license agreements recorded on the Software Media. These limitations may include a requirement that after using the program for a specified period of time, the user must pay a registration fee or discontinue use. By opening the Software packet(s), you will be agreeing to abide by the licenses and restrictions for these individual programs that are detailed in Appendix D, "What's on the CD-ROM," and on the Software Media. None of the material on this Software Media or listed in this Book may ever be redistributed, in original or modified form, for commercial purposes.

5. <u>Limited Warranty</u>.

   (a) IDGB warrants that the Software and Software Media are free from defects in materials and workmanship under normal use for a period of sixty (60) days from the date of purchase of this Book. If IDGB receives notification within the warranty period of defects in materials or workmanship, IDGB will replace the defective Software Media.

(b) IDGB AND THE AUTHOR OF THE BOOK DISCLAIM ALL OTHER WARRANTIES, EXPRESS OR IMPLIED, INCLUDING WITHOUT LIMITATION IMPLIED WARRANTIES OF MERCHANTABILITY AND FITNESS FOR A PARTICULAR PURPOSE, WITH RESPECT TO THE SOFTWARE, THE PROGRAMS, THE SOURCE CODE CONTAINED THEREIN, AND/OR THE TECHNIQUES DESCRIBED IN THIS BOOK. IDGB DOES NOT WARRANT THAT THE FUNCTIONS CONTAINED IN THE SOFTWARE WILL MEET YOUR REQUIREMENTS OR THAT THE OPERATION OF THE SOFTWARE WILL BE ERROR FREE.

(c) This limited warranty gives you specific legal rights, and you may have other rights that vary from jurisdiction to jurisdiction.

6. <u>Remedies</u>.

(a) IDGB's entire liability and your exclusive remedy for defects in materials and workmanship shall be limited to replacement of the Software Media, which may be returned to IDGB with a copy of your receipt at the following address: Software Media Fulfillment Department, Attn.: *JDBC™: Java™ Database Connectivity,* IDG Books Worldwide, Inc., 7260 Shadeland Station, Ste. 100, Indianapolis, IN 46256, or call 1-800-762-2974. Please allow three to four weeks for delivery. This Limited Warranty is void if failure of the Software Media has resulted from accident, abuse, or misapplication. Any replacement Software Media will be warranted for the remainder of the original warranty period or thirty (30) days, whichever is longer.

(b) In no event shall IDGB or the author be liable for any damages whatsoever (including without limitation damages for loss of business profits, business interruption, loss of business information, or any other pecuniary loss) arising from the use of or inability to use the Book or the Software, even if IDGB has been advised of the possibility of such damages.

(c) Because some jurisdictions do not allow the exclusion or limitation of liability for consequential or incidental damages, the above limitation or exclusion may not apply to you.

7. <u>U.S. Government Restricted Rights</u>. Use, duplication, or disclosure of the Software by the U.S. Government is subject to restrictions stated in paragraph (c)(1)(ii) of the Rights in Technical Data and Computer Software clause of DFARS 252.227-7013, and in subparagraphs (a) through (d) of the Commercial Computer – Restricted Rights clause at FAR 52.227-19, and in similar clauses in the NASA FAR supplement, when applicable.

8. <u>General</u>. This Agreement constitutes the entire understanding of the parties and revokes and supersedes all prior agreements, oral or written, between them and may not be modified or amended except in a writing signed by both parties hereto that specifically refers to this Agreement. This Agreement shall take precedence over any other documents that may be in conflict herewith. If any one or more provisions contained in this Agreement are held by any court or tribunal to be invalid, illegal, or otherwise unenforceable, each and every other provision shall remain in full force and effect.

CD-ROM Installation Instructions

Most of the programs included on this CD are stored in compressed archives. For some programs, you will need to run `setup.exe`. For others, you will need to decompress the archive. Refer to the `ReadMe.txt` on the CD and the instructions associated with each program for specific installation instructions. For example files, copy the appropriate directory to your hard drive. Some of the examples need to have access to the Marimba GUI classes. Install the Marimba software on your hard disk (see the `ReadMe.txt` file on the CD for instructions). The `PATH` environment variable should contain `<jdk-installation-dir>/bin`. The `CLASSPATH` environment variable should contain at least the following:

`<jdk-installation-dir>/lib/classes.zip:<bongo-installation-dir>/lib/marimba.zip`. Note that it is advised to have the JDBC Driver classes for your DBMS in your `CLASSPATH` as well.

For native non-Java JDBC Drivers, the DLLs or shared libraries should be in the `PATH` or `LD_LIBRARY_PATH` environment variable. Refer to the driver documentation for more information.

See Appendix D, "What's on the CD-ROM," for a complete list of CD contents. Please note that the first time this CD is inserted on a Macintosh, it might display an error message and rebuild the desktop.